OBSTRUCTION OF JUSTICE

FOREWORD BY NEWT GINGRICH

OBSTRUCTION OF JUSTICE

HOW THE DEEP STATE RISKED NATIONAL SECURITY TO PROTECT THE DEMOCRATS

LUKE ROSIAK

REGNERY
PUBLISHING
A Division of Salem Media Group

Regnery® is a registered trademark of Salem Communications Holding Corporation

Cataloging-in-Publication data on file with the Library of Congress

ISBN 978-1-62157-943-4
ebook ISBN 978-1-62157-944-1

Published in the United States by
Regnery Publishing
A Division of Salem Media Group
300 New Jersey Ave NW
Washington, DC 20001
www.Regnery.com

Manufactured in the United States of America

10 9 8 7 6 5 4 3 2 1

Books are available in quantity for promotional or premium use. For information on discounts and terms, please visit our website: www. Regnery.com.

For my daughters Olivia,
who was born when I began this investigation,
and Avery, who was born as it ended.
Their natural joy and directness kept me grounded
as I was immersed in a world that seemed
self-preservationist, hypocritical, and
cynical at every turn.

CONTENTS

FOREWORD

NEWT GINGRICH

I am delighted to write this foreword for Luke Rosiak's remarkable book, *Obstruction of Justice*, which exposes corruption and a coverup by the United States House of Representatives.

President Trump wrote: "The Democrat I.T. scandal is a key to much of the corruption we see today." This book shows how right he is; in fact, it exposes three different parallel scandals:

1. The actual, alleged illegalities involving Democratic members of the House of Representatives, including the system that IT aide Imran Awan and his associates created for stealing money, equipment, and, potentially, information from the House.

2. The failure of the Republican leadership to investigate aggressively and expose the various aspects of the scandal.

3. The failure of the liberal media to cover what is
   possibly the biggest scandal in the history of the
   U.S. House of Representatives.

All three scandals would have remained hidden if it was not
for the remarkable, persistent, and courageous work of one
reporter: Luke Rosiak.

When I first noticed Luke's stories, I thought they made
interesting assertions but were not a part of a particularly big
scandal. The facts seemed so improbable—more than forty
Democratic House members involved; the former chair of the
Democratic National Committee protecting the alleged crooks
less than a year after the DNC offices had been hacked under
her watch; the loss of hundreds of thousands of dollars in equipment and possibly millions in wages for no-show work; a former
McDonald's manager being paid by House Democrats as an IT
specialist; five Pakistanis led by Imran Awan who had question-
able business dealings in the U.S. and Pakistan; the list went on
and on.

At first, I shrugged off the stories as the exaggerations of an
ambitious reporter eager to make his name. After twenty years
in the House, the last four as the first Republican Speaker in forty
years, I concluded that I was curious but unconvinced. It all
seemed too bizarre, too complicated, and too far-fetched.

After all, I reasoned, if the scandal was that big, the major
media would be all over it, and the House Republicans would be
demanding investigations, holding hearings, and turning it into
a major liability for the Democrats in the 2016 (and 2018) elections. After all, a party that had almost one out of five of its

elected members connected to a scandal would be a party on defense.

Instead, there was amazing silence.

Luke would find another amazing piece of evidence and write another remarkable story, yet nothing would happen.

The liberal media, busy chasing every possible rumor about President Trump, apparently had no time or energy to report on a scandal involving Democratic congressional members.

What finally convinced me to take this scandal seriously was Luke's persistent hard work that produced a steady and consistent drumbeat of new, fact-based stories with reputable sources. I asked my team at Gingrich Productions to pull together all of Luke's articles and I shared them with former House members who had been part of the Majority when I was Speaker. One of them, Congressman Bob Livingston, was a former prosecutor who read the material and said, "Luke Rosiak has persevered successfully where traditional law enforcement dropped the ball. His conclusions are shocking."

Another House colleague of mine, Congressman Bob Walker commented, "The U.S. House of Representatives was disgraced by the use of Pakistanis to run internal IT networks and then by the failure to hold those who hired the Pakistanis responsible for jeopardizing our national security and misusing taxpayer money."

Then I went to Capitol Hill and met with a group of Republican House members who were deeply frustrated by their leadership and were convinced that a lot of bad things had happened—and that the fix was in to protect the Awan associates and the Democrats.

Congressman Louie Gohmert wrote to me, "Imran Awan seems to have been at the center of what was likely the biggest scandal in Congressional history. Yet, with the motto of House Republican elected leaders being, 'When there's no drama, we win,' they were not only blatantly wrong, but they did enormous damage to the country. Luke Rosiak did an amazing job while being stonewalled by House leadership, as misrepresentations were apparently being made within the FBI to the attorney general about this whole matter."

Every American who is concerned about corruption in Washington should read Luke's book on what is possibly the largest scandal and coverup in the history of the United States House of Representatives.

Here are the facts.

There was a familial syndicate of five Pakistanis offering IT services to one-fifth of the House Democratic Party.

Congresswoman Debbie Wasserman Schultz, the former Democratic National Committee Chair, protected, defended, and continued to employ IT leader Imran Awan even after he had been removed from the House network. In fact, she was so protective of the IT scandal that at one point, Congresswoman Wasserman Schultz, member of a committee in charge of the Capitol Police's budget, threatened the Capitol Police with "consequences" if they did not accede to her demands.

With more than forty House Democrats implicated in hiring or dealing with the Awan associates, they put such pressure on the House Republicans that the entire mess has, until now, been hushed up, covered up, and minimized.

Luke captures this entire disaster in two brutally honest paragraphs:

> This is not a partisan book. What it exposes is the "Uniparty"— a core of entrenched, establishment, career politicians and bureaucrats whose overriding goal is to preserve their power and the status quo.
>
> Establishment Republicans might be more embarrassed by this book than Democrats. The Democrats portrayed here are scheming, dishonest, and cutthroat; but at least they are good at it. They work with their allies in the media and the bureaucracy to accomplish their self-serving goals with Machiavellian precision. The Republicans, meanwhile, are apathetic, myopic, gullible, and cowardly.

Based on Luke's reporting, I knew that House members, staff, the Awan associates, and others needed to be held accountable. I waited until after the 2018 election—to avoid any taint of politics—and then wrote to U.S. House of Representatives Inspector General Mike Ptasienski.

In my letter, I noted that:

> As a former Speaker of the U.S. House of Representatives and a concerned private citizen, I am alarmed by the appearance of a cover-up of serious crimes committed by a former House employee and his associates, as well as, potentially, members of the House of Representatives themselves ...

To help reassure the American people that our nation's leaders stand for honesty, accountability, and transparency, this letter is a formal request to ask for the release of the two PowerPoint presentations given on September 20, 2016 and September 30, 2016 by your office to House leadership.

The presentations provide critical information pertaining to the possible invoice manipulation, equipment theft, illicit cyber activities, irregular cyber-related login and usage patterns, and outside storage of House data by Imran Awan and his associates.

The plea agreement for Mr. Awan, court appearances, and reported conversations with witnesses connected to the FBI's investigation of Awan and his associates' activities suggests that the FBI (while working with the United States Capitol Police) and the Department of Justice have avoided conducting a thorough and meticulous investigation.

For example, in the July 2018 plea agreement, the DOJ stated that approximately forty witnesses were interviewed throughout the duration of the investigation. Upon further examination, this number seems substantially inadequate for an investigation potentially involving so many individuals. While employed by the House for thirteen years as shared IT employees, the Awan associates worked for more than sixty members, and in 2015, 2016, and 2017, the Awan associates were on the payrolls of approximately forty members each year. When taking into account the members, the staff of each member, fellow House IT colleagues and peers, and additional business associates, the forty interviews that were conducted appear to be remarkably insufficient to support the argument that an investigation of this magnitude was conducted thoroughly.

In connection with the investigation, it has also been reported that key witnesses were only contacted days or hours before the plea agreement was signed. In another case, a witness was asked to be interviewed by the FBI but was prohibited from bringing any documents. Conducting investigative interviews in this manner suggests that the FBI investigators merely wanted to be able to say that they contacted witnesses and raises significant questions as to whether these interviews were actually conducted in good faith.

Aside from the alleged criminals themselves, this apparent collective effort of willful negligence sought to protect the involved members of Congress and their staffs—at the expense of the American people who they were entrusted to protect in the first place.

The sheer scale and size of the alleged criminal activity, the potential damage it could have caused, and the continual threats it potentially poses for the United States, raises significant questions that every American deserves to have answered.

In just one of the dozens of offices where one of the Awan associates were employed, almost $120,000 worth of equipment was written off of the House inventory, after he was unable to produce the equipment. An unofficial transcript of your office's PowerPoint presentation from September 20, 2016 asserts that the "shared employee stated that the items were never received, shouldn't have been inventoried, or the staff lost the equipment." The flaw in this claim is emphasized by the transcribed statement that follows: "However, equipment could not be on inventory or have [an] asset tag unless it had arrive[d] in office and EIN had been signed."

The member of the office in question is a member of the Committee on Ethics.

Additionally, more than $111,000 was paid by the House Democratic Caucus to one of the Awan associates throughout the duration of her employment. Members on the Committee of Foreign Affairs issued payments to associates totaling more than $950,000. Members of the Permanent Select Committee on Intelligence paid the associates over $530,000, while the Committee on the Judiciary paid more than $446,000. The Committee on Ethics paid more than $221,000, and the Committee on Homeland Security paid upwards of $175,000.

Close ties between Pakistan and the Awan associates were also identified, including large amounts of property that were owned but not properly disclosed in House documents. A $165,000 home equity line of credit loan received in January 2017 was wired in its entirety—almost immediately—to

two individuals in Faisalabad, Pakistan. Imran
Awan pleaded guilty this summer to obtaining this
exact loan illegally.

These allegations and the accompanying investigation have been kept under such secrecy that tℓ American people have been denied their fundamental right
to know what happened, who is responsible, and what
actions have been taken to ensure the fair and trans-
parent administration of justice.

The American people expect better than this. The
United States Congress should be better than this.

Releasing the requested documents is essential to
show that the U.S. government will require every member of Congress to answer to his or her constituents
and fellow citizens for his or her actions.

If you choose to deny this request, I will appeal to
the House membership to pass a resolution that will
make public the two documents, and all additional
documents that are related to the claims made against
Imran Awan and his associates, investigators and law
enforcement, and the House members and staffers
who may be involved.

Americans deserve truthful, complete answers to
the questions that have been raised surrounding these
extensive allegations.

I could never have written this letter outlining the scale of
this potential scandal without the years of hard work that Luke
Rosiak has put into this case.

His book is a must-read for everyone who wants to clean up corruption in Washington.

INTRODUCTION

The story you are about to read is like something out of a Hollywood movie, only it is all true. A family of Pakistani nationals gained access to all the files of one in five House Democrats. These IT aides—some of whom had dubious, at best, credentials, and had never been properly vetted—were caught funneling data off the House network, stealing the identity of an intelligence specialist, and sending electronic equipment to foreign officials. The manipulative mastermind of this operation had a penchant for extortion, and before he tried to flee to Pakistan with a suitcase of cash, he mysteriously left a congress-woman's laptop in a phone booth at midnight.

In the heat of the 2016 election's Russia fever, Democrats, Republican Speaker Paul Ryan, and the Department of Justice had a choice to make: protect national security or cover up a politically inconvenient scandal. They chose, of course, to cover up the scandal, and in the process, evidence disappeared, witnesses were threatened, and the press ignored the story.

Except, essentially, for me and my employer, the Daily Caller News Foundation. For two years, I doggedly investigated this story, and what I found convinced me that the so-called "Deep State" absolutely exists, because I saw it in action. In this book, I will show you how it works.

The most egregious actions in this scandal—documented in undeniable detail in this book—were taken by obscure bureaucrats who engaged in backstabbing, lies, and manipulation to ensure that justice was not done and the media was kept quiet. These actors have little to fear from civil service laws, and their near anonymity, not to mention their hold on a supposed watchdog press, shields them from scrutiny.

When President Trump said, "The Democrat IT scandal is a key to much of the corruption we see today," this is what he meant: this one momentous case reveals the Deep State in action to such a degree that it might as well be a blueprint for its insidious techniques. It is a case you may have never heard of, and if you have heard of it, most everything you heard was probably wrong, precisely because of the Deep State's efforts.

This is not a partisan book. What it exposes is the "Uniparty"— a core of entrenched, career politicians and bureaucrats whose overriding goal is to preserve their power and the status quo.

Establishment Republicans might be more embarrassed by this book than Democrats. The Democrats portrayed here are scheming, dishonest, and cutthroat; but at least they are good at it. They work with their allies in the media and the bureaucracy to accomplish their self-serving goals with Machiavellian precision. The Republicans, meanwhile, are apathetic, myopic, gullible, and cowardly.

When national security is jeopardized, as it was in this case, who can we trust? The sad answer, when it comes to Washington scandals, is no one. Not the Democrats, at least not when the fault lies with them; not the establishment Republicans who value their images and bipartisanship over truth; not the bureaucrats who profit from the status quo; and not the Department of Justice, the interests of which are not justice, but the same self-serving agenda of any other bureaucracy—to go along and get along with the permanent powers that be.

This book's heroes decided not to go along. They bucked the system, took their responsibilities seriously, and tried to act even if it put their livelihoods at risk. For their trouble, they were threatened, abused, harassed, mocked, ignored, shot at, given ultimatums, and run out of their jobs.

I hope this book will be, in some ways, their reward. It is the true story of the most successfully concealed of the 2016 election's many scandals. It is a story that the media missed. It is a story that congressional Democrats, Republican Speaker Paul Ryan, and the Justice Department do not want you to know. I know this story because I lived it. You will know it because you will read about it here fully, in the pages that follow, for the first time.

ONE

"ONLY GOD CAN HELP ME"

(FOURTH OF JULY, 2018)

Sumaira Siddique can never go home again.

Not to Pakistan, where she was a civil court judge and the daughter of a wealthy politician.

She is stranded in government housing in Virginia, at least as long as her green card is valid, in a country where no one loves her and whose government will not protect her.

It is the Fourth of July 2018, and I'm watching fireworks crackle like machine gun fire over the Capitol dome faintly visible on the Virginia skyline, talking and thinking about the events that began two years ago nearly to the day.

Sumaira tells me: "The funny thing is now I believe that even in America, law and order is also in politicians' pocket. Now the notorious criminals are getting fame. This is how I figured out that the system here is not very much different than the Pakistani system."

And the worst part is, she is right.

I'm just a regular guy. A thirtysomething investigative news reporter. With a baby daughter at home and another due any day, and my colleagues hitting the bars in Washington, D.C.'s Chinatown, never in my life would I have guessed that I'd spend America's birthday seeing it through the eyes of this outsider who was positioned to see things that many of us haven't. That I'd spend it with this woman who so truly believed in the American dream that she immigrated to this land of opportunity and rebuilt her life from nothing, going from riches to a homeless shelter to law school only to lose it all in a betrayal by the legal system to which she'd dedicated her career. America is everyone's last hope, but for the first time, she felt hopeless. Everyone had failed her. All was in Allah's hands now.

She is hiding from people in the United States, though it is Pakistan where she dares not go. The people she fears were until recently some of the highest-paid and most privileged staffers in Congress—and may soon be again.

One of them was her husband, Imran Awan, a computer systems administrator of unremarkable skill who wielded unexplained influence over a fifth of the Democrats in the House of Representatives. He had an air of upper-crust respectability to preserve here, and that, more than whatever semblance of the rule of law is still intact, is what would keep her safe.

But what he might do in Pakistan is a different story. For months at a time, Imran administered the United States Congress' computer servers from Pakistan while he received unexplained protection from armed Pakistani government agents. A well-connected and morally depraved person, as she believes Imran to be, could have her or her family put down with a snap of his fingers.

He told his wife all about how he used money he earned in Congress to pay police in Pakistan to torture his enemies—the same stories he bragged about to coworkers in a House cafeteria. "He actually gave money to a police officer and said, 'Rape the guy. How many times you will rape him? I will pay you,'" Sumaira told me. He was paying a corrupt cousin on the Faisalabad police force, Azhar Awan, but "the cousin is a low-level cop, it's higher up."

He was clever about it, sometimes making it seem to be an accident. She saw what happened after his stepmother called the police on him. "He would always say, 'Oh the stepmother, you will see what I will do to her brother. I will get someone to hit him with a motorbike. I will pay people to start a fight and teach a lesson.'" Now this retaliation would be directed at her.

Sumaira's social worker had promised her that Imran would be in jail by now. After all, the social worker had seen in the news how shortly before the 2016 election, House investigators discovered that Imran was using his position to make "unauthorized access" to House data. It was only a few weeks after the election when she rode with Sumaira up the narrow escalator at the Fairfax County Courthouse to renew a restraining order against Imran, only to be greeted in the lobby by a short woman with curly hair who said she was from the Federal Bureau of Investigation. This federal stakeout wasn't unprecedented to the social worker, who advised Sumaira that she had rights and didn't need to cooperate. The federal agent replied that this wasn't about a run-of-the-mill crime, it was a matter of national security. Sumaira already knew that, and she also knew—at least at the time, she was sure—that she wasn't the target. She wanted to talk.

The agent showed Sumaira pictures of congressmen and, more often, congresswomen: Representatives Yvette Clarke and Gregory Meeks of New York; Representative Jackie Speier, a Californian on the Intelligence Committee; and Florida Representative Debbie Wasserman Schultz, who had resigned a few months earlier as head of the Democratic National Committee. Had she heard Imran communicate with these people? Yes, often. Imran could be heard at all hours picking up the phone and saying, "Hey, Jackie!" As for Representative Wasserman Schulz, he even traveled to Florida to meet with her and boarded a horse in Lorton, Virginia that Representative Wasserman Schultz's daughter rode weekly. When it came to congressmen, she overheard one (as a non-native English speaker, she couldn't remember all the names) tell Imran that his mistress had his House iPad and it could end badly. Only Imran could fix this situation for him.

Fairfax County police reports show that Sumaira had called the cops on Imran three times since their 2015 marriage in Pakistan, but that only included instances when a report was filed; they had been to her apartment in Alexandria, Virginia, more often than that. The second time a report was filed, police found her bloodied after Imran tried to wrestle the phone from her. On another occasion, Imran told a police officer that he was a senior staffer for the United States Congress. Imran dialed a number and Sumaira heard a female voice on the other end. Imran told the cop a congresswoman was demanding to speak with him and handed him the phone. The local cop left without filing a report.

The last time she called police, two years ago on July 18, 2016, the officer recorded that Sumaira said Imran "keep her there like a slave." Sumaira wanted to get a restraining order, but rather than wait for that, she fled with her two children to her father's house in Pakistan. Shortly after her arrival, two gunmen rode up on motorbikes and shot through the windows of the home. She told me what she told the FBI: to her, it was attempted murder to prevent her from bringing added law enforcement scrutiny to what was already a brewing investigation in the House of Representatives.

As a former judge, she knew how these things worked, and she had evidence. A Pakistani police report filed by Sumaira's father on August 3, 2016 stated that "around 2 a.m., between August 1 and August 2, unknown gunmen shot multiple fires at my house and fled." According to an August 8 report in a local newspaper, a copy of which she also offered the FBI agent "a week after a Pakistani-American female lawyer's home in Pakistan was attacked by unknown gunmen, the police have still not taken action."[1]

The curly-haired FBI agent said she didn't want these documents, but she handed Sumaira a business card. When Sumaira got home, she hid the business card, but Imran found it and took it. "My life to him is an open store where everything is free," she told me. Later, he seemed to know everything she had told the FBI, reciting her statements almost word for word. Even if she still had the card, that was enough to keep her from opening her mouth again.

By the time the FBI approached Sumaira again two years later, Imran had had rigged her home with high-tech surveillance equipment and was blackmailing her with a hidden-camera sex tape; one he knew would cause her to be exiled from Pakistan's rigid society if he posted it on Facebook, as he threatened to do. "He said, 'If you ever try to leave me, the bullet will go into your ankle and then you will lose your leg and who else will accept you after that?' I said, 'You will ruin everyone attached to me?' And he said, 'If I have to.'"

Imran told her something else: that he was a "mole" in Congress.

Sumaira asked him what that meant and he clammed up. But later, he said he "knew too much" to have any chance of going to jail. "Sumaira, you think you can do anything to me? I fool the U.S. government. You're just a judge. I am invincible."

She told this to the FBI, knowing it was relevant evidence. Imran's job afforded him unrestricted access to all the emails and files of one in five House Democrats and their staffs; what House officials called the "keys to the kingdom." Given that he had been caught violating nearly every congressional cybersecurity rule and funneling data off the House computer network, and that the affected lawmakers were not doing anything about it, the prospect that he was extorting or blackmailing members of Congress loomed large.

Only yesterday, July 3, 2018, she had told FBI Special Agent Spencer Brooks that she wanted Imran charged for his threats and blackmail against her. Special Agent Brooks, however, was not on her doorstep to hear her complaints.

That same day, Imran pleaded guilty to one count of bank fraud in a plea bargain arrangement. He told the *Washington Post* that he was a victim of Islamophobia and President Donald

J. Trump had taken his career and his family from him. The *Post* reported that Imran "questions whether the case would have been pursued if he did not have a Pakistani name."

That morning, Imran's attorney, Chris Gowen, a former aide to Hillary Clinton, gave reporters an unusual letter from the Department of Justice which defended Imran against charges the department had never brought. The document stated that the "government has uncovered no evidence that your client violated federal law with respect to the House computer systems," dismissing—without explaining the obvious discrepancies—hard evidence gathered by nonpartisan House investigators.

There's an old expression: if you're going to shoot the king, you better not miss. Sumaira had enraged Imran by going to the FBI, but he would go unpunished, leaving her more in danger than ever. I had tried for months to protect Sumaira as best as I could after everyone else had ignored or abandoned her. I couldn't help but feel that I'd failed. When Special Agent Brooks showed up at her door yesterday and told the polite, burka-clad woman, incredibly, that he was there to make sure she didn't try to go to Imran's court date—something she had no desire to do—it was me who she called for advice. After the initial interview with the FBI and everything that had happened since— or more to the point, failed to happen—Sumaira was convinced she must not understand what types of things were relevant to the FBI. The agents hadn't cared when she offered a police report about a shooting that could have killed her children, so why would they care that Imran had surveilled, threatened, and blackmailed her, and described himself as a "mole" in Congress?

What did I think, as an American? They will care, I advised her. Tell them everything.

There is much to say now, but there isn't much that can be done. Tonight, now that it's all over, I suggest the only concrete step I can think of: put any documentation she has in a secure location, like a safe deposit box. If the last two years have taught me anything, it's that in this case, evidence has a way of disappearing.

She doesn't seem to follow. "I have shown all those documents to FBI," she responds.

I explain my thinking about preserving evidence and try to keep her spirits up about what happened yesterday.

"I think it was important that you told the FBI what you did, even though they didn't help, because now the FBI can't say they didn't know certain things." Now, this is about holding the Federal Bureau of Investigation and the Department of Justice to account for their demonstrably corrupt handling of a politically charged case.

But the truth is, I'm the one who isn't following. How would that help her any?

"The FBI knows. I guess they are on Democratic payroll. No one cares. Only God can help me," she says.

She continues to say that even a Pakistani lawyer who had been working to secure a divorce from Imran was now afraid to help her. "People are frightened… You just don't get it, in Pakistan you can just kill people like dogs. My whole family is back there. There is so much he can do. He knows how to cover his tracks."

If, after publication of this book, anything happens to Sumaira Siddique or her family members in Pakistan, you'll probably know who ordered the hit.

And so will the United States Department of Justice.

———

The crowds are out for the Fourth of July, teeming masses of humanity spread across the National Mall, but I can't help but feel as lonely as Sumaira.

The first time I spoke with her on the phone, I took the call from the lobby of my apartment building to avoid waking my baby. A pair of young Mormon missionaries dressed in neatly pressed white shirts were resting there beside their bicycles. I wondered what they must have thought as they overheard my end of the call: "So the congressmen are paying for this Hillary Clinton lawyer?... He said he was going to shoot your legs off?... What did he want you to do with the bars of gold?"

The events surrounding the case of Imran Awan were so surreal and so inadequately covered by the press over two years that one could be forgiven for dismissing them as impossible, which is exactly the reaction sought by the dozens of Democratic congressmen and women, congressional staff, and others who know the evidence but have publicly dismissed it all anyway. It was a "gaslighting" campaign massive enough to make a person second-guess everything he'd ever thought he'd known to be true. One so concerted that only skilled political operatives could pull it off.

The two-year odyssey, playing out against a backdrop of a media and political environment that claimed to care about cybersecurity in politics, pitted tribal loyalty against integrity and made for strange bedfellows. Democrats protected aides who had apparently victimized them; Republican House Speaker Paul Ryan and Attorney General Jeff Sessions sided with Democrat Nancy Pelosi and against Republican President Trump; Bernie Sanders-supporting liberals joined forces with Freedom Caucus conservatives to demand justice; and the Capitol Police force appeared to go to lengths to guard the reputation of a member of Congress who publicly threatened their own chief.

In the course of the unfolding scandal, congressional authorities documented a key piece of evidence going "missing;" congressional computers turned up in an elevator shaft and multiple Democratic staffers lost their jobs for whistleblowing on Imran.

The FBI had followed a hacking suspect to the airport, found $12,000 in undeclared cash in the suspect's suitcase, and filed papers saying it believed she was fleeing for good—but first it allowed her to board the flight to Pakistan. Prosecutors granted Imran a sweetheart plea bargain while he was soliciting others to buy bricks of gold and create straw companies. A white male lawyer mocked a burka-clad widow, while press releases implied that Sumaira and three other Muslim women who separately alleged that Imran was guilty of wiretapping, extortion, or death threats were Islamophobes. The press gladly ran with the storyline offered to them: this was all part of a diabolical plot by President Trump to get a Democratic family man.

In this topsy-turvy world, a major cybersecurity breach in Congress was ignored lest it distract from the alleged Russian hacking of the computers at the Democratic National Committee, and the well-documented crimes of Imran Awan were dismissed as a "conspiracy theory." One that would require believing that a vast array of people who didn't even know each other and who had neither the power nor the motive worked together over two decades and across two continents to frame Imran—itself a fantastical claim.

I'd met the forgotten men and women struggling to be heard—people like Sumaira and so many more like her, including rank-and-file Democratic staff in the House of Representatives who were ripped from their ordinary lives by extraordinary events of no choosing of their own. But mostly, I'd met powerful elites who would rather remain silent: Democrats and Republicans who knew what was going on but were too afraid to do anything about it, all of them hoping someone else would step up.

This scandal began with one astonishingly manipulative, cutthroat, and depraved family. But I soon realized that the cover-up was much bigger. That I'd followed a trail that risked implicating both political parties and their enablers in the justice system and the media. I saw firsthand that what's been called the "deep state" exists. It has one goal: to maintain the status quo that gives its members power and influence. Yes, this 242nd birthday party for the United States of America is well attended with an eclectic crowd. But as the fireworks sputter into a slow crackle, it is a lonely one indeed. And it is not only Sumaira's faith in American justice that is being tested; it is my own.

TWO

FRAUD ON CAPITOL HILL

(2014-2016)

Since 2014, Eddie Flaherty, a Democratic staffer for the Committee on House Administration, had tried to blow the whistle on IT aide Abid Awan for stealing cell phones. Stout, jocular, and graying, Eddie took seriously the committee's important if unglamorous work of "oversight of federal elections and the day-to-day operations of the House of Representatives." His desk was wedged in the few feet behind the office door of Jamie Fleet, the lead Democratic committee staffer and his boss, and was bounded on a third side by a closet. His alcove was barely bigger than a phone booth; so small that every time the door opened, it almost slapped him. As the entryway proceeded past the alcove and closet, the room opened to Jamie's plush, spacious office—the site of many high-powered meetings. The alcove was a degrading place for a middle-aged white-collar worker to do business, so comically cramped that only Eddie's short physical stature seemed to make it possible. It conjured images of a

Chihuahua sleeping at the foot of its owner's king-sized bed. Eddie labored just as many hours as Jamie and was twenty years older, yet made less money. But Eddie was fiercely loyal to Jamie and never complained, except about one thing. He constantly harped on the issue of Abid Awan's stolen cell phones even though no one seemed to care.

There was a Verizon kiosk in the Longworth House Office Building, and, as at many Verizon stores, if you signed up for a new phone plan, you could get a new phone. But because of the way the House subsidized phone lines, this one worked a little differently. The plan could be cancelled soon after it was set up. Abid appeared to have figured out how to exploit the loophole to get dozens of new iPhones, which Eddie assumed he was reselling. But the clerk at the Verizon kiosk wouldn't disclose statistics and claimed he couldn't tell whether a phone tied to a given contract was actually activated and operating on that line. It was hard to get angry at the low-level Verizon worker because the truth is the safeguards set up by Eddie's own committee were just as unhelpful. It turned out that the House Committee on Administration itself didn't track cell phones by serial number. No matter how damning the circumstantial evidence, technically, "I couldn't prove it," Eddie told me.

————

In late 2015, the outlines of a more substantial scheme emerged thanks to the efforts of one brave woman.

Wendy Anderson is a forty-one-year-old African American with an easy ability to strike an outward balance that made some women on Capitol Hill envious. She wore understated but elegant jewelry tucked under power suits that seemed to leave no doubt that she was aware of the import of the position she had.

She'd bounced around Florida and Brooklyn before landing her post as deputy chief of staff to Representative Yvette Clarke, a Brooklyn congresswoman, and, having run into some money problems that led to tax liens being placed against her in New York State in 2009 and 2010 as well as an eviction, understood the plight of the impoverished constituents in Clarke's district. But she also understood that being in this high position, in the seat of power where laws were made, meant that laws must be followed. She agreed wholeheartedly with Representative Clarke—who got her start in politics by inheriting her mother's seat on New York's City Council—that the government needed to spend more on the social welfare of struggling people like those in Brooklyn. She knew that with that commitment to greater resources for the needy, those like her and other top managers in Clarke's office—with their $160,000 salaries—had all the more duty to ensure that every penny of taxpayer money went as far as possible. Like in other congressional offices, an annual budget of $1.2 million had to make do for representing 600,000 citizens. Considering it had to fund D.C. and district offices, travel, expenses, and fifteen staffers to get the job done, that sum wasn't as much as it sounds like. In fact, it wasn't nearly enough. The best Wendy could do was pledge that Representative Clarke's little section of the House was a well-oiled machine. The people of Brooklyn needed it and deserved it.

It was this kind of work ethic that had her in the office on a Saturday in the waning days of 2015 to put in hours without distraction. Representative Clarke was back in Brooklyn for the weekend as usual, but Wendy noticed the door to the congresswoman's office was ajar. When she swung it open, her first thought was that it looked like Christmas. There was an incredible assortment of boxes of new merchandise strewn everywhere. Much of was the kind of thing you'd see at home, not the office: Apple TVs, iPod music players, and other consumer electronics. Alone by the congresswoman's desk was Abid Awan.

His presence in the inner sanctum was inappropriate to say the least. Abid handled routine IT matters like setting up a new staffer's email account or resetting a password for a handful of congressional offices, each on a part-time basis. He was technically a direct employee of Representative Clarke's staff, a W-2 employee in IRS parlance, but he wasn't really part of the team. With just over a dozen staffers, all from policy backgrounds, there was little necessity for an IT guy to be embedded in the culture, nor too involved. Certainly, there didn't seem to be any reason he should have keys to the office locks. And in an environment where you paid your dues and acknowledged your place in the pecking order, there was even less reason he should feel comfortable letting himself into the congresswoman's office like he owned the place.

That was to say nothing of the boxes, which were far more numerous than her office could ever need. The Capitol Hill work environment is pretty ascetic once you got past the high ceilings and ornate molding. There was no such thing as perks like these in any congressional office she'd seen, and she'd never heard of any office in the world that would need an iPod.

She asked Abid what was going on.

"These aren't your items," he said. "They belong to another office."

She had never had a good feeling about Abid. This equipment certainly smelled like stolen goods.

"Whatever they are, get them out of here," Wendy hissed.

A few weeks later, Clarke's chief of staff, Shelley Davis, quietly departed the office's employ. Before he was hired by Clarke, Shelley, a skinny black man with a shaved head, had worked as the travelling assistant for the Reverend Jesse Jackson Sr. (his replacement filed a lawsuit alleging that part of that job was discretely arranging the reverend's rendezvous with mistresses[1]), and for Congresswoman Sheila Jackson Lee of Texas, who was known for such abusive tirades that half of her staff quit or was fired each year.[2] Though he was paid well, he had money problems, and had once even been evicted from his residence in D.C. He was Congresswoman Clarke's closest and most trusted confidant, and now he was leaving with no new employer listed on his LinkedIn page. When I called him and asked about the circumstances of his departure, he declined to answer and blocked my number.

Wendy Anderson was promoted to chief of staff. One of her primary duties was managing the office's money. She found that the office had long been paying for huge amounts of extraneous electronics, and when she looked around, she didn't see them. Yet, the payments had been authorized by Shelley.

She knew from her chief of staff training that under House rules, members of Congress were personally financially liable when their offices went over budget or if money couldn't be accounted for. She'd been working toward this job for years, and now it was her ass on the line—hers and Representative Clarke's. To ensure her smooth transition to chief of staff, she had access to an archive of Shelley's emails. She searched them for Abid's name and what she found troubled her. Shelley and the part-time IT guy seemed far closer than there was any reason they should be. The emails seemed to show Abid ordering items for Shelley with no business reason. In February 2016, Wendy ordered an audit of the office's equipment, matching it with the official inventory record. The audit found that $118,416 worth of equipment was missing. That was one-tenth of the office's annual budget, or enough for two hundred iPads or 120 laptop computers—ten to twenty for each staffer.

She took these findings to Representative Clarke. The congresswoman was oddly defensive, not only of Shelley, but also of Abid. She seemed to simply want the problem to go away.

Wendy called the hotline of the chief administrative officer, who kept track of the House's assets. When a small item went missing or a laptop was accidentally broken, they could be "written off" of the inventory, but a six-figure write-off was unheard of. Nevertheless, Wendy received permission to simply remove the massive trove of equipment from the House's records as if it had never existed.

Still, as Wendy pressed Representative Clarke about the importance of the issue, something about the congresswoman's response didn't feel right. Representative Clarke was a member of the House Committee on Ethics, the very body charged with levying sanctions against wrongdoers in the House. Didn't she understand how this looked? The Shelley problem had been taken care of, even if there were no real consequences for him. But with

Representative Clarke refusing to fire Abid despite one of the most dramatic and inexcusable events that could be associated with someone from whom the office asked so little, what's to say something wouldn't go wrong again? A chief of staff normally has wide latitude over hiring and firing. But Congresswoman Clarke refused to let Wendy fire Abid. So, she printed out the suspicious emails between Shelley and Abid and took them to the House's Office of Inspector General, which polices waste, fraud, and abuse inside the chamber.

Months passed and there was no mention in the media or the House Ethics Committee about major theft in the congresswoman's office. Then Wendy got a call from Jamie Fleet, the top Democratic staffer who ran the Committee on House Administration, alerting her that officials would be reviewing financial activity connected to Abid Awan and other Awan family members in each of the congressional offices that employed them. Wendy thought Representative Clarke now had no choice but to fire Abid. It would look bad enough that she had waited so long. She was stunned, however, that Clarke remained adamant that she would not fire Abid, a part-time worker whose job could have been done by nearly anyone. In some offices, the IT duties are performed by a legislative assistant who sets aside a few hours a week.

Clarke did begin cooperating with investigators. She and Wendy began meeting with them to go over everything that had happened. The investigators would fill them in on the latest progress in the investigation. But Wendy soon came to believe that someone was "backdooring" this information to Abid. District Director Anita Taylor, the head of Clarke's New York office, seemed to know everything the investigators had said. The information could only have come from Clarke. Wendy told investigators that Taylor seemed to be funneling it straight to Abid.

Wendy confronted Abid and asked him to explain the $120,000 worth of missing inventory. First, Abid said the equipment was never received, which was a blatant lie because items were listed on the inventory only *after* they were received and a bar code was affixed to them.

He conceded that items were received, but argued that they shouldn't have been added to the inventory, which exempts items costing less than $500. This was a bizarre quibble. One that seemed to assume that Wendy would be okay with equipment going missing as long as she could fend off investigators by invoking a technicality. Its premise was also incorrect; the purchases at issue were large.

Finally, he blamed Clarke's staff, saying they had "lost" the equipment. A lawyer representing one of the Awans later singled out Shelley and said, "I think there was potentially some issues there." Abid also said some equipment had been inexplicably discarded. A new 65-inch TV, he claimed by way of example, had been thrown away because there wasn't enough space for it.

Finally, Clarke relented and agreed to fire Abid.

But a fear brewed in the office. In any small company, the hostile firing of the sole IT administrator leaves the company vulnerable. The IT worker may be the only person who knows the ins and outs of the office's particular computer setup, giving him inordinate leverage. A vengeful IT aide could sabotage the system on his way out, or simply decline to facilitate a transition.

Here, it was worse as it turned out that Abid had the passwords not only to Clarke's House accounts, but to all of her personal logins for things like banking, credit cards, and personal email. Why, no one seemed to know. Was it because Clarke was so tech-illiterate that she had enlisted him as an unpaid personal assistant, helping her navigate the web for basic tasks? Or something even stranger?

Wendy believed, and House officials concurred, that Abid might retaliate if he were fired, inflicting untold damage onto the congresswoman's personal life or simply rendering all of the office's computers inoperable. A careful operation was planned. Just before the firing was set, a House information security specialist sat down with Representative Clarke, reset all of her personal passwords, and locked Abid out of Representative Clarke's House computers. Abid was fired on September 19, 2016, and Wendy was shaken by the ordeal. She returned to the office late that night to pick something up and the door to the congresswoman's inner office was open a crack. She sensed that Abid might be behind it and ran out of the office, frightened. It was just a gut thing and there is no indication that he was, but Wendy was not feeling quite at home in Representative Clarke's office anymore.

That feeling was cemented later that week when Representative Clarke told Wendy she was having second thoughts and wanted to undo the firing.

She never did it, but just a couple months after Abid was fired, Wendy's brief ride at the helm of Clarke's office was over too. She took a job as chief of staff to Val Demings, a newly-elected congresswoman from Florida, in many ways a step down because the freshman member lacked the seniority and committee assignments of Representative Clarke, who had been, ironically, the top Democrat on the Homeland Security Subcommittee on Emerging Threats, Cybersecurity, Science, and Technology. When I ran this whole saga by Clarke's spokeswoman, she wouldn't tell me whether Wendy would have had the option of staying on. But she only denied one element: Anita Taylor's alleged involvement.

———

Remarkably enough, the impetus for Jamie Fleet's call to the Democratic chiefs of staff didn't seem to have anything to do with Representative Clarke's office. Around the same time that Wendy became concerned about equipment that was on the inventory but missing, staffers for the chief administrative officer (CAO) had discovered a different fraud scheme designed to keep equipment from showing up on the inventory in the first place. They found that in some of these offices—all of which employed Abid or one of his relatives—everything seemed to cost exactly $499.99. Not coincidentally, any item that cost more than $500 was assigned a CAO bar code. Periodically, CAO employees inspected the offices, scanned the bar codes, and ensured everything was still there. A depreciation schedule was incorporated that allowed old electronic items to rotate off the list. Anything less than $500, on the other hand, was deemed not worth tracking and essentially treated as petty cash.

The Awans had invented clever ways of making it appear that expensive items cost $499. For example, an iPad costs $799, and it is common to spring for an $88 Apple Care warranty. The Awans billed the iPad at $499 and then added $300 to the cost of the warranty. The vendor got his full price and the Awans did not have to add the items to the official inventory. Dozens of invoices using similar creative math, and totaling tens of thousands of dollars, had recently been submitted. In March 2016, the CAO brought this information to the Committee on House Administration, and in April, the committee referred the findings to the inspector general.

One wrinkle in the scheme is that the Awans weren't generating the invoices. The goods were purchased from two major companies, CDW-G and More Direct, which had to rig the numbers. Ted Rambo was the salesman listed on the CDW-G invoices. When Rambo was brought in for questioning, he was scared. He brought a CDW-G executive with him. Rambo said Imran Awan essentially told him if he wanted to continue doing business anywhere in the House—a massive account—he'd need to play ball. They were the customer, after all. One thing eventually caused investigators to inform CDW-G that it was not a target of the investigation, despite the troubling truth that the company had knowingly and systematically falsified government financial records. Rambo convinced them that he, too, was a victim of the Awans.

While keeping prices under $500 kept items off the chief administrative officer's House-wide inventory, it didn't hide them from the congressman or his chief of staff who still had to pay the vendor. In some cases, as with Shelley, getting the chief of staff to sign off wasn't a problem. But in other cases, the Awans relied on a third scheme. They charged hundreds of thousands of dollars of equipment to congressional offices, sometimes delivered straight to their homes, but never took the invoices to chiefs of staff. They simply let congressmen accumulate debts that became delinquent. Five offices had unpaid invoices more than five hundred days old.

Clearly, the purpose of these schemes seemed to be to facilitate the disappearance of equipment. Investigators made the rounds to the affected offices to look for the items, and sure enough, they could not be located. A December 6, 2016 memo by the Department of Justice said that "some of the equipment either disappeared or never made it to the member's office for whom the equipment was purchased."[3] The Congress members couldn't tell investigators where the equipment on the invoices was because they didn't have it. The Awans claimed ignorance as well until after weeks of excuses, they finally led investigators to an abandoned elevator shaft in the basement of the Longworth House Office Building, now walled off and turned into a closet. Inside was a massive stockpile of equipment, vaguely matching what was missing.

The investigators concluded that the Awans had retroactively purchased similar equipment and placed it there to throw off investigators after learning they were onto them. With House budgets as lean as they were and technology improving and becoming cheaper, there was simply no reason to purchase electronics in such large quantities and let them sit, especially in such an odd place. If it was there all along, why hadn't they just said so?

Democrats convinced investigators that unless they had exact serial numbers for all the missing equipment and were prepared to match it up with the elevator cache, they couldn't prove that this was evidence tampering. It was a catch-22; the paperwork fraud ensured that equipment never went through the process by which serial numbers were recorded, but the Republicans involved in oversight of the case threw up their hands, conceding that perhaps this evidence wouldn't hold up against aggressive lawyers in a court of law.

So that's how, after tips from two Democratic aides, an investigation into procurement fraud and theft wound up in the hands of the Democrat-appointed inspector general, Theresa Grafenstine. It was clear that the Awans were versatile fraudsters and Theresa knew that people willing to break rules don't typically confine their predatory behavior to one area. One major aspect of the Awans' work had thus far not been examined at all: the Awan family had access to more congressional data than almost anyone on Capitol Hill. Once her investigators looked at the server logs documenting the Awans' network activity, the theft scheme hardly seemed to matter.

THREE

THE ELECTION SEASON HACK YOU NEVER HEARD ABOUT

(CAPITOL HILL, 2016)

As I sit here speaking with Sumaira on this humid Fourth of July night, I can't help but think about the disquieting cast of characters surrounding the case of House of Representatives systems administrator Imran Awan, and how it seems the only people in Washington who have balls anymore are women. Like Wendy Anderson, none of them craved the public eye. Yet, of these two male-dominated worlds that had somehow collided for me—the U.S. Congress and Pakistani-American culture—it seemed that only a handful of people were able to put their egos aside and do the right thing, even if it meant being in uncomfortable situations. And almost all of those were of the supposedly gentler sex.

Among them was Theresa Grafenstine, a spunky woman with kind eyes and the impossible job of policing corruption in Congress as the House's inspector general, a position that made her one of only eight official "officers of the House." Most people, even House staffers and reporters, had no idea the House Office of Inspector General even existed. That was by design. Unlike inspector generals at federal agencies, her bosses in Congressional leadership mandated that every one of her reports be secret, keeping any wrongdoing she discovered from the public and even from those in Congress. Since 2010, when then-House Speaker Nancy Pelosi appointed her, Theresa had led a team that toiled in near obscurity.[1]

By training, Theresa was an auditor, studying financial irregularities and following millions of dollars. She rapidly rose to the top of her profession by having a talent few number geeks seemed to have: people skills. She was the rare extrovert in a male-dominated field of auditors who, even if they had the mathematical prowess of Albert Einstein, tended to be bookish and a little socially awkward. Given that they were making determinations that could amount to accusing high-profile Republicans of waste, or do-gooder Democrats of fraud, it was these men who hit a glass ceiling. They couldn't survive a day at the higher levels of management, which required navigating an environment as daunting as the House of Representatives, with its backstabbing and competing factions.

Theresa's people skills came in handy, or perhaps were developed through her other capability. She was also a hard-nosed investigator who could read a suspect's face and determine if he was lying, and could set traps with lines of questioning but also knew it was sometimes better to sit in an interview room in silence, letting the awkwardness build until the suspect started spewing forth in a nervous free association.

She made this rare combination a trifecta with expertise in a subspecialty of the investigative field: computer skills. These days, a crime, deception, or theft was as likely to involve an IP address as a fingerprint. If the Watergate break-in were to occur in the modern era, the investigator who caught it would be one who could recognize an SSH key that was out of place, not a flashlight. The problem was that, at least in the government, most gumshoes came from cop-like backgrounds, many of whom had spent decades knocking on doors and ruffling through papers. They lacked digital literacy.

Theresa was an essential weapon for an institution under such constant cyberattack as the House of Representatives. In Washington, everybody is somebody, and Theresa's qualifications as an undisputed queen in the field of cyber sleuthing were almost comically sterling. On the side, she led the worldwide council of cybersecurity professionals.[2]

That made it all the more alarming when, in summer 2016, Theresa and her team of investigators realized that something was seriously amiss on the House computer network.

———

Somehow, a man named Imran Awan, his younger brothers Abid and Jamal, his friend Rao Abbas, and his wife Hina Alvi (Imran was a polygamist married to both Hina and Sumaira) were all on the congressional payroll as computer systems administrators. Each worked part-time for around eight members of Congress, forty-four in total. Their job was to configure servers, set up email accounts, and purchase phones and desktops for the offices.

The problem is they were also logging onto the servers of other members of Congress who they didn't work for. They were logging in using members of Congress' personal usernames. They were funneling massive amounts of data off the network. They were accessing the House Democratic Caucus server with a bizarre frequency—five thousand times within a few months. And they used elaborate digital techniques to conceal what they were doing.

Representative Michelle Lujan Grisham of New Mexico had terminated Abid in 2015, before these other problems became known, but he kept logging into her servers after he was fired. In early 2015, Representative Kyrsten Sinema of Arizona had fired the youngest of the three Awan brothers, Jamal, for "incompetence." He was a well-paid incompetent, joining the congressional payroll at $165,000 when he was only twenty years old and still employed by many of her colleagues. And why had the Awans' elderly father Muhammad, a religious cleric who spent much of his time in Pakistan and had not a lick of IT skills, been briefly on the congressional payroll as the systems administrator for then-Congressman, now-Senator, Joe Donnelly of Indiana?

It was July 25, 2016, three days after WikiLeaks threw a bomb into the presidential race and permanently brought politics' dirty tricks into the modern age by publishing the first of the DNC's emails, when Theresa brought the first results of her months-long cybersecurity probe to the body that oversaw her work, the Committee on House Administration. The timing of the discovery of the server logs documenting their behavior made the seriousness of it all impossible to miss. WikiLeaks was publishing the DNC's emails on a weekly schedule, reminding politicians that cybersecurity breaches were a real and omnipresent threat. The threat of malicious actors inside the highest levels of the government itself should have made the infiltration of the DNC, a private fundraising group, pale in comparison assuming Democrats valued data from their country's government above that of their party.

Republican Congresswoman Candice Miller of Michigan chaired the committee, but in practice, congressional staff runs much of Congress, especially sleepy minor committees like this one. Theresa reported her findings to the committee's Republican staff director, Sean Moran.

Sean is a mild-mannered veteran congressional staffer with a short, slight frame and one of the rare gray-haired heads in a complex dominated by youngsters. He found the specifics hard to follow. After all, he only had two apps on his iPhone and it took his wife to install them. When he echoed his understanding of the findings to people later, it showed, saying "terabits" where he meant "terabytes," and saying the Awans used "codes" rather than "scripts." But the significance wasn't lost on him. It was obvious that the committee needed to bring this to the top—Speaker Paul Ryan and Minority Leader Nancy Pelosi—and fast.

Speaker Ryan's office told Theresa to continue her investigation, but there was a complication. While many IT aides worked for members of both parties, the Awans worked exclusively for Democrats, so the investigation had to be done in a way acceptable to Democrats. A meeting was set up in the office of Kelly Craven, Ryan's chief for internal affairs, about how to get to the bottom of it. The answer was very slowly or not at all. Craven heard viewpoints offered on one side by Nancy Pelosi's counsel, Bernie Raimo, and on the other, Mark Epley.

Raimo said, "These are our employees. You can't look at any files or interview them without getting permission from their bosses first."

Theresa protested, "That's forty-four members!"

"Oh, and you can't ask any members because that will disclose the case," Raimo added.

When Theresa complained that it was impossible to conduct an investigation under those restrictions, Raimo yelled, "You're not the policeman of the world!"

That meant Theresa was tasked with doing a cybersecurity investigation in which she was banned from talking to the suspects or their employers and had to watch data fly off the network without knowing what it was. Theresa considered where that left her. The Awans' fraudulent billing of congressional offices for computers and other equipment wasn't as critical as the cybersecurity breaches, but the falsified receipts contained easily provable lies. Those lies might enable police to put the Awans behind bars before they dismantled more evidence and did more harm. She just needed to learn how the falsified receipts were generated. She could at least search the Awans' government email accounts, right?

Raimo said no. The initial complaints named only Abid, so including the other family members would amount to a "fishing expedition." On top of that, Raimo cited the "speech and debate clause" of the Constitution. That clause states that members of Congress "shall in all Cases, except Treason, Felony and Breach of the Peace, be privileged from Arrest during their attendance at the Session of their Respective Houses, and in going to and from the same; and for any Speech or Debate in either House, they shall not be questioned in any other Place." The clause is part of the Constitution's separation of powers and is intended to protect members of Congress from the executive branch. Raimo argued that it extended to IT support staff like the Awans, and implied that it protected them from Theresa's investigation even though she was part of the legislative branch.

Theresa offered a concession: have a third party use a computer command to pull only those emails sent to or about the federal contractor CDW-G. Authorities could then learn whether the Awans were running a fraud scheme, CDW-G was responsible, or the Awans had a man inside CDW-G. Whatever they found would be significant because CDW-G was a multi-billion dollar company that did business throughout the federal government. This was classic government accountability work.

Even that was too much for Pelosi's man. Craven looked at Ryan's general counsel, Mark Epley, a former aide to the Deputy Attorney General at the Department of Justice, to settle the dispute. He wasn't making much of an effort to push back. Internal matters were different than the hard-fought legislative battles that played out along party lines each day on the campus. Such issues inside the House were more personal and routinely defined by bipartisan agreement, with a lack of consensus defaulting to inaction. Epley offered a meager, but classically bureaucratic, compromise: the House would preserve the Awans' emails, but for now, no one would look at them. When the meeting adjourned, no such bargain was reached for accessing data that held the key to what by all appearances were major cybersecurity violations.

Paul Ryan wasn't just the head of House Republicans, he was the leader of an institution with hundreds of years of precedent and a reputation to preserve. The Democrats were in the minority, but they were far more invested in shaping this case than the Republicans, who didn't seem to know much about it.

For all Craven, Epley, and Raimo knew, the Awans might have been working for a foreign intelligence service, selling sensitive information to the highest bidder, or dealing in extortion or blackmail. Neither party in Congress seemed interested in finding out, at least not before the 2016 elections. Politics took precedence.

FOUR

THE PUPPETEER

(CAPITOL HILL, 2016)

The staff director of the Committee on House Administration's job involves coordinating and brokering between various congressional offices, but it takes Sean Moran ten times longer to walk down the lengthy Capitol corridors than anyone else. It's not because of his seasoned nature, having worked in Congress for as long as a large fraction of staffers have been alive; physically and mentally, he is spry. Rather, it's because he knows and loves everyone. He can't get from point A to point B without hugging every janitor, lunch lady, and Democratic and Republican assistant approaching from the opposite direction. Sean is a reliable and knowledgeable congressional aide, and this easygoing nature has helped him do his job. But if he has one downfall, it may be his trusting kindness.

You don't last as long as he has on Capitol Hill without the constant friction of opposing parties doing one of two things: leaving you jagged and broken or sanding off all your edges. By now, Sean was smooth as silk. But you also didn't survive so many battles in the trenches without contracting a characteristic world-weariness. For that matter, you didn't make it to his age, making peace with a divorce and life's other various curveballs and inadequacies, without a certain amount of resignation.

In a job like this, you had to go along to get along. If he was the kind of guy who drew a red line on every issue and refused to budge, he'd probably still be stuck somewhere in the 1990s. Hell, by his age, it seemed like a detached compromising was the only way to keep moving forward. Maybe that's what maturity is.

All of this left Sean's sprite frame saddled with layers: a spark in his eye behind spectacles. The clean-cut, rule-following look of a military man, where somewhere along the line his buzz cut had begun giving way to baldness. Alert posture, propping up the rumpled dress of a bean-counting bureaucrat counting down his days to retirement.

The top guns at the inner-circle meeting remanded the issue to Sean Moran and Jamie Fleet, his Democratic counterpart on the Administration Committee, for executing their orders. But Sean was so troubled by the scandal that the sparkle in his eye had him considering doing something he'd never done before: going public. "I'm really afraid that they might be Pakistani ISI," he said. "No investigation has been done to show that they aren't...We need to shout this from the rooftops."

The problem was, while the notion that Congress gets nothing done is a cliché, at no time is that more true than in August. The House's month-long summer recess is a humid, languid time, when the bigwigs are home glad-handing in their district, staffers trade suits for more casual attire, and all of Capitol Hill transforms into one big national park where tourists gawk and staffers bring their dogs to work. Sean would do nothing without the approval of his boss, Representative Miller, and she was checked out more than most. She was retiring from Congress and already had her sights set on her next gig, one that spoke volumes about what she thought of Congress: she was leaving to oversee the drains in Macomb, Michigan, as county water commissioner.

In the end, neither party's leadership would dare publicly take the position they were taking behind closed doors: that the existence of unknown data improperly flying off the House network wasn't worth looking at. But before Sean could ask Representative Miller for permission to bring the facts to the public eye—triggering attention that he knew would force the House to examine what had happened with more urgency and intensity—he took a long trip to Latin America, where his wife lives. When he got back, he caught up with Jamie and felt him out on the idea.

Jamie, like many Democrats, understood the way the media works far better than Republicans, so feeling this out would be informative. He might even agree with Sean. After all, Jamie had volunteered repeatedly that the cybersecurity findings kept him up at night.

Sure enough, Jamie responded that the idea had already occurred to him. He found it so necessary that he'd even met with Theresa about it while Sean was gone. The problem, he said, was that Theresa had been stern that it simply must not be done. There were highly sensitive, intensive operations taking place and unless the pair wanted to be responsible for ruining the whole case, they needed to stay quiet, as difficult as that would be. This absolved him of an anxiety-ridden decision. But more importantly, the good news was that this meant somewhere, someone was treating the whole mess as the matter of national security it clearly was. Sean was a loyal soldier and he had faith in the nation's institutions.

But while Sean was jetting overseas and biding his time until retirement, Jamie was busily shaping the case behind the scenes. The moves had already been under way for some time, and now, one of the most critical pieces had been secured. There was no ban from Theresa on talking about the case nor any conversation about high-level, thorough investigations too top secret to reveal. Jamie had made it up out of whole cloth.

————

The tall, blond Jamie Fleet is nearly two decades younger than Sean, but was arguably more accomplished on Capitol Hill.

He was a political prodigy who landed a spot on the Gettysburg Borough Council at the age of eighteen. He wasn't even on the ballot; he won on a write-in campaign as a Gettysburg College freshman after convincing his fellow students that they deserved representation on the town council.[1]

The teenage councilman soon started his own political consultancy group and made inroads into Philadelphia politics. He hitched his wagon to Representative Bob Brady. When Brady, an Italian-American machine politics operator who has clung to the chairmanship of the Philadelphia Democratic Party since 1986, wanted to move from Congress to the Philadelphia mayor's office, he enlisted Jamie to work his magic. That mayoral bid was unsuccessful, but in 2007, just five years out of college, Jamie was at Brady's side in Congress, and Brady as then-chairman of the Committee on House Administration, chose Jamie to run it. That position put Jamie on the platform with Barack Obama at the forty-fourth president's inauguration, it had him tossing a football with Obama in the Rose Garden, and it placed him on the House floor for the passage of Obamacare.

If Sean was well-known and well-liked throughout the Capitol corridors, Jamie's light shined brighter, even though he was now in the minority party. "He's probably the most recognized person here, and that includes the Speaker of the House," Representative Brady said. Jamie worked so hard that, for years, he often slept in his office—something not uncommon among congressmen, but virtually unheard of for a committee staffer.[2] There was a reason Jamie was as recognizable to insiders as then-Speaker Nancy Pelosi herself: he'd become a top operator for her. Talking to him was a stand-in for speaking with Pelosi. Jamie spent so much time in the foyers of the House Democratic leadership that he wound up marrying an aide to House Democratic Whip Steny Hoyer.[3] Jamie excelled in exerting pressure in ways that accomplished the Democratic leadership's goals without leaving their fingerprints.

This required a rare personality. Good-looking, Jamie came across as gregarious, light-hearted, and an honest broker, while in fact he was restrained, calculated, and rarely gave a political inch. He'd let on that he harbored ambitions to run for Congress himself and was confident he could win, even in Representative Brady's overwhelmingly black district.

When I first came across Jamie, someone called him "the biggest puppet master who ever walked the Earth," pulling on invisible strings and manipulating people and events.

Chief Information Security Officer John Ramsey was summoned to the offices of the Appropriations Committee Subcommittee on the Legislative Branch, where the counsels for Speaker Ryan and Minority Leader Pelosi, a Capitol Police lawyer, and others, were waiting. It was the kind of high-level meeting at which busy people want concise summaries, and Ramsey was asked a simple but carefully crafted question about the Awan scandal: "Were we hacked?"

The Harvard-educated and somewhat nerdy Ramsey had been asked this before, and those who'd heard him knew his answer always came down to the arcana of technical terms. He'd explain that the academic definition of hacking required two things: breaking in and then escalation, a term that meant moving from one user account with minimal privileges to a higher-level one. The Awans were House employees and had access to the servers, so there was no break in, and as IT administrators they already had super-user accounts, so there was no "escalation." Then he'd go on, in his bumbling manner, explaining that this was more accurately described as an "insider threat" every bit as severe.

He was a behind-the-scenes kind of guy and these kinds of meetings with political powerhouses made him nervous. He told the attendees, "No, this isn't hacking." Though he had more to say, someone else interjected. That seemed to be all they needed to know, and the meeting was quickly adjourned. Ramsey quit his job not long after in August 2017, leaving the House with no chief information security officer at all. What lingered was the misleading impression left by this truncated version of a pedantic answer.

It was one a savvy operator could elicit from Ramsey as if by pulling a string.

In early October 2016, Theresa updated the Paul Ryan-Nancy Pelosi crowd with a briefing which had no purpose other than to shout: "Everything I told you about is still going on! They're still on the network! It's only gotten worse!" Under a header one word longer than the last briefing—"CONTINUED UNAUTHORIZED ACCESS"—Theresa told the leaders that "during September 2016, shared employees continued to use Democratic Caucus computers in anomalous ways," logging in using seventeen different accounts that they had no business using, including "credentials [that] belonged to members." There was no doubt that rules were being broken.

Worse, there was "possible storage of sensitive House information outside the House." Files were being copied to Dropbox, which uploaded them to cloud servers and synced them with external devices. Dropbox was not permitted in the House, so this was a secret account and out of authorities' control. It is a "classic method for insiders to exfiltrate data from an organization," the presentation said. Not only did files appear to be aggregated from various congressmen's computers onto the House Democratic Caucus servers, files were jumping from that server onto the internet. Theresa and her investigators could see the lists of folders and files. "Based on the file names"—one of which was "credentials"—"some of the information is likely sensitive."

Without looking at the files themselves, no one could know exactly how severe the breach was. "We have not been permitted to view content of the files on these workstations," Theresa reminded the House leadership.

Theresa was not a political person. She had been appointed by Nancy Pelosi and retained by Speaker Ryan. She was there because every training session, textbook, and professional development course underscored that the actions she discovered were against every tenet of basic cybersecurity practice, and hallmarks of exactly the type of nefarious behavior she was sworn to sniff out. She was there to do her job, and her job involved protecting the United States of America.

But for members of Congress, politics was always at the forefront. Democrats wanted to protect the United States of America too, and to them, that meant protecting it against what they felt was the inexperienced and rash personality of Trump, who they couldn't imagine having possession of the nuclear "football." This obviously concerning breach wasn't happening in isolation. The very words "emails" and "servers," when combined with the word "Democrat" were radioactive. Even though Democrats appeared to be the victims of these IT aides, the disclosure of this scandal would be an embarrassment for the Democratic Party.

For months, some of the most tenacious and barbed press coverage of Hillary Clinton's presidential campaign revolved around her homemade email server, run for a time out of a bathroom. In some instances, classified information was stored on the server, which lacked the high-grade firewalls necessary to prevent hacking from foreign powers. Clinton had elected to use this server anyway because it allowed her to dodge oversight from Congress or from journalists who could oth wise seek her official emails under the Freedom of Information Act.

Then there were the separate hacks of both the Democratic National Committee and the personal email of Clinton's campaign chair, John Podesta. The Democrats had a PR strategy in the works: pivot from the embarrassing content of the emails exposed by the DNC breach to the fact that the disclosure was a crime inflicted by foreigners. If America's focus could be turned to a common enemy—and Russia, with its communist history, seemed to make a particularly viable enemy for conservatives— then Americans of all stripes might actually band together against this outsider. One who, the storyline went, wanted Trump to win. The result would be sympathy for the victimized DNC and antipathy for Trump.

But adding another Democratic cyber scandal to the list so close to the election, this time in the House, seemed to conjure a version of every father's admonition: hack me three times, shame on you. Hack me four times, shame on me. It begged the question: how could the highest-level officials of the world's most advanced nation be so sloppy?

Worse, the Awan breach was eerily similar to the DNC hack. First, they happened at the same time. Second, the House breach involved the House Democratic Caucus, a group that voters could not be expected to differentiate from the Democratic National Committee. Lastly, both involved Representative

Debbie Wasserman Schultz, who chaired the DNC until she resigned because of the fallout from the WikiLeaks breach, and who was one of Imran Awan's earliest and most supportive employers. Though everyone in the room assumed the two incidents to be unrelated, as political operators, they knew the truth didn't matter so much as the public perception. If it got out that Representative Wasserman Schultz's IT aide hacked the House, the average swing-state American would very likely conflate that with the DNC breach. The "Russia" narrative would be diluted to a more complex one about various hacks, at best.

The House scandal involved Pakistani nationals, and some of their employers, like Representatives Yvette Clarke, Hakeem Jeffries, and Andre Carson, were among the most vocal in denouncing Donald Trump's plans for "extreme vetting" of immigrants from largely Muslim countries. The idea that Democrats had been victimized by Pakistani-born staffers after failing to vet them might make some Americans feel that Trump was right, and that could not be tolerated.

It might seem unbelievable that anyone would fear bad publicity more than the consequences of leaving malicious actors on a sensitive network, but Democrats had made the exact same calculation weeks before. The DNC had found that the Fancy Bear malware, which included an IP address registered to a company in Pakistan called CrookServers, had hopped over from the Democratic Congressional Campaign Committee, or DCCC. As the *New York Times* reported: "Though DNC officials had learned that the Democratic Congressional Campaign Committee had been infected, too, they did not notify their sister organization, which was in the same building, because they were afraid that it would leak."[4] And just as Democrats were thwarting a vigorous investigation into the Awans, Wasserman Schultz had forbidden the FBI from taking the DNC server as evidence, preferring to have a private company present their analysis of the hack to the Washington Post.

If the Democrats had much to lose from the exposure of the Awan scandal, President Trump had something to gain. It was early October and Trump was lagging in every poll. Paul Ryan had just been given information about a cybersecurity breach in the House that reflected very badly on the Democrats. But Ryan, like many Republicans, was unenthusiastic about Trump. Privately, he called Trump a "joke," and three weeks before the election, he told Republican members of Congress to jump ship and distance themselves from Trump. Some speculated that Ryan looked forward to a Clinton victory in 2016 so that he could run against her in 2020.

Even if this were a small company selling paperclips rather than the U.S. Congress in the days before a major election, the aides' removal would be following the most basic cybersecurity practices: ban them immediately. Put them on paid leave if you're concerned about due process. Ninety-nine times out of one hundred, when activity like this was detected, the systems administrators responsible wouldn't last a day.

On the other hand, didn't the politics of it all call for special sensitivity? The FBI's director, James Comey, had been faced with similar decisions about how much to say about his ongoing investigation into Clinton's email practices, and he had gotten pilloried for his choices. After all—putting out of mind that it was the leaders' foot-dragging that led to this result—so much was still unknown. Quiet law enforcement action that could stem any damage without making the incident public was not an option. The arrest or forcible removal of a group of five people from the House network would almost certainly make the news. Would Ryan take decisive action by ordering immediate arrests, which would no doubt have the side effect of creating an October surprise? Or would he leave his institution open to an ongoing infiltration of unknown severity?

Ryan chose the latter. He was prepared to let Republicans lose the White House while Democrats talked nonstop about cybersecurity. He sat on findings that, coupled with the Democrats' response, seemed to expose those laments as empty posturing.

The systems administrators would stay on the network.

Still, something had to be done. The Office of Inspector General had a mandate to conduct exactly this type of probe, and Theresa was by far the House's most knowledgeable cybersecurity expert. Democrats knew that, but they're also masters of political posturing. They said: why not take the investigation away from the IG and refer it to the police? It gave them a sound bite that was hard to argue with: we referred it to law enforcement, what more could we do?

But it was not an escalation. In previous cases, the IG had worked directly with the FBI and prosecutors. But when Democrats said "police," they meant the Capitol Police who man the metal detectors at congressional office buildings and whose mission is to protect members, not cause problems for them. As part of the legislative branch, they're beholden to the House leadership, not the Department of Justice.

The day a lone Capitol Police officer met with Theresa to conduct the hand off, he joked about how little he understood about computers. "This is the case I'm going to get fired over," he grumbled. He was wrong. It was Theresa who would soon be out of a job.

FIVE

PANIC

(ELECTION DAY 2016 TO INAUGURATION DAY)

Democrats everywhere assumed Hillary Clinton would be the certain victor in November 2016. But she did not win, sending D.C. into turmoil. No one was scrambling as frantically during that period as the Awans, who appeared to be so worried about what a competent investigation would find that they were making plans to flee the country.

AshLee Strong, a spokeswoman for Speaker Ryan, would tell me a year later that the purpose of leaving the Awans on the House network for so many months after cybersecurity violations were detected was to conduct a sting. "The [Capitol Police] requested that the shared employees be allowed to continue to use their IT credentials until February because they didn't want to tip off the employees," she said. There was just one problem. Even if it was somehow reasonable to let a cyber-security breach of unknown severity continue through the election in order to catch them in the act, the Awans already knew about the investigation.

Jamie Fleet's garrulous and gossipy assistant, Eddie Flaherty, told people that Abid Awan was popping in to see Jamie on a regular basis about how he was under investigation. Not only that, but as part of the Representative Clarke investigation, Abid had been forced to answer questions.

On September 7, 2016, as the House investigation was in full swing, Imran flew to Pakistan. He was there for months, but all of his House employers kept paying him anyway, and server logs showed that he and his relatives were still logging into congressional computers. While Imran was in Pakistan, his wife Hina began liquidating their possessions. She listed her possessions such as a piano for sale online. The couple also owned a rental property a block away from their residence, and on November 1, 2016, Hina "sold" it to Imran's brother Jamal. It netted a handsome sum in quick cash, as the house was sold at a high price, and almost all of Jamal's money was financed by a mortgage company; a scenario banks would virtually never permit for a rental property. The house was rented by a military family. The wife told me Imran is "a very charming guy, charismatic, you'd like him. He's brilliant, he's very smart, knowledgeable about everything." But when it came to money, his behavior was suspicious. "I would write the rent to all sorts of different people," or pay in cash, she said. The November sale seemed to be on paper only. She never met Jamal, and when Imran later had her sign a new lease with Jamal's name instead of his, something was different. "He was desperate for us to sign with Jamal. He was a very different person than we'd met two years ago. If he killed himself, I wouldn't be surprised," she said. Imran's daughter was friends with their child and in the same class at school, and out of the mouth of babes, something slipped: the youngest Awan told her friend she was moving to Pakistan.

———

On November 18, an eviction notice was issued against an apartment rented in Imran's name in the slums of Alexandria, Virginia. It was the home of his second wife, Sumaira. He stopped paying her rent after she called police and said Imran kept her "like a slave." Sumaira was granted a restraining order against Imran, with a judge ruling that "either the petitioner is in immediate and present danger of family abuse or there is sufficient evidence to establish probable cause that family abuse has recently occurred," where "family abuse means any act involving violence, force, or threat that results in bodily injury or places one in reasonable apprehension of death, sexual assault, [or] bodily injury."[1]

On December 9, Imran returned to the United States after being accused of unrelated fraud in Pakistan. Three days later, he approached the Congressional Federal Credit Union to take out a home equity line of credit against one of Hina's several rental properties. The bank approved because the application said it was for "home improvement," which meant the bank's equity would be enhanced. He filled out the form impersonating his wife, though he listed his House phone number and personal email as contact information. The bank didn't offer lines of credit against properties used as rentals, so a signed affidavit was submitted swearing that the property was Hina's principal residence.

The application acknowledged that the couple owned a different property that they did rent out, a small run-down townhouse in Alexandria, which he said brought in $1,650 in rental income. But the couple's jointly-filed tax returns, included as part of the application, showed that they had not paid taxes on any rental income. On January 3, 2017, the loan officer wrote to Imran asking him to explain this apparent tax fraud. Imran responded: "Property was not on my 2014 and 2015 tax returns as a rental because it was not rent out during those years. Regards, Hina Alvi." As evidence, he enclosed a lease claiming it had been rented out to someone named Suriyah Begum on March 1, 2016. Imran was in a hurry to get the money. Two days later, he wrote: "When will you have an answer on both of our HELOC approval? And what are the soonest closing dates please?" On January 12, the loan went through.

The evidence was fake. Suriyah Begum is Hina's mother, and she did not live in the apartment. A young black couple told me they were paying $1,800 a month in rent for the property and had been since 2014. The vacancy had opened up for them after some drama with Imran's last tenant. "The lady living here before us, he said she fled, and he was going to take her to court. She said it was because he was a creep and involves his whole family," the current tenants said. They soon found their own situation to be similar. Imran took extensive and frequent trips to Pakistan, during which they would deal with Hina. They had to do their own repairs and drive rent payments to Imran across the county in Lorton. Like the other tenants, they said instead of traceable payments, "he only wants cash—security deposit, everything."

Imran's intense hunger for money is why they found it so suspicious when, around the election, Imran tried to evict them with two weeks' notice so that he could sell the house at a fire-sale price. "He was gonna make us move out in two weeks, and he wanted $110,000 for the apartment. Now he wants $200,000," they told me in March 2017. It went on the market again after a strange call they got in February. Imran "called me and said he lost his job. But I looked at the caller ID and I said, 'then why does it say he's calling from the House of Representatives?'"

When the renters saw Imran next, something was different. "He said 'life is changing, I've realized the importance of life.' He saw two holes in the wall and said, 'don't worry,' something he never would have said before." His kindness was coupled with one demand: Imran ordered the couple not to cooperate with any law enforcement, should they come around asking about him.

On January 5, the Awans' stepmother called the Fairfax County police on the Awan brothers, saying they were preventing her from seeing her husband in the hospital. On January 16, the Awans' father, Muhammad, died of cancer in the hospital in Reston, Virginia, and Jamal, his youngest son, filed a death certificate falsely swearing that Muhammad was divorced. The next day, Abid removed their stepmom as the beneficiary of Muhammad's life insurance policy and replaced her with himself, then filed a claim for the $50,000.

On January 18, Hina applied for a "financial hardship with-drawal" from her federal retirement account in the amount of $202,000. She lied that it was for "medical expenses." On the same day, an international wire request form was submitted in Hina's name to the congressional credit union to send $283,000 to two individuals in Pakistan. The form had Imran's phone number and email. Later that day, a bank employee called and asked to speak to Hina. Imran pretended to be her. The bank employee asked the purpose of the wire.

"Funeral arrangements," Imran said. The bank employee understandably balked at the idea of a nearly $300,000 funeral and said that reason wasn't acceptable. Imran told the bank teller to hold while he Googled for a reason they'd have to accept. After a long pause, he had a new reason: "Buying property." The Congressional bank employee dutifully accepted this and put the wire through. Much of the money went to a police officer in Faisalabad, Pakistan.

The FBI was watching—kind of. It assigned a first-year rookie, Brandon Merriman, to the case. The Bureau did nothing as Imran got on a plane back to Pakistan, a free man, this time with his father's corpse.

All of this happened *after* the House was in possession of evidence that ordinarily would have triggered a dramatic response, and any of these additional facts alone would seem to have been enough push an ambivalent investigator over the edge.

The House waited until Imran was already gone again before they bothered to do anything about it.

SIX

A "THEFT INVESTIGATION"

What happened in the House soon after the election could only affirm to authorities that the suspects not only knew of the investigation, but were taking elaborate steps to dismantle evidence.

Then-Representative Xavier Becerra, an outspoken Democrat who is now the attorney general of California, was chairman of the House Democratic Caucus in 2016. When he learned of problems on his servers, he barely took action and concealed it from the public afterwards, even as Democrats talked incessantly about the concurrent hack of the DNC. His staff director, Sean McCluskie, now the deputy attorney general of California, *had* noticed suspicious behavior by Abid and became worried. Something about the middle brother just didn't seem right. Ordinarily, the fact that Abid was doing *anything* involving the office should have been a problem considering he wasn't employed by the office, his sister-in-law Hina was. But apparently, Becerra didn't mind that people who weren't on his payroll had full and unrestricted access to his congressional server. McCluskie responded to his suspicions by asking Imran, who was also not on his payroll, to stop Abid from accessing the caucus's computers.

Abid did not stop. The IG could see it in the server logs and noted it in her September presentation to the House leadership. After the inspector general flagged the caucus server as a primary target of unauthorized access, Jamie Fleet, Nancy Pelosi's operator on the House Administration Committee, told Representative Becerra not to cooperate with the IG probe. When the Capitol Police took over in October, Congressman Becerra agreed to work with them, but as he later acknowledged to the media, he did not proactively approach the police, they approached him.

In October, Representative Becerra granted Chief Administrative Officer Phil Kiko permission to make a copy of his server for analysis. Working over a weekend so the Awans wouldn't notice, Chief Information Security Officer John Ramsey made a bit-for-bit clone of the server's hard drives and recorded identifying information such as its serial number. No one examined this evidence for months—until well after the election. No one could explain the dilly-dallying. What did these House cybersecurity professionals have to do that was possibly more important than this?

On December 1, Representative Becerra announced that he was resigning from Congress to become the top lawyer for the largest state in the country. With his departure, Sergeant at Arms Paul Irving and Chief Administrative Officer Kiko moved in to collect the Caucus' computer equipment on Christmas Eve. They immediately documented their findings in the draft of a letter.

One finding should not have been surprising: Representative Becerra's "request," as the IG report described it, for a criminal suspect to stop meddling with key Democratic servers—without banning his family from the network, changing the locks, or arresting him—had not been effective. "The server in question was still operating under the employee's control," they wrote. But there was more. What appeared to be "the server" that December night wasn't the server at all. It was a decoy, a looka-like machine in place of the one that had been collecting data. "While reviewing the inventory, the CAO discovered that the serial number of the server did not match that of the one imaged in September. The USCP [United States Capitol Police] inter-viewed relevant staff regarding the missing server." Officials were in agreement that the Awans had realized the server had caught the eye of the IG and planted false evidence to trick the police, swapping it with something innocuous.

Nevertheless, the Capitol Police did not seek a warrant to search the Awans' homes, ban them from the network, or arrest them. Instead, with the memo still unsent, they waited another month before taking the decoy equipment from the Awans' con-trol. Four days after Trump's inauguration, on January 24, 2017, "the CAO acquired the server from the control of the employees and transferred that server to the USCP," the final memo from CAO Kiko and Sergeant At Arms Irving to the Administration Committee said.[1]

A week later, the Office of Inspector General got a call from the Capitol Police asking a comically obtuse question for a police force that had supposedly been investigating the situation for four months: "How many members did these guys work for again?" They needed to know because the Awans were finally being banned from the House network and the Capitol Police needed to explain why. The problem was that they didn't seem to know even the basic details of the case. At a meeting a few days later, the Capitol Police Chief briefed staffers from the congressional leadership on the invoicing scam that had been uncovered nearly a year before; he didn't mention the cybersecurity breach. Theresa also attended the meeting, and while no questions were permitted, she said, "That seems like the data I gave you four months ago. Are you talking about additional invoices?"

The chief obfuscated: "It's very complicated, you have to look at the transactions and trace them to the paper records and it's a lot of work. I really can't say anything about it because it's active."

"Why have a briefing then?" Theresa asked. "You all need to understand: I don't care about them stealing a couple hundred thousand in laptops. This is about cyber insider threats. This is the exact recipe."

The chief glared at her, and Sergeant at Arms Paul Irving intervened: "Let's take this offline and not get in the weeds." Afterwards, he said sternly: "This is going to be a theft investigation."

Irving isn't a political animal, he's a pragmatist. He had no interest in a cover-up, per se, but he'd been around the block in Congress enough to know when there was simply no appetite for something, and that fighting it would only make it worse. Perhaps the best he could do is adopt what law enforcement types call a harm reduction strategy and try to contain the damage.

On February 3, 2017, the Irving-Kiko memo was finally sent under the header: URGENT. "The House OIG and HIR cybersecurity have documented multiple procurement irregularities, IT security violations, and shared employee policy violations by five shared staff employed by multiple House offices," it began. "Based upon the evidence gathered to this point, we have concluded the employees are an ongoing and serious risk to the House of Representatives, possibly threatening the integrity of our information systems and thereby members' capacity to serve constituents."

That same day, Kiko, Irving, and Jamie summoned the chiefs of staff to a meeting to inform them that the Awans were being banned. No Republicans were allowed to attend. Sean Moran assumed that Jamie told the chiefs of staff about the cybersecurity concerns, which the letter clearly laid out as the cause of the ban. But members later denied that, saying they were merely told there was some sort of theft. A rare press release sent out by the House Administration Committee, approved by both parties, made that denial possible. The headline read: "Statement on the House Theft Investigation." It said no other information would be provided until the probe was concluded.[2]

SEVEN

NEWS DUMP

It was no coincidence that, long after the evidence was clear, the belated ban and cryptic press release went out two weeks after the inauguration of President Donald J. Trump. If authorities had picked that date in advance, it was almost certainly for a different reason: they believed that by that point, Hillary Clinton would firmly be ensconced in the White House. That included her picks for the Department of Justice, who could deal with this breach— or not. But developments happen quickly in politics, and savvy political operatives know how to pivot.

There's a dark art practiced in Washington known as the "news dump," the strategic release of embarrassing or incriminating information at a time when it's likely to go unnoticed. The classic standby is a Friday afternoon. Another is when reporters are in a feeding frenzy over a different story.

When the House Administration Committee released its vague "theft investigation" press release on February 3, 2017, virtually every news reporter in Washington was consumed with Trump news. I was one of the only reporters to show even a smidgen of interest in the "theft investigation." If others had, events might have taken a different turn.

I had previously worked as a computer programmer, so when a friend sent me a curious little Buzzfeed article about how four House IT guys had been arrested, it caught my attention. The story quoted an anonymous Democratic congressman who feared his data could have been compromised.[1]

I looked up at the TV screens mounted on the wall of the Daily Caller newsroom, with chyrons linking Trump in unspecified ways to Russia; a media obsession that began when Democrats blamed the Russians for hacking the emails of the Democratic National Committee.

During the heat of the presidential campaign, the entire newsroom had gathered to watch FBI Director James Comey give an extraordinary speech faulting, yet declining to charge, Hillary Clinton for her use of a private server to store classified information. That server was discovered only because longtime Clinton confidant Sidney Blumenthal used the comically insecure AOL and had his emails hacked, revealing Clinton's secret email address. Then, there was the release of Clinton campaign chair John Podesta's emails, and the DNC's as well. *I'm old enough to remember when cybersecurity in politics was a big deal,* I thought.

I reloaded my browser and saw Buzzfeed begin to walk back the story. Now it said the aides hadn't been arrested, only banned. It included quotes from the Capitol Police emphasizing that members of Congress were *not* being investigated. It repeated that the investigation centered upon theft, not cybersecurity, and revealed that the IT aides were related.

All of this struck me as odd. As an investigative journalist specializing in data analysis, I'd studied how the House spends money on itself, and the truth is that while Congress is good at wasting taxpayer money on executive branch programs, their own office accounts have precious little padding, making it difficult for a sizeable theft scheme to go unnoticed. If so little was known that they couldn't make an arrest, why had they ruled out investigating members, and why dismiss the possibility of a cybersecurity breach?

I used my own IT skills to update a database I'd programmed a few years back to monitor the House's expenditures and ran a query that showed me systems administrators who shared the same last name; a good way to detect nepotism. A short surname flashed on my screen: Awan. Three first names were listed underneath it: Imran, Abid, and Jamal. While most of the other IT aides listed in the spreadsheet made around $55,000, these three made $160,000 or more, almost the same amount as congressmen themselves. While other IT aides only seemed to have time to serve several members, these aides had been hired by eight members each, with each Democrat paying them $20,000 a year.

House officials refused to confirm their names. I almost forgot about the story and moved on, joining the rest of Washington's press corps in writing about the latest Trump tweet. But late that night, I couldn't sleep thinking about how systems administrators could read the emails and files of congressmen, and all the damage we'd seen stem from those materials in the last few years. I opened my laptop to see what I could learn about the Awans through basic public records. I saw some immediate red flags. Abid had three minor misdemeanor convictions. He was arrested for alcohol-related offenses shortly before and immediately after the House hired him, and had filed a one million-dollar bankruptcy while drawing a $165,000 House salary. Massive debts are the number one reason security screenings bounce applicants; people with money problems have an incentive to steal, either directly or through selling data. His brother Jamal had joined the House payroll at age twenty, and he too was making $165,000.

Then there was Imran Awan. I saw that his wife's name was Hina Alvi and she was also on the House payroll. That made her the fourth person banned. The family members were linked to a dozen limited liability companies between them—little corporate entities with the stench of shell corporations—even though they were full-time, individual employees of Congress. They hadn't listed these companies or Abid's bankruptcy on House ethics disclosure forms, designed to detect security risks and self-dealing.

I was certain these were the banned employees. I got confirmation by emailing their House addresses and getting bounce-back notices that the accounts had been closed. But there was still a fifth accomplice outstanding. I could see that Imran often appeared on the payroll of a member of Congress for a token amount of money—enough to trigger the creation of logon credentials—before handing the job off to a relative. I coded an algorithm to see if the Awans' limited liability companies were receiving payments from congressional offices where they were the IT aides. But no, the Awans appeared to buy equipment from big companies like IBM or CDW-G, companies that were unlikely to participate in one family's scam.

The algorithm did, however, identify payments to several other individuals: Nataliia Sova, a name I recognized as Abid's Ukranian wife; Haseeb Rana, whose online resume had him searching for work in the defense industry; and Rao Abbas. Abbas popped up on the House payroll immediately after Abid revealed in bankruptcy documents that he owed Abbas money, as if Abid was using the House payroll to repay a personal debt. The first two departed the House payroll a few years ago, so he was our fifth guy. He was an IT specialist with no IT training, which made me wonder if the theft was putting no-show employees on the House payroll. If so, it was a major heist. Between them, the group had been paid seven million dollars in taxpayer salaries over the last decade or so.

Their individual salaries alone made them some of the highest-paid employees on the Hill, and the cybersecurity risk was real: their employers included a disproportionate number of members of the House committees on Intelligence, Foreign Affairs, and Homeland Security.

As the news cycle was dominated by coverage fueled by Democrats suggesting that Trump was an illegitimate president because of a hack on the DNC, I'd learned that a sizeable portion of the highest-level Democrats in the U.S. had for a decade entrusted all their data to one family of Pakistani citizens with deeply troubled backgrounds and few apparent qualifications.

I wrote a story for the Daily Caller News Foundation revealing the names of the banned systems administrators and delving into their troubled financial backgrounds. I figured that might be the end of it. If the Awans hadn't frightened and angered so many people on Capitol Hill with their behavior over the years, it might have been.

Rank-and-file legislative staff *hated* Imran Awan. Of those I could get to talk to me, low-level aides recounted what they described as incompetence and inattentiveness. They also recalled feeling beat down when they sensed that somehow, this random part-time repairman seemed to have far more influence with their chief of staff and congressman than they did. A legislative aide to Ohio Democrat Tim Ryan, for example, said Imran is the "creepiest guy" he'd ever met. "He had all our passwords, and I came into the office late at night and his sister was logged into my computer. They always had some excuse. Another time, my computer needed more RAM, so I gave it to him and three days later, he gave me back a different laptop. He said, 'Oh, that wasn't yours?' He just played dumb and made me use it. I never found where my laptop and all its data went."

Staffers in the House's central IT, known as House Information Resources, said Imran had for years badgered them to give him extra permissions without leaving any clues. "In order for certain permissions to be granted, a form was required to ensure that there was a paper trail for the requested changes," one said. "Imran was constantly trying to get people to process his access requests without the proper forms. Some of the permissions he wanted would give him total access to the members' stuff. Correspondence, emails, confidential files—if it was stored on the member system, they had access to it." Central tech workers saw that the Awans ran IT for more offices than anyone else on the Hill, yet never attended weekly House-wide IT meetings nor participated in the chatter on a mailing list used by the department. They'd come to believe Imran might be running a kickbacks scheme in which some members paid his relatives for no-show jobs in exchange for getting part of the wages back in cash. No investigators ever bothered to talk to these rank-and-file workers, which they took as a clear sign that they didn't want to know. The employees knew better than to stick their necks out by proactively taking their testimony to their supervisors or the police.

The official reaction I got from chiefs of staff, congressmen, and their spokesmen was different, almost uniform and militant in their silence. But a few days after publishing my first story, I got an email from someone named Stephen Taylor, a congressional IT contractor, asking me to call him about Imran Awan.[2] Taylor told me detailed stories about Imran and the bizarre influence he seemed to exert over congressmen. "It is so much more than theft. Several members should be kicked off the Hill. Everyone knows that all of this is going to unravel, what they're hoping is it unravels slowly," he said.

On at least two occasions, it appeared that Congress members fired legislative aides at Imran's request. "Imran would come in and only help the member—he'd tell me this—because 'staff come and go.' There was one staffer whose computer was broken and who was in charge of paying bills, and she said, 'I'm not going to pay my invoices until you fix my computer.' He went to the member and they fired *her* that day. Imran has that power."

He and numerous other contractors I spoke to were befuddled when Imran's employers refused their offers to do the same work for a fraction of what they were paying Imran and his relatives. Why would they be so adamant about losing money for poor service? "Staffers would say 'Imran said he'd get our copier fixed and it's been nine months,' and I'd offer to do the work Imran was doing for a quarter of the price. The members said 'no, he's our man.' I can't articulate how loyal they were to him," Taylor said.

Imran solicited a cash bribe from Taylor in order to sell access to a Florida congresswoman's office. If he paid, Imran would ensure that Taylor's company got work from newly elected Congresswoman Gwen Graham. "Imran said, 'There is this new member from Florida named Graham, let's make a deal and I'll get you into this office.' He showed me a letter and I said, 'Look, Imran, I can't do that, it's not legal.'" The letter was a commitment to award a contract. "And at 8 a.m. the next morning, he had another signed letter rescinding it and said, 'Let's go with Lockheed instead.' How the hell did he have enough control over a member that by 8 a.m. the member has done his exact bidding? If you were a new member who just got elected, don't you think they'd be like, 'Why are we switching, you told me yesterday the other was better?'"

Imran would go to Pakistan for months at a time, Taylor said. He recalled eating lunch with Imran and two other colleagues in a cafeteria in the Cannon House Office Building when Imran told him frightening stories about his supposed power in Pakistan. "I have these guys that work for the Faisalabad police department, and all we have to do is pay them $100 a month and they take [people] over to the police station, strip their clothes off, hang them upside down and beat them with a shoe," Imran told the crew.

"We were all like, 'what the fuck,'" Taylor said. "We said, 'he's a fucking monster.'"

Of the forty-four Congress members that the Awan group worked for, I'd focused on those with sensitive national security positions. But Taylor said other lawmakers were the keys. "Gregory Meeks is buddy-buddy with Imran. Andre Carson or DWS [Debbie Wasserman Schultz] will tell a member you need to use this person, and Imran goes over there and helps people and Imran will say, 'put this guy on the books,' [referring to one of his relatives] and the member will say okay. DWS is always causing problems. This is one more time when her data was made vulnerable." Representatives Meeks and Carson are both members of the Congressional Black Caucus representing inner-city districts. Carson is one of two Muslim members of Congress and also serves on the Intelligence Committee. Debbie Wasserman Schultz, of course, had led the Democratic National Committee from May 2011 through July 2016.

Taylor told me that Imran was frequently at the Democratic National Committee. From payroll records, though, I discovered that he had only been on Debbie Wasserman Schultz's congressional payroll, not that of the DNC. The law requires a strict separation between taxpayer-funded entities and donor-funded entities so that government funds aren't used for the benefit of incumbents. This raised further suspicions. Taylor said, "I was a member of the DNC Club"—a private restaurant for Democratic insiders on the first floor of the DNC building, a block away from the Capitol—"and would always see him walking through the little alley and he'd always tell me, 'Oh, the chairwoman's really busy.' He'd always call her the chairwoman. His phone would ring, and he'd show me it'd say 'Schultz' and he'd answer, 'Madam chairwoman,' because he always treated her like that. She'd call him all the time. That goes to show he must have been doing some work at the DNC too. Those things are so disorganized, I have no doubt he was doing something there. Anything Imran does is for money." If Imran was secretly working at the DNC, it raised the question of whether he was involved in the hacking of the DNC emails. But I didn't spend any time thinking about that possibility, and focused on the well-documented breach documented in the House server logs.

Nevertheless, a simple search of Imran's name on the WikiLeaks site revealed that Imran was on a first-name basis with DNC officials and had access to Wasserman Schultz's electronic devices at the DNC. On May 4, 2016, DNC Assistant to the Chair Amy Kroll wrote: "I do not have access to her iPad password, but Imran does."[3] A DNC spokeswoman did not deny that Imran frequently went to its headquarters but would not explain why. The WikiLeaks emails also highlighted the kind of access an IT aide could have. In a May 12, 2016 exchange, Rosalyn Kumar, an aide to Wasserman Schultz, wrote: "Pelosi is doing a closed door meeting. No staff or anyone allowed. Kaitlyn come to Rayburn room and get [DWS'] iPad for Imran."[4]

Putting the DNC aside, if even half of Taylor's other allegations checked out, this was an explosive story. I assumed other reporters would be fighting to get it, so I asked Taylor not to speak to any other journalists. He told me he had already emailed much of what he'd told me to the *Washington Post*, ensuring it wouldn't go overlooked by having a friend who worked as a science reporter there, Brady Dennis, send it directly to his political-beat colleagues. Given his credentials and what seemed to be the obviously newsworthy topic of cybersecurity issues on Capitol Hill, Taylor was shocked that he never heard back. So, he reluctantly agreed to be my exclusive source. In retrospect, this competitive posturing was a mistake on my part. He told me, "I really want to see this story through." I promised him I wouldn't let it go.

I went through my database, calling House IT aides until I found one willing to speak with me. After Congress banned the Awans, many members suddenly needed IT aides. Pat Sowers took over the office of Don McEachin, a newly elected Democrat from Virginia. Sowers had, in fact, been originally slated to set up the office after the election. "Within a week of the election," however, "McEachin's chief of staff called me and wanted to hire me, but they were told to hire Imran. By who I don't know, but they were very clear on it," Sowers said. This meant that even though the Awans had, according to Buzzfeed, been under investigation for "months," they'd been allowed to expand their roster of clients and configure the entire computer networks of newly elected members, including two new members of the Congressional Black Caucus, McEachin and Lisa Blunt Rochester of Delaware, and three new members for Florida, Charlie Crist, Darren Soto, and Stephanie Murphy. They weren't merely allowed to do so—someone pushed them onto these members.

What Sowers found when he arrived in February as Representative McEachin's second-choice IT aide is that all the computers were configured to be nothing more than "thin clients" that pointed to an external server, meaning all of Representative McEachin's data was being stored somewhere else. The computers also lacked the most basic precautions, such as antivirus software mandated by the House. The most troubling part is that no one seemed to have documented or cleaned up the configuration before his arrival. The House simply assigned him to bring the system into compliance with the House rules. No investigators ever asked him what he'd found. Sowers told me that other IT aides had shared similar stories, and worse. What it came down to, they said, is that the Awans were funneling all the data off of members' official servers and onto one computer in an unknown location; a massive security violation.

"I love the Hill, but to see this clear lack of concern over what appears to be a major breach bothers me," Sowers said. "I don't know what they have, but they have something on someone." Sowers added, "Everyone has said for years they were breaking the rules and it's just been a matter of time" before there was public scandal. The House had, over the years, issued rules that IT aides thought were aimed at dealing with the Awans without having to publicly acknowledge their suspicious activities.

I talked to other IT aides who wanted to remain anonymous and told similar stories. One had warned a member of Congress that the Awans were putting his data at risk but had been rebuffed. After the Awans were banned, he figured he was a shoe-in as a replacement for that office, but he said the member seemed to believe that he was a "snitch." Why would a congressman be unhappy with someone for identifying computer violations?

Another aide taking over an office configured by an Awan found that all the staffers' phones were connected with a single Apple account that wasn't even tied to the House. He couldn't understand why the Awans were treated so favorably. "If I was accused of this, I'd be in jail the same day. I'd be hauled out in handcuffs and never work in government again."

I was beginning to think I was on to something big.

EIGHT

FRIGHTENING CONNECTIONS

(2017)

I found two groups of people who knew Imran: those who vocally described vicious behaviors tantamount to extortion, and those on Capitol Hill to whose emails he had unrestricted access to, who were strangely and rigidly silent despite plainly troubling facts.

Outside of Congress, Imran Awan was known as a predator who would stop at nothing for a buck. In my interviews with people who knew them, the Awans were repeatedly accused of extortion, greed, and possible money laundering. Their schemes ranged from petty to frightening. Their public records footprint was easier to follow than most because Imran Awan was an extraordinarily busy man. Virginia corporation records showed about a dozen purported companies running out of the Awans' homes, or established in their names, that weren't disclosed on their mandatory House ethics disclosures. His lawyer later told me he had "no idea" what these companies did, implying that police never asked. Operating out of Imran's home in Lorton, for example, was New Dawn 2001 LLC. Considering it was created not in 2001 but in 2011, part of me wondered: What happened in 2001 that a Pakistani might consider a "new dawn?"

Their extensive real estate holdings also provided a road map to interview those who had dealt with them. In one marathon day, I put about 100 miles on my 2007 Corolla, hitting addresses associated with the Awans' complex web of rental properties, LLCs, and lawsuits.

At what I had guessed was Imran's actual residence in Lorton—an exurb of D.C. synonymous in local parlance with a now shuttered federal prison there—a marine named Andre Taggart had recently moved in. He said someone named Alex had listed the home for rent on a military housing website. I later learned that all of the Awans went by aliases. "When we first moved in, a guy came with certified mail from the House of Representatives. We were trying to be nice and signed for it. We went to take it to [Imran] and he lost his shit, saying 'Why did you sign for it, this is illegal.' The postman came a second time with a certified letter and I called Imran on the spot: 'What do you want me to do?' He said, 'Just send him away, I'm homeless,'" Taggart told me.

Soon after, he received a call from a D.C. law firm demanding he return electronic devices left in the home. "He threatened to sue us; it was unbelievable," he said. The aggressiveness of the demand piqued his curiosity, and in the garage, he found a cache of hard drives and phones that he recognized as government equipment. There were "Blackberries, print servers, wireless routers, hard drives that look like they had tried to destroy, laptops, [and] a lot of brand-new expensive toner," he said. Taggart'd had enough. First, Imran had used a military-geared website to find renters, then tried to remove a legally required provision from the contract allowing that if the military deployed the family, they could break the lease without penalty, he said. Next, he pressured him into signing an unusually long three-year lease, but immediately after having him sign, he listed the house for sale and demanded that the family constantly leave for a few hours at a time so realtors could show it to prospective buyers. Now Imran kept showing up trying to get these electronics, but Taggart didn't feel comfortable letting him in, and the intensity with which he wanted them back let him know that something wasn't right. He called the military police to report suspected stolen government equipment and was surprised when two different agencies—the Capitol Police and the FBI— responded instead to interview him and collect the items.

Even the backstory to the Awans' many homes involved fraud. The middle brother, Abid, owned two homes, one of which was deeded to him by Imran. The other had been used in a mortgage fraud scheme between a corrupt real estate agent from the firm Fairfax Realty and an illegal immigrant who fled the United States to escape a felony charge. Government licensing documents show that Imran also worked at Fairfax Realty at the same time he was earning $165,000 from Congress. In fact, he wasn't just a real estate agent, he was a broker; a designation that typically signified someone who oversaw large financial transactions and supervised others. To get this license, one had to swear that he was working forty hours a week in the real estate business. This second full-time job was another thing Imran didn't list on his House ethics disclosure form.

Some of Imran's homes were previously tied to Johar Mirza, who is the same age as Imran and emigrated from the same city in Pakistan. He is also on the FBI's Most Wanted list. He fled to Scotland to avoid mortgage fraud charges in Virginia, raped a woman there, and then—facing deportation to Pakistan—claimed he'd converted to Judaism and sought refugee status, saying Pakistan killed Jews.[1] In the Virginia suburbs, Johar and his brother Gohar ran a mortgage scheme that involved creating fake IT companies and pretending unqualified buyers worked there.

Another rental property tenant was Laurel Everly. She told me Imran said the home was actually his, but it was officially owned by Hina. The lease said she was renting it from Imran's father Muhammad, and Imran instructed her to give him rent checks made out to another relative, Hina's mother Suriyah Begum. Imran was frequently in Pakistan, so she had to drive checks to Imran's friend, Rao Abbas. The house was run down, but Everly was separated from her husband, her small business had just failed, and she told Imran she needed a short rental while she tried to reconcile with her spouse. He tried to make her sign a three-year lease anyway, and, she said, would do anything for a buck. "The property was trashed. The cabinets in it were twenty years older than the house. When he bought the house, he sold the cabinets in them and brought in older ones. Think about that, it's a crazy thing to do. The dishwasher was on wheels and hooked up to the sink," Everly said.

"He became very abusive and threatening. He was trying to get me to pay for all kinds of different made up damages." He demanded she pay him $350 because the flowers in the home's garden were dead... in January. These demands came under threat of lawsuit. "He's an extortionist, a horrible, horrible person. You want to wonder if he's capable of doing something bad in Congress? Absolutely. He threatened me, all these attempts to get money from me in different ways. He probably knew I was vulnerable and that's why he took advantage of me."

When the basement flooded after a storm, Imran demanded that Everly pay $10,000 to replace the drywall. She pointed out that the basement flooded because Imran had not bought a sump pump. "How dare I question his integrity, he was a high-ranking federal employee who had passed a background investigation," she recounted Imran saying. He even set her up, she said, creating a situation where she agreed in writing to handle replacing a filter in an air conditioner, and then later falsely said she'd broken the entire unit by installing it wrong and would have to pay for a new one. He knew the AC was always broken, and she saw his efforts to create a liability-shifting paper trail in advance as a petty example of a strategic, months-long con where "the whole thing was telegraphed."

Imran took half of her security deposit for supposed repairs and, after Everly documented that there were no damages, he said he was in Pakistan and could not return the money. "He emailed me from his House email address, which is "123@mail.

house.gov" to say that he was in Pakistan and wouldn't have his cell phone, but would be using that work address.

When Imran wasn't in Pakistan, he was a frequent visitor to the rental. "Imran came all the time to get stacks and stacks of mail for all different people," including an invitation to the White House Christmas party, Laurel said. She suspected that he might be stealing people's identities, and worried that he could have stolen hers. He also used these visits to check on some sort of equipment that was running in a shed. "He insisted the power had to be left on to keep what's in there cool. I'm pretty sure he was running computer equipment on my property. I do believe that shed with the light and the fan that he was always coming and going from was probably a server." Of course, Everly had to foot the electricity bill for whatever was in the shed. Meanwhile, the house appeared to have a second internet connection in addition to the one she paid for, but she wasn't allowed to use it. Imran's lawyer later claimed that the prior owner had locked the shed and Imran had never tried to open it in all those years, implying police never looked.

The Awans' commercial dealings often led to legal disputes. They were frequently sued, and they frequently sued others. Cristal Perpignan, a high-level federal IT executive at the General Services Administration, got locked in a landlord-tenant lawsuit with Imran after he attempted to make her pay for water damage caused by old leaking pipes. The legal paperwork included photographs of what appeared to be Imran's entire family calling attention to a tiny nail hole in the wall, the kind left by hanging a small picture frame. The whole thing was laughably petty from a family that cleared the better part of one million dollars a year.

Wasn't their time worth more than this? The most chilling part was, because they went to such lengths to document things and knew how to work the system, they won the lawsuit.

Perpignan lived on the top two floors of the townhouse, while Rao Abbas, who Imran told her was his best friend, lived in the basement. Rao was on the payroll of the House of Representatives, ostensibly running IT for congressmen including Emmanuel Cleaver of Missouri and Ted Deutch of Florida. But Perpignan said Rao was "home most days." She added, "At one time Imran told me and my partner that Rao worked at McDonald's and had lost his job." It was enough to blow your mind: members of Congress were paying a McDonald's worker and giving him access to all their data, even though he wasn't actually showing up.

Imran was loyal to few. He "would periodically talk bad about his best friend in the basement or the previous renter, and I am sure he did the same about me," she said. "Imran is very cunning and shady, and I noted this throughout the time I lived there. He is very persuasive and well-spoken. He gives you a sob story and you believe him." She recalled him "lying about giving me authorization to paint a room in his home, lying about the condition of the home when I moved in and out."

"He put the lease in his wife's name although I only interacted with him and seldom saw his wife. He also asked me to give my rental payments and write my checks out to Rao Abbas," she told me. "He did take my security deposit without merit." Imran was so unwilling to lose a single day of rent that he scheduled her move-in for the same day the previous tenants were scheduled to move out, leaving Perpignan's movers waiting.

There was not a single person I spoke with that didn't have stories just like this. I'd never encountered someone whose behavior had so concerned everyone he interacted with in my life. But the take of numerous tenants was only one part of the picture available to any investigator who cared to look. Most of the Awan court cases were at the Fairfax County, Virginia courthouse. The files were so voluminous that I couldn't copy them all. They hadn't been viewed in years and had to be brought out of the archives. I raced against the 4:30 p.m. closing bell to try to take in as much as I could, jotting down notes in pencil. More frightening associations emerged.

While the Awans worked for congressmen who sat on the Intelligence, Homeland Security, and Foreign Affairs committees, Abid Awan managed a car dealership that took money from an Iraqi government minister wanted by U.S. authorities. The purported car dealership was called "Cars International A," but most of the time, they called it "CIA." Few people seemed to actually buy cars from CIA, but those that did tended to be vulnerable. In 2010, a woman from the slums of Southeast D.C. sued Abid, writing that he sold her a car and the engine went out two months later. Abid reneged on a promise to fix it and was summoned to court, but he never showed up, and she never got her money. He told another woman she could return the defective car he sold her and get her money back. He took back the car but never refunded her money. The same story played out a handful of times. Court-ordered financial judgments simply went ignored.

The contempt for the legal system when they were in its crosshairs was coupled with a strange but seemingly justified confidence that it could be deployed as a weapon at the Awans' disposal. The unbridled predation made it hard to believe that congressional data could be safe in the Awans' hands.

Brian Jenkins of Silver Spring, Maryland, said the dealership sold him a car that would not even start without jumping the battery. According to the court records, "rather than replacing the battery, Defendant merely informed Plaintiff that he should keep the vehicle running and not use the lights or radio." Apparently rather than provide him with a forty dollar part, Abid expected Jenkins to leave it idling in his driveway each night. Abid had told him the car came with a warranty, so Jenkins brought the car back. Abid stalled him at the dealership, telling him he was working on his problem. After five hours, he suddenly told Jenkins he would not be receiving any assistance and should leave. When he went to the parking lot, he found that Abid had summoned police cars to block Jenkins' car in, leaving him stranded far from home with neither a car nor his personal possessions that were trapped inside. Under these conditions, Jenkins was browbeaten into agreeing to pay Abid even more than he had previously agreed to for the broken car (and his possessions).

But there was no reward for his concession. When Jenkins left, Abid called the police again and reported the car—which Jenkins had now paid for twice over—as stolen. "Defendant is aware of the falsity of this report to law enforcement," Jenkins' lawyer said in the court case.[2]

On paper, Abid and a man named Nasir Khattak each owned fifty percent of CIA. Khattak also owned a longstanding car dealership called "AAA Motors" directly across the street. This partnership, like so many Awan business dealings, quickly descended into accusations of fraud and double-crossing.

CIA never seemed like an ordinary car dealership, with inventory, staff, and expenses. On its still-existent Facebook page, its "staff" were fake personalities such as "James Falls O'Brien," whose photo was taken from a hairstyle model catalog, and "Jade Julia," whose image came from a web page called "Beautiful Girls Wallpaper." If a customer showed up looking to buy a car, Abid would simply go across the street to AAA Motors to get one. "If AAA borrows a car to Cars International and they have a customer, it was simply take the car across the street and sell it, and then later on give the profit back or not," Khattak testified. "There was no documentation. ... If you go and try to dissect, you will not be able to make any sense out of them because there were many, dozens and dozens, of cars transferred between the two dealerships and between other people."

Khattak did not explain why he would ruin his existing business to help the Awans. "All of those transactions was to support Cars International A from AAA Motors," he testified. "That's why I did not make any money from my dealership, because my resources were supporting Cars International A."

Khattak said in court documents that after the business racked up massive debts, Imran somehow convinced a variety of creditors to draw a distinction between the two partners, Khattak and the Awans, and to turn on Khattak, making him the fall man.

Abid incorporated Cars International A in 2009 while he was working for Congress, even taking out loans from the

Congressional credit union. His Ukranian wife, Nataliia Sova, was also involved. A few months before the dealership was incorporated, she created a different mysterious company, Alain LLC.

It's not clear where the dealership's money was going—it was sued by at least five different people for not paying its rent, not paying wholesalers for its cars, and cheating its car buyers. The predation spared no one.

But we do know the source of some of its investment capital. In 2010, the CIA dealership took a $100,000 loan from Ali Al-Attar, described in the lawsuit as a doctor who could not testify at trial because he was a government official in Iraq. When I searched his name online, I saw that he is currently a fugitive from the Department of Justice, and that an officer for the actual CIA had connected him to Hezbollah.

In 2003, while living in wealthy McLean, Virginia and practicing medicine, the post-Saddam Hussein Iraqi government asked Al-Attar to establish the Iraq Ministry of Health.[3] It might be said that he helped create the opening. In the leadup to the U.S.-Iraq War, Al-Attar had been the head of a group of Iraqi expatriates on whom Pentagon official Paul Wolfowitz relied for guidance, even though Al-Attar's parents were Iranian.[4]

Al-Attar eventually returned to the United States and ran a sprawling, and as it turned out, criminal, medical practice. In 2009, the FBI concluded that he and his partner bilked more than two million dollars out of insurance plans like Medicare, including by stealing the identities of diplomats. He would use stolen Social Security numbers to bill nonexistent surgeries against patients. They recorded one man as having four hundred surgeries. The insurance scam worked by splitting the bills among numerous purported medical offices in multiple states. He refused to cooperate with investigators and would not even tell them where his office buildings were. In 2012, he was indicted for tax fraud and he fled the country. With Al-Attar in Iraq, money was moved from him to the car dealership through accounts intended for high-end real estate in McLean. A former Central Intelligence Agency officer wrote contemporaneously that in 2012—shortly after the loan was made—Al-Attar "was observed in Beirut, Lebanon conversing with a Hezbollah official." As I was digging through these court records, *Politico* reported a bombshell story that Hezbollah deployed used car dealerships in Northern Virginia to launder money, but that law enforcement was hamstrung from acting by political considerations involving President Obama's pending nuclear deal with Iran.[6]

I was starting to see the Department of Justice—which, like most people, I'd always assumed was on top of things, and worried when I thought I might be risking the slightest infraction—in a new light. How could a figure like Al-Attar continue moving money into the Washington suburbs without consequence? For that matter, how were the Awans still free months after the findings of "unauthorized access" to congressional servers? Could the car dealership be some sort of money-laundering entity connected to Hezbollah? Was it possible that the government would look the other way at potentially dangerous crimes for political expediency?

Abid Awan's car dealership continued to rack up massive debts. In 2010, Abid declared personal bankruptcy, discharging $1.1 million in obligations.

Just as Imran seemed to use others as his cutouts when it came to owning homes and receiving paychecks from the House of Representatives, Khattek said, "It was Imran…who was running the [car] business in full control." Only Imran, he said, knew where CIA's money went. Even though Imra was actually in control of CIA, since it was listed in Abid's name, Imran kept his abundant assets.

IT aide Stephen Taylor told me, "I've known people who declared bankruptcy and they're stressed out, but they [the Awans] were the same. It was BS to clear their assets. They didn't care."

Even Abid kept ownership of both of his houses through the bankruptcy instead of having to sell the second one to pay his suffering creditors, because he swore "under penalty of perjury" that he was separated and living apart from his Ukranian-born wife, Nataliia Sova. But as soon as CIA folded, Nataliia created two more, apparently fake, car companies based out of the house where Abid lived. Years later, Abid and Nataliia were still living together.

They knew how to rig the system.

NINE

PLAYING DUMB

There was one more court record that caught my eye: an eviction notice dated October 2016 and filed against Imran for an apartment in the slums of Alexandria. It was odd that someone who owned multiple homes and made such a high salary would be renting an apartment. It turned out to be where he kept Sumaira, his second wife.[1] After she called the cops on him for keeping her "like a slave"—which occurred just as House investigators were closing in on him for cybersecurity breaches—he stopped paying rent, leaving her to be evicted. The landlord said Imran had been quick to note that he worked at the House of Representatives and that his email address was "123@mail.house.gov."

I did a double take when I saw the email address. When tenant Laurel Everly told me Imran said he could be reached in Pakistan at that address, I figured it must be some kind of misunderstanding and that she was using it as shorthand for the

convention that every House staffer uses: firstname.lastname@
mail.house.gov. Now it was clear Imran actually used that bizarre
address, which removed the accountability that comes from having one's name attached to an email bearing the House domain
name. Can you imagine the terror one could strike, particularly
in someone unfamiliar with U.S. government such as an immigrant, by emailing from that address and purporting to be some
all-powerful official?

Emailing imran.awan@mail.house.gov had triggered a
bounce back that said the account was shut down. Now I tried
this address. The email didn't bounce back. That meant the
username was still active and providing a backdoor into the
House system months after Imran had been banned. My email
program told me the name attached to the address was "Nathan
Bennett."

A big part of Imran's job was setting up email accounts for
others, so creating extra accounts would be easy for him. Yet,
even when it came to the one action authorities had actually
taken— blocking his account to prevent further access to House
data—they hadn't done basic due diligence. There was still a
gaping hole in the House's cybersecurity, which was even more
frightening considering Imran now had his back up against the
wall.

Worse, "Nathan Bennett" is not just any name. Of the ten
thousand staffers on Capitol Hill, very few have anything to do
with national security information, but Bennett is one of those
few. Bennett, who studied military strategy at the United States
Army War College, works for Representative Andre Carson of
Indiana, one of two Muslim members of Congress. "My

individual legislative portfolio covers national security and foreign affairs, including the House Permanent Select Committee on Intelligence," Bennett says on LinkedIn. "As [Carson's] national security staffer, I developed and executed a plan to successfully secure the congressman's appointment as a member of the House Permanent Select Committee on Intelligence (ranking member of the Subcommittee on Emerging Threats) and the House Armed Services" Committee. Imran worked as Representative Carson's email administrator, giving him the perfect opportunity to steal his identity.

I was sure Representative Carson would be apoplectic to learn what had occurred: the suspect in an ongoing criminal investigation had assumed the identity of a key intelligence staffer. I printed out the eviction paperwork proving Imran used the 123 account and took a screenshot of Bennett's name attached to the account. Before I reported this story, I wanted to alert Representative Carson so he could close the account and prevent further harm.

But when I took the printouts to Carson's office, his spokeswoman wouldn't let me see Bennett. She didn't seem interested in taking the papers or hearing what I had to say. She simply said it wasn't Imran's address and that the chief administrative officer, Phil Kiko, would give me a statement waving me off the story. I told her that Kiko's office had always told me policy forbade it from providing information about any aspect of this investigation, but she said, "Don't worry, they'll do it for us." The statement never came.

On the way out of the office, I got lost in the Pentagon-esque halls of the Rayburn House Office Building. I was lost in my thoughts about something the early tipster, Stephen Taylor, told me: Imran was so close to Representative Carson that he played video games with him in his office, and Carson's chief of staff, Kim Rudolph, knew Imran was up to no good but couldn't break Imran's hold over the congressman.

Kim Rudolph, he told me, is "very to the letter; kind of uptight, but every penny was accounted for." When she was chief of staff for Representative Carolyn Cheeks Kilpatrick, they "had an old printer go missing and Kim Rudolph called the Capitol Police and did a sting operation. It turned out it was a House employee that was taking things slowly."

The office's muted reaction to something far more serious told you everything you needed to know. "Kim Rudolph would tell me Imran would go in his office, wouldn't even talk to the receptionist, and hang out with him for a half hour. The congressman would then tell Kim, 'You need to do this, this, and that for Imran.'" It was highly unusual for a congressman to be so concerned with routine computer administration of his office rather than delegating that to the chief of staff.

I found myself in front of Representative Carson's office again and decided to press his spokeswoman a second time. I finally convinced her to let me talk with Bennett through email.

Bennett seemed more interested in separating himself from the story than in getting to the bottom of what had happened. He said the records must be a "fabrication," and he meant by *me*, without even once expressing concern that this could stem from nefarious conduct by a systems administrator. "I do not, nor have I ever, had control of the 123@mail.house.gov email account or any other account connected with Imran Awan or his family," he said.

"Regarding your screenshot, this is the first time that I have seen this. I'm not sure how or why my name is listed, but I can assure you that what you see is either an error or fabrication."

Didn't he see that the entire problem was that he didn't have control of an account in his name? Why was he so sure it was an "error" rather than a deliberate act by the person who had been banned from Congress by the police because server logs proved that he was making unauthorized access to Democrats' servers? *My God*, I thought. Is this what the state of U.S. politics has come to, that a Democrat would rather take the word of a criminal suspect who'd been banned from Congress for egregious cybersecurity violations, if he was associated with their party, than look at crucial, independently-verifiable evidence if it was in the hands of a reporter from a conservative-leaning news organization? Or was the office taking this hostile posture because they knew exactly how bad the truth was? I had approached the congressman not for comment, but as an American doing my duty. It seemed the intelligence committee member had other allegiances.

When I emailed the 123 address again a few days later, it still didn't bounce back, and I published the story. Representative Carson never talked to me, but he did give interviews to local media in which he stood up for Imran and attacked me. "The Daily Caller is not a reputable entity," Carson said. "I think that they've proven themselves to be very bigoted, Islamophobic, and anti-black. I think it goes along with their narrative of anybody who is foreign, who happens to be a Muslim, who happens to be black, happens to be Latino, who conducts unethical acts, they want to condemn the entire Congress."[2]

Taylor was angered by the brazenness of the response when I filled him in. "That really pisses me off," he said. Representative Carson "was friends with Imran. They were really freaking close," Taylor said. He had worried that his fellow Democrats might try to hide behind identity politics to make the whole thing go away, but it seemed so unbelievably cynical. Now, everyone was playing dumb. House Minority Leader Nancy Pelosi told reporters that she hadn't followed the House cyber breach "very closely."

"I'm not sufficiently understanding the situation to make any concern about it, but there are plenty of people who are under an investigation who still have their jobs," she said, naming Attorney General Jeff Sessions as an example. She didn't mention that her own top staff had tried to block a hacking probe into the Awans. One day, outside the Capitol after votes, Joaquin Castro of Texas, a member of the intelligence committee who employed Abid Awan, said there never was any cybersecurity investigation, swearing he was only told it was about money. "Do you have evidence that there's anything more?" he asked. "If someone's given you a document to that effect, please give it to me." When I did exactly that and provided his office with detailed information, they refused to accept the documents or respond.

The truth is that Democrats knew about the cybersecurity incident and were so worried about what it might find that they tried to make a law that could keep the FBI from investigating it. In May 2016, a few weeks after the Awan investigation had been referred to the inspector general, a cryptic paragraph titled "Cybersecurity Assistance" turned up in an unrelated bill thousands of pages long. "Cybersecurity is quickly emerging as one of the most important aspects of the House of Representatives' security platform," it read, but "constraints" on the executive branch's ability to investigate are necessary. "It is intended that the Speaker, in consultation with the Minority Leader, outline the type of infrequent executive branch assistance that may be required, including... resources provided by the executive branch, actions and constraints on those resources necessary to protect the Separation of Powers, privileges under the Speech or Debate Clause, and other constitutionally-derived powers and rules."[3]

The goal of that paragraph was to make it illegal for the FBI to investigate the hack on their network without Democrats' acquiescence. The bill into which the provision was slipped dealt with topics that typically fall under the domain of the Appropriations Committee's Subcommittee on the Legislative Branch, a panel on which Representative Wasserman Schultz is a senior member. The language was stripped out before it became law. But a year later, days after Imran Awan left Wasserman Schultz's laptop in a phone booth triggering a furious Democratic effort to block prosecutors from looking at it, similar language was inserted in a different bill.[4] In fact, the language in the bill that became law is stronger, requiring "the concurrence of the Minority Leader."[5] Nothing would happen without the Democrats' consent.

TEN

POWER OF ATTORNEY

The strangest email I've ever received came not long after I published the first stories about what had occurred on the House network. "My name is Samina Ashraf Gilani. I am stepmother of Abid, Imran, and Jamal Awan. My step children captivated me in house for a long time and during illness of my husband," it began. She said the brothers were using their technology skills to wiretap and extort her. Gilani speaks only Urdu, and the first time I heard her voice, it was on a phone call with her cousin Syed Ahmed in Canada, where she'd fled to escape the Awans. I heard her sobbing in the background as she told her story to Syed, who translated for me. "They kept their stepmother in sort of illegal captivity from October 16, 2016, to February 2," he explained.

They installed a listening device under her kitchen counter. She took pictures of the sticky gum residue that remained after Imran finally agreed to remove the devices, and another contraption "behind the printer" of her computer. "She was told that her movements were under constant surveillance and conversations within the house and over the telephone were being listened to. They would repeat what she had told people to prove that they were really listening," Syed said. They took her cell phone, but her sister smuggled her a burner phone in the mail, and she'd stand in the backyard to call extended family in Pakistan, begging for help.

She wasn't chained to the radiator; they kept her confined through high-tech surveillance and threats. It was a prison built around her status as a vulnerable immigrant and devout Muslim, using those traits to prey on her. Gilani was acculturated to a life of deference to male family members, she didn't drive, and isolation meant she had nowhere to turn.

Lying in a bed at Georgetown hospital dying of cancer, Muhammad cried out for his doting wife. Imran gave a bizarre response that stood out in the minds of multiple witnesses: "She said she can't be bothered to come to the hospital. She is busy writing a book." Then they told Gilani that Muhammad was refusing to see *her*.

Gilani finally called the Fairfax County police. The officer who responded to her call recorded that her stepsons had "denied access" to her husband. Though it was the middle of a weekday, "her stepson Abid responded to location and was obviously upset with the situation. He stated he has full power of attorney over his father and produced an unsigned, undated document as proof. He refused to disclose his father's location."[1] Police gave her a tracking number on a form she couldn't read and left her alone with three grown men who were now seething.

As part of a civil lawsuit, Gilani reported what happened next: "Right after the police left, Mr. Ashraf's other son, Imran Awan, showed up and threatened me for calling the police. Imran Awan threatened that he is very powerful and if I ever call the police again, Imran Awan will do harm to me and my family members back in Pakistan and one of my cousins here in Baltimore. Imran Awan threatened that he has the power to kidnap my family members back in Pakistan. Worth mentioning here that Imran Awan introduces himself as someone from U.S. Congress or from federal agencies," she wrote.

She never saw her husband again and did not attend the supposed $300,000 funeral in Pakistan. I don't know that I'd put Gilani in the category of a brave, independent woman, like Sumaira, Wendy, and Theresa. She's guarded, as if the cloth burka that shrouded her body was wrapped around another invisible one that shielded her innermost thoughts. When she begged me for help at various times over the course of a year, I pointed out the obvious—that she could file criminal charges—but then she'd go silent. Other times, she'd ignore my requests for details about Imran's activities that I was certain she'd know. One thing is for sure: by the very fact that she had survived all this, she'd exhibited a strength and perseverance greater than most of us will ever have to summon. Who was I to judge? If I were in her position—worn down by repeated failure, abuse, and expectations of subservience, the way Sean Moran was beat down by two decades of Capitol Hill skirmishing—would I do any better?

On top of everything else, she was struggling to understand the United States, where she had spent the better part of the last eight years. The corruption and violence that defined her home-land wasn't supposed to exist here. In America, you were supposed to be able to count on authorities.

Speaking to Gilani through emails clumsily decoded to English using Google Translate was like receiving heartbreaking missives from another world. "Luke, my son," one said. "You can't imagine how they had captivated me. My husband gave me an iPhone which they ravished from me. It had pictures of my husband. They even took my diary, one of my husband's memory. Can you get my diary back?"

Muhammad Ashraf Awan's final moments were not spent reminiscing with loved ones, but being pestered to sign his possessions, down to his 2004 Camry, over to his sons. After Muhammad died, the Awan brothers entered Gilani's home and cleared it out of her two laptops and important papers, including her husband's will.

The title of Muhammad and Gilani's Springfield residence listed Abid as a secondary owner and Gilani not at all, ensuring its ownership automatically transferred to him immediately following his father's death. Gilani had no job, virtually no friends in the United States, no driver's license, and now no spouse and no home. Imran and Abid owned six houses between them, but they took the home. When they changed the locks, they planted a flag like pirates: a blue decal, three feet in diameter, affixed immodestly facing outwards in a first floor window. It was an official seal surrounded by the text that read: "United States House of Representatives."

Gilani was homeless but knew that her husband had a $50,000 life insurance policy that named her as a beneficiary.

When she called the insurance agent, he was alarmed. He told her that within hours of Muhammad's death, someone else had claimed the money. When Muhammad died, Jamal, his youngest son, filed a death certificate falsely swearing that Muhammad was divorced. The next day, Abid used the certificate to file a claim, all before Gilani even knew her husband was dead.

Muhammad had never consented to removing his wife as the beneficiary, but Gilani's lawsuit eventually produced evidence documenting how the brothers had pulled off the caper. It was a video the brothers recorded in which they laughed while their heavily medicated father, hooked up to IV tubes, groggily signed a form making Abid the administrator, but not the beneficiary, of his $50,000 life insurance policy.

I was struck by how every move the brothers made appeared to be plotted three steps in advance. What they were about to do would bring accusations of fraud and the video built an evidence trail to use in their favor. Abid used his administrative powers to modify the plan, removing Gilani as beneficiary and replacing her with himself.

The callousness and greed inherent in this plot was sick. The brothers had little need for $50,000—the three cleared half a million a year in federal pay alone—and even less for a 2004 Camry. But that's how Gilani wound up sleeping on Syed's floor in Canada. Syed told me a little bit about Gilani's upbringing and how happy she was to land in the U.S. Now, life with the Awans was so torturous that she chose to leave for another strange country to get away from them. As Democrats used talking points about cruelty in the immigration process in their war against Trump, he asked: "Can you imagine a lady left the United

States to take refuge in a different country?" And it was all because of her treatment at the hands of congressional aides.

I understood how much of a lifeline $50,000 would serve for a homeless widow, but I could tell there was more to the story. The insurance company suspected that Abid might be guilty of fraud and submitted the case to the Fairfax County courts to resolve. In court documents, Gilani wrote that the wrath she had incurred was leverage to force her to do something else. Imran "demanded me to sign a power of attorney for my Pakistani matters and was forcing me over the phone and through other people to sign power of attorney. I was put under tremendous pressure."

Imran wanted that power of attorney because Muhammad had vast wealth stored overseas. He owned two real estate developments the size of towns, known as the Gulshan-e-Moeen and Gulshan-e-Fareed in Pakistan.

For a decade, Imran had been intimately involved in these big-money deals, but his name had been carefully kept off the paperwork. Among the benefits of storing their proceeds in their father's name in Pakistan was that the FBI would not see the money and not be able to seize it. But that plan only worked as long as their father was alive. After his death, some of those assets were legally Gilani's. Muhammad had made sure of that in his will. The brothers needed a Pakistani power of attorney to take ownership of his property and assets, and Gilani refused to grant it.

Gilani was a simple woman who at times sought refuge in superstition—she said the number sixteen had special significance to Abid, implying that he might have pulled the plug on his father January 16 to get the money—but she wasn't stupid. The Awans had taken her husband's will and financial papers, but she knew his assets in Pakistan were valuable. She also knew that Imran's threats weren't bluster. In Pakistan, she'd seen how he received protection from armed government agents, and in America, he seemed to have important influence as well. She was smart enough to recognize that a meek, burka-clad woman stood little chance of navigating the easily corruptible Pakistani legal processes against savvy and rich stepsons who were cutthroat and singly focused like no one she had ever met.

Even if she could afford a plane ticket to Pakistan, trying to claim the money herself was too risky in multiple ways. That $50,000, and the prospect of the chance to lay her head again in that Springfield, Virginia home was tempting. Sure, it's a bad deal, but what's the alternative? The brothers had calculated right again, and the widow, in a moment of weakness, told Imran she would sign the Pakistani power of attorney. Imran turned sweet, called her "mom," and removed the listening devices in front of her. But the manipulation was a little too overt. She thought: "If you say you are my son, then why are you keeping my phone conversations listened to?" At the last moment, her sister convinced her it would be the wrong thing to do, and she didn't sign it.

Gilani, so she told me, knew giving in was wrong and that this wasn't just about the money, but about how those boys had gotten it. Syed also convinced her to look beyond her immediate survival. "I am fighting to protect the country," he said. "These are very bad people with such a greedy mentality. They can do anything for a single penny. This is what their nature is. If they had any opportunity to get some information from Congress, they would sell it to somebody."

Syed—who knew the brothers well and had even loaned Abid money—told me that Abid was sending iPads and iPhones to government officials in Pakistan. Imran "would entertain people from Pakistan, send gifts to the government officials. He used to come home and tell the dad 'I sent such and such to the police or an official in Pakistan,'" he said. "A few months ago, Abid gave them so many iPhones to distribute."

With the life insurance dispute tossed to the Virginia civil courts to decide, a judge set a deadline for Gilani to plead her side. It was a civil case and, just as the brothers had architected, she couldn't afford a lawyer to handle it for her. Precisely because the brothers had so thoroughly fleeced her, it looked as if they'd get away with it. Gilani begged me—whether because she thought I had some sort of Washington connections, or simply because I was one of the few American-born people she knew—to connect her to a lawyer who'd work free of charge. But I'd just met her and didn't think that was my role. If I knew the stakes back then, and how outgunned one side would be at every turn, I would have made a different choice.

She missed the deadline. Soon after, a relative referred her to a lawyer who would take the case for what she could afford. But you get what you pay for. Gilani's lawyer was Michael Hadeed—a convicted felon who had just had his law license reinstated after a long disbarment. Now, he was basically a small-time lawyer who'd take whatever work he could get—DUIs, divorce, traffic tickets—working out of an old rowhouse alongside his wife.

If there are alpha males and beta males, Hadeed may be the first omega male. As I got to know him, I concluded that he committed his crime not because he was a bad person, but because he was a bad lawyer. Cheating was the only way he'd ever win a case. The way he wound up a convicted felon started with a former client who owned the King of Pita Bakery in Virginia. He didn't pay his bill, so Hadeed let him work it off by arranging a ghost employee scheme in which the restauranteur would place visa applicants into fake jobs at the bakery. The bakery wrote paychecks to create a paper trail, but the money was returned in cash.

Processing a work visa was easier than litigating real immigration petitions. When one man sought political asylum—a legally interesting and emotionally meaningful case—Hadeed said it would be "easier and faster" just to get him a work visa through the pita place. When the jig was up, Hadeed had a breakdown. "They're coming for me next. I should have known. I shouldn't have been in this," he cried.

On the surface, the Awan insurance tort was a family dispute one step above small claims. That made Hadeed think he could handle it, and he was willing to do so for the meager amount of money that Gilani was able to borrow from a friend. But Hadeed raised his eyebrows when he saw that Abid had enlisted Jim Bacon, a powerhouse white-shoe attorney whose defense practice specialized in major international money laundering cases. What few realized is that, as Imran's wife Sumaira told me, Bacon had been helping the Awans structure their money moves for years.

Who among us doesn't have an ongoing engagement with a money-laundering attorney? Hadeed had crossed paths with Bacon before, and Bacon was the kind of man who, a few decades earlier, might have beaten him up on a playground.

Hadeed thought it was recklessly arrogant of the Awan brothers to pursue a lawsuit against their own stepmother for chump change at the same time they were subjects of investigations by the media, Congress, and the FBI. The civil suit opened them up to the legal process known as "discovery," in which they would have to turn over almost any documents Hadeed demanded, including banking records, that were relevant to the case. The brothers knew that, but assumed Gilani would not fight back.

I'd already come to the same realization, which is why I needed Hadeed so badly. By the time the wheels of justice rolled forward, I'd begun to realize that this story was bigger than I first thought, and the discovery process could be used to unearth crucial information about Congress' inner workings. The Awans and Congress members had all refused to speak to me, but under oath in a deposition as part of this civil case, Abid would have no choice. I'd also realized that Gilani—whose wild stories told through broken English at first seemed over the top—wasn't making this up and needed help. I'd never seen a woman so helpless, and so rightfully in despair, in my life.

The timing of the life insurance move, coming during a critical moment of a high-profile criminal case, illustrated that Abid had motive to defraud. And the long history of deception by Abid that could be readily demonstrated with public government records—from tax fraud to bankruptcy fraud to lying on his House ethics disclosures—showed a past pattern of behavior that even I, as a non-lawyer, knew could be helpful to Hadeed as far as his task at hand, which was showing whether Abid had swindled his stepmother out of $50,000.

Gilani gave me Hadeed's contact information and asked me to brief him, so I did. But he seemed disinterested. Of all the possible reactions to what I was telling him—involving congressional servers, suitcases of cash, and FBI investigations—I could understand excitement or disbelief, but not disinterest. I had to find some way to make him understand how these two cases related, and how a rigorous discovery served both our interests. A few days before the court date, I happened to watch an Amazon TV series *Goliath,* in which a disgraced alcoholic lawyer played by Billy Bob Thornton salvages his reputation by pulling the thread of misconduct in a $50,000 case until it blossomed into an award of half a billion dollars. Gilani was a meek, broken woman, and the person she was counting on to advocate for her, Hadeed, was a meek, broken man. But he was also someone I imagined was searching for redemption and triumph. He had to be convinced that this case could resurrect his career and put his name back in the headlines—for a positive reason this time. Given the amount of money Gilani was indicating she might be entitled to in Pakistan, there could even be big money for Hadeed if he played his cards right. I thought a rousing, in-person speech could do it. On the escalator ride up to the floor that housed the civil courtrooms for the initial hearing, I mouthed the motivational speech to myself. But when I actually gave it, its effect was deflated by Hadeed repeatedly dropping his papers on the ground and bending down to gather them up while saying, "Oh, geeze." I couldn't understand how the balding man with chest hairs sticking out through a rumpled shirt didn't seem to find a thrill in the twists and turns of chasing down new leads and pursuing justice wherever it took us.

Technically, the lawsuit was only between Abid and Gilani, but the entire family, except Hina, who had already fled the country, showed up to present a unified front. When I walked by Abid outside the courthouse, he smirked and told me I wasn't "authorized" to take his picture. Just before the parties were summoned into the courtroom, Abid offered to settle the case with Gilani by splitting the money. But Gilani wouldn't settle. She later told me, "I didn't do the deal because they had been adopting bad behaviors. I cannot agree to that. It wasn't about the money."

In the hearing—which was to address a motion for default filed by Abid's lawyer within minutes of Gilani missing the deadline—Abid's lawyer told the judge he was poor and needed the $50,000 to pay the bills, omitting the fact that the immediate family had long cleared the better part of a million dollars a year. The judge admonished that whatever the law might say about deadlines, he found it unusual that Abid filed an insurance claim the day after the death and then used the widow's period of mourning against her. Most people are too busy grieving to think about money for a while after the death of someone they love.

The judge denied Abid's motion for summary judgment and gave Hadeed more time to prepare. The life insurance dispute would live to see another day, and with it, the fate of vast sums of Pakistani wealth, for which no power of attorney had been assigned.

Hadeed was a striking example of a phenomenon I'd encounter again and again. One in which, even when people saw what was happening, they stood by passively. "Good luck with your stories," he told me, as if this was *my* bizarre, frightening series of events. But I didn't ask for this. I just did what I assumed anyone would if they'd peeped through this astonishing porthole. In the end, I came to see that most people are reluctant to believe their lives could harbor the vividness and stakes of a Hollywood drama right there in front of them. It's a strange tendency, the urge to believe the interesting stuff only happens to someone else, to bigshots and celebrities, or behind TV screens. That an ordinary person like you or me could never and should never get caught up in something wild and major. But I'm here to tell you that the thing about ordinary people is there's a lot of us, and when those wild things occur—and they do— statistically speaking, we're *exactly* the people who'd get caught up.

Faced with the moment when you risk just a little to make a big difference, most people recoil. They all hope the next guy will do it. And Hadeed was unlikely to become our Billy Bob Thornton lead. When I told him I suspected that his client, who was literally homeless, actually had millions of dollars in assets that she could obtain with the right legal assistance, he looked at me like I was crazy. A few months and a 15,000-mile round trip to Pakistan later, when I tried to tell him I'd obtained the documents proving that Gilani was entitled to a portion of two massive real estate developments, he didn't return my call.

ELEVEN

"ROB YOU WITH THEIR TONGUES"

Who was this exceptionally manipulative person named Imran Awan and how did he come to command such influence over so many people? For that matter, how does an entire set of brothers manage to turn out this way? The answer seemed to lie in the father, Muhammad.

In the U.S., Muhammad collected a disability check, and on insurance records, he said he made only $1,200 a year working as a religious adviser. Yet 7,000 miles away, he somehow controlled assets sufficient to unleash a cutthroat game of cat and mouse among a sordid cast of Pakistanis. Incorporation records showed five different LLCs running out of Muhammad's modest home in Springfield, Virginia, including "Vienna Real Estate Corp.," a financial lender named "Express Services Corp.," and a nonprofit, the "International Sufi Educational Organization." Many of these LLCs mentioned the name Sampson T. Winfield.

Winfield was a real estate assessor who had been blacklisted for inflating home values. Public records suggested he had multiple wives in Ohio, went by multiple names, and had conducted mortgage fraud. Now he lived an hour outside of D.C. in Bristow, Virginia. Despite the obviously suspicious businesses that linked the elder Awan and Winfield, the FBI never bothered to talk to him. I did. Like so many of the people who'd dealt with them, Winfield had come away with the notion that even in a world of thieves, the Awans had no honor.

Winfield told me that he had discussed several business ideas with Muhammad Awan, but when he realized the Awans "were not good people," he stopped.

"The father is a crook, every time I help him, he was not a good man," Winfield said.

Muhammad told him he had made a fortune in admittedly stolen Pakistani real estate, which he was willing to invest in Winfield's businesses, Winfield said. "He was a big fraud. They took a lot of people's land. I told him on judgment day you're going to be in trouble."

He summed up the Awans' modus operandi: "They rob you with their tongues."

———

Even as a teenager in Faisalabad, Pakistan, Imran pulled the strings in the family.

In 1997, Imran Awan applied to immigrate to the United States under the diversity lottery. He won. The family—Muhammad, Imran, Abid, Jamal, sister Adeela, and their mom, Tahira—borrowed money for the plane tickets to the United States, and when they arrived, stayed with distant relatives: Nasim Akhtar, who owed the federal government six figures in outstanding taxes, and her husband, who was indicted on charges of Medicaid fraud. Akhtar told me the Awans were not exactly grateful, and "the relationship was ruined over money." The Awans ripped them off, something that surprised her since "there was an expectation of trust given the relationship."

The Awans acquired a garden apartment of their own in the same development on Manitoba Drive in Alexandria, Virginia, a complex full of Pakistani nationals. For whatever else might be said about Imran, no one has ever called him lazy. His pursuit of money—in the early days simply to support the family—knew no bounds. He'd run home from high school, toss his backpack inside, and work at the McDonald's across the street until midnight.

His father was more interested in manipulating the system than in working. He took a series of jobs, but only as an excuse to get disability payments.

"He doesn't like to work. He was working for a while for me at KFC and he told me his knee was broken, so I said, 'Don't pick up anything heavy.' Then he said, 'My knee got hurt at work, do you have insurance?' I said, 'You lied to me; you told me you hurt it back home playing football,'" Winfield told me. "He got a job in Washington, D.C. and sued the company for hurting the same knee; then he got disability from it. It was a maintenance company. He retired from there and said he hurt his knee shoveling snow."

I was starting to see that, at best, Gilani had a blind spot when it came to her husband. I'd discovered in court documents that he'd changed his name from Muhammad Awan to Haji Shah, and when I asked her why, she told me it was because Imran had stolen his disability money and he wanted to distance himself from his criminal sons. But that wasn't the full truth. To Pakistanis, the last name Shah indicates one is a descendant of the holy prophet of Islam. Haji has similar spiritual connotations. To Pakistanis I spoke with, falsely fashioning himself as a member of that caste amounted to fraud, and he used it to represent himself as a faith healer selling snake oil to the uneducated masses of Manitoba Drive. "He became a fraud priest. He puts in newspaper: 'I can make you heal if you give me money,'" Winfield said. "He takes money from people with his talking."

Imran, the eldest child, was trained as Muhammad's apprentice. Lithe, handsome, and charismatic, Imran was a good talker, especially with women. Muhammad would find men who were suffering from cancer and other deadly ailments and send Imran to convince their wives to exchange their life savings—sometimes as much as $20,000—for the continued life of their spouses. The pair learned as much as possible about their targets, and Imran would talk his way in with flattery. "So many naive people, they got entrapped. He was making a lot of money," Winfield said. Relying on Muhammad's spells in lieu of medical procedures, the clients often died.

Within a few years, and after working his way through community college and even Johns Hopkins University at a frantic pace, Imran used that charm to talk his way into an arena where the stakes were much higher: Congress. In his early twenties and while still not a U.S. citizen, he began working in congressional IT through a contractor, InterAmerica Corp., now iConstituent, which managed data about people who requested help from their Congress members; data that could include Social Security numbers and other sensitive information. One of the people he worked for through the contractor was Florida Representative Robert Wexler, who in 2004 hired Imran directly. An InterAmerica executive told me that Imran had signed a non-compete agreement to prevent Imran from cutting out the middleman, but Congressman Wexler warned the company not to try to enforce it.

Imran became a citizen sometime that same year and his client list soon expanded to include Representatives Debbie Wasserman Schultz of Florida and Representative Xavier Becerra of California.

His early employers encouraged newly elected members to place him on their payrolls and was soon making the maximum salary allowed under House rules. That's when his relatives began appearing on the House payroll. As soon as more dollars could no longer be attributed to that person under the House rules, another relative appeared, then another. You could see it in the salary records: the Awans spread like a virus, capturing key influencers, then percolating out through their ranks. The Awans' employers include four of the last five chairs of the House Democratic Caucus, four of the last five chairs of the Congressional Black Caucus, and the two most recent chairs of the Congressional Hispanic Caucus. Immediately after Imran gained citizenship, he married his first cousin, Hina Alvi, automatically conveying citizenship onto her. She joined the House payroll as well.

He'd always had his eye on another Pakistani woman, Sumaira, but she was married. Sumaira's husband was murdered, and Imran wed her in Pakistan, taking her as a second wife under Sharia law.

Imran and Hina moved to a single-family home in the suburbs but kept Sumaira in an apartment on Manitoba Road. According to a police report, he also kept a third woman a few doors down in the same complex, and after that woman called the police on him, the officers found her bloodied. Imran sometimes spent the night with Hina, sometimes with Sumaira, and occasionally with other women, including Sumaira's cousin.

Even while working for Congress, the brothers spent significant time in Pakistan. In 2007, their mother died in a car accident there. The youngest Awan, Jamal, was thirteen years old, and he fell under Imran's wing, eagerly doing whatever his older brother asked. Though Jamal still had a father, Imran legally adopted his youngest brother and used the paperwork to put him on congressional health insurance as a dependent. Jamal was Imran's eager gofer—his duties included ferrying papers between Imran and the Pakistani embassy—while balancing a normal life enrolled at George Mason University. When Jamal was twenty, he joined the House payroll at $160,000 a year.

There was also an Awan sister, Adeela, who wed Naeem Shah, her next-door neighbor in Springfield, Virginia, in an arranged marriage. Naeem didn't trust the brothers, and they apparently didn't trust Adeela. They refused to arrange for congressmen to place her on their staffs. Instead, like many of the Awans' associates from the Manitoba Road apartments, she found employment in government, in her case, administering car and real estate taxes for Fairfax County.

After growing up in Faisalabad with fourteen people crammed into a three-bedroom house, and his grandfather commuting to farmers' fields on horse-drawn cart, no amount of money seemed to be enough for Imran. He amassed a stunning amount of wealth, controlling the family's assets as one pool of money while maintaining a superhuman ability not to spend a dime. He told Sumaira that—though I assume it was a wildly inflated boast—the assets he had squirreled away in Pakistan were worth $77 million, eleven times what the family was paid by Congress. Either way, from the outside, no one would guess the income he had coming in.

The middle brother, Abid, lacked those superhuman abilities. Imran needed him to serve as a lieutenant, but he was always the weakest link. Abid had only a high school degree when he was placed on the House payroll at $165,000 a year, while simultaneously running the CIA car dealership. The cocky Abid was a schemer like Imran, but wasn't as good at it. Most of the evidence of wrongdoing that authorities discovered on Capitol Hill involved him, and like any normal person, he felt that the purpose of having lots of money was to enjoy it. While Imran drove around in a rusted-out sedan that a fellow IT aide described as an "oxidized piece of shit," Abid had a black BMW M3, lowered like a rapper's. It must have cost $100,000.

Ajmad Khan, a business partner at the car dealership, told reporters from the Daily Mail that when Abid went into D.C., he "would spend $3,000 or $4,000 a night" at nightclubs. "Abid would say, 'I work for the government, I don't care. I have a

$120,000 job and my wife is working, my brother's working, this one's working, that one's working.'"[1] Abid couldn't restrain himself from unorthodox transactions, with money flying in every direction. He loaned $30,000 to a Hispanic man on the terms that it be repaid a few days later, then sued him when he failed to pay. When Abid declared bankruptcy to discharge one million dollars in debts, his documents revealed that his creditors ranged from a possible stripper to a wealthy student from the United Arab Emirates.

The most out-of-place appearance was the Abid's wife Nataliia Sova, a bombshell blonde from the Ukraine who seemed to have no public-record footprint in the U.S. whatsoever until she married him.

———

Between Imran's real estate broker job, Abid's purported car dealership, Jamal's college, and Rao Abbas' burger flipping, it's hard to imagine that the members of the Awan clique were actually earning their $160,000 salaries as IT experts on Capitol Hill. No one was pretending people like Sova had any IT qualifications. "Whether they had formal training or not, they were trained on the job by Imran," Imran's lawyers said.

A car dealership associate said Abid "would just go in [to Capitol Hill] a couple times a week for a couple of hours, just to show his face. On paper I think [Abid and Imran] were both working, but in reality, only one was working." When Gilani's cousin Syed asked Abid what he did for work, Abid said he'd have to ask Imran. When Abid did show up on the Hill, he told people he someday hoped to work for himself rather than his brother—an acknowledgement that even though on paper he was hired and employed directly by congressmen, the House paychecks were all being aggregated by Imran, who then dished out a cut to his proxies.

For a time, Haseeb Rana, a man of Indian heritage whom Imran knew from high school and had bona fide IT qualifications, was "hired" by Imran and forced to do the work of several high-paid aides for a fraction of the salary. His father told me that at first he was proud of his son for getting in with Imran because Imran's home was full of portraits of prominent politicians, and he projected success. But Rana quit angrily after only a few months, unwilling to be taken advantage of.

There are no timecards to punch in the House and no way of proving who was actually working, short of having members of Congress testify that they'd been signing paychecks month after month to people they never saw. Members were unwilling to do this. Rana would have made a key witness in a prosecution into taxpayer dollars going to no-show workers, but investigators didn't even appear to know about him because their review didn't go back in time. By the time investigators got around to approaching him, if they ever bothered at all, Imran had hooked Rana up with his lawyer, Chris Gowen, bringing their interests into alignment and ensuring Rana wouldn't talk. Gowen wouldn't say who paid Rana's legal bill.

Until 2014, Representative Ted Deutch of Florida curiously paid Imran a few hundred dollars a year, enough to make him technically a staffer. More money went to Abid's wife, Nataliia Sova. In recent years, the only member of the group on his payroll was McDonald's employee Rao Abbas. Deutch also had another IT employee based in Florida, and he wouldn't say what the purpose of all these aides was or whether he'd ever seen Abbas.

With fierce competition for limited staffing slots, there is little reason for members of Congress to spend scarce salary funds on no-show workers unless there was something in it for them. The idea of a "ghost employee" scheme—where a congressman pays a no-show employee taxpayer funds in exchange for cash back under the table—is well known to Congress, and the idea that Democratic members of Congress might be involved in such a scheme with the Awans would have been enough for the Democratic leadership to want to block any investigation.

Former Democratic Representative Corrine Brown of Florida is currently in prison for indulging such a scheme. Other current members of Congress have raised eyebrows, if not been prosecuted, for the people they have put on the congressional payroll.[2]

A sizeable contingent of representative-elects come to Washington with notions of wealth and power only to find that they were unrecognizable back-bench members who suddenly had to maintain two households. The Awans' most vocal advocates tended to be Congress' poorest members. In 2008, as the Awans cemented their inroads in Congress, the Awans' original patron, Robert Wexler, was deeply in debt. So was Andre Carson. Gregory Meeks, Yvette Clarke, Kendrick Meek, and Debbie Wasserman Schultz all ranked among the House's most financially struggling.[3] In later years, newer Awan employers, like Joaquin Castro, also were in debt.

As of 2015, Representative Emanuel Cleaver of Missouri had the second-biggest money problems in the House, with two million dollars in debt.[4] He also paid Rao Abbas as his only IT employee. When my colleague Kerry Picket asked him about the cybersecurity implications of the Awan investigation, Congressman Cleaver said it had never occurred to him that the criminal investigation into his IT aide could mean his emails were at risk. He tried to dodge the question about the McDonald's worker by saying, "Imran is the guy who worked in our office. I don't know this other guy." Since Kerry got the whole thing on tape, an ethics group filed a complaint. "Cleaver used taxpayer dollars to pay over $60,000 to Abbas, who he did not know, and the evidence indicates did not do work for him," it said. "There is no logical or reasonable explanation for Cleaver to affirmatively identify Awan as his employee unless Awan was the individual actually providing IT services. Cleaver accepted IT services and incredibly would have given full access to his data and files to someone who was not on his staff." The complaint was filed by the Foundation for Accountability & Civic Trust, which was headed by Matthew Whitaker, who would go on, when it was too late, to replace Jeff Sessions as acting attorney general. But then, he was just a little-known attorney.

And the ethics committee did nothing with the complaint, even though congressmen are in violation of House rules when they pay people who don't actually work for them and let non-staffers access their data.[5]

The liberal group, Citizens for Responsibility and Ethics in Washington, has named Representative Gregory Meeks of New York on its annual list of corrupt congressmen more times than almost anyone else.[6] A New York state bribery sting that brought down state lawmakers failed to implicate him after the person whose house was outfitted to record incriminating admissions found that Meeks "only meets in parks." In 2007, Meeks took $40,000 from Queens businessman Edul Ahmad. When confronted by officials, he claimed it was a loan. But he "received the money without any discussion of interest rates, due dates, or collateral requirements," and made no effort to repay the "loan" until 2010, after the FBI questioned Ahmad about the money. Though Meeks never disclosed any loan on three years of ethics statements, the House gave him a pass. Ahmad's lawyer told the ethics body that there was no loan paperwork, but Meeks told them he'd "misplaced" it. Meeks turned his association with criminals—Ahmad was a convicted mortgage fraudster—into something that worked in his favor. "The committee found the credibility of the lender, Edul Ahmad, insufficient against the word of Representative Meeks because Mr. Ahmad had pled guilty to fraud charges in an unrelated case," Citizens for Responsibility and Ethics in Washington wrote. "Apparently, if members are caught illegally pocketing cash, they need only claim to have made an honest mistake and the House Ethics Committee will take them at their word."

Congress protects its own. The FBI had circumstantial evidence that the Awans might be involved in a kickback scheme with congressmen or chiefs of staff, in part because the Awans had been the subjects of hundreds of bank-generated suspicious activity reports flagging possibly criminal large-dollar transactions over the years.

Proof was lacking, but so was a desire on the part of the Democrats in Congress to search for it.

In the early 1990s, an investigation into embezzlement by a single House employee grew into one that found a large portion of congressmen systematically manipulating House finances. The leadership covered it up, and congressmen blamed incompetence by the institution's back offices. But the chairman of the Ways and Means Committee eventually went to prison, in part for paying ghost employees. The scandal led to the replacing of the House bank with a credit union that was supposed to be less willing to do favors for insiders, and the creation of the inspector general's office.

TWELVE

PAKISTAN

An advanced investigative technique, "Googling it," might have helped authorities learn everything they needed to know about Imran Awan if they had wanted to know.

A 2009 article in the Pakistani newspaper, *Dawn*, available online in English, revealed that Imran was a serial fraudster who surrounded himself with other morally compromised individuals, systematically exploited the vulnerable, double-crossed his partners, routinely extorted and threatened witnesses, framed his victims for crimes, and used political influence to get away with it.[1]

The story was headlined "Influential expat shields father from long arm of law," and centered on Muhammad Awan's real estate development. According to the story, Muhammad had purchased "huge chunks of land from different farmers," but his checks had bounced. A dozen farmers filed a criminal complaint against Muhammad and he was arrested. "The police high-ups," however, "are 'ominously' indifferent to proceed against Awan," because Imran, mistakenly identified as a White House employee, had intervened. "Sources said that some 'power muscles' in the federal capital as well as in the provincial capital had phoned the local police to lend all sorts of help to the U.S. national and his father," *Dawn* reported, saying it was "noteworthy" how fervently they were "complying with the desires of the U.S. national."

Imran influenced the police to charge the victims with crimes instead, according to *Dawn*. The police "harassed" the farmers, who had lost everything they had to their names, and implicated them in "frivolous" cases. Imran filed outlandish claims, with police alleging that five elderly farmers had stolen four million rupees from *him* and subjected the then-twenty-seven-year-old to "severe torture." The farmers swore they were nowhere near where Imran said this improbable beating had occurred. Nineteen people were subjected to retaliatory charges. Even the victims' lawyer was arrested.

"Muhammad Abid, a victim of Awan's alleged high-profile swindling, said that Awan's son had easy access to the corridors of power and that's why he was able to [pressure] the police to dance to his tunes," *Dawn* reported.

But that wasn't the worst of it. Not long before, there was a car wreck on the side of one of Pakistan's dangerous, winding roads. The car was carrying both of Imran's parents as well as Shabbir Ahmed, one of Muhammad's two business partners on the land deal. Ahmed and Imran's mother Tahira were killed. Muhammad was injured, but survived. In the hours after his own mother tragically died, Imran appeared to have one thing on his mind: how to gobble up Ahmed's share of the company before Ahmed's relatives could inherit it. According to the *Dawn* reporters, Ahmed's grieving

widow said that "Imran was threatening her with dire consequences for not transferring the remaining properties to his father's
name." He also tracked down Ahmed's brother in Lahore, who
worked for the government, and harshly retaliated.

The third business partner in the real estate deal, Rashid
Minhas, had been arrested alongside Muhammad, and the paper
commented that Muhammad Awan "distanced himself from
Minhas," leaving him to take the fall for the land fraud.

I had seen Minhas' name before. In the litany of Awan-
related calls to the Fairfax County police that I obtained under
Freedom of Information laws, there was an entry for alleged
threats between Muhammad and Minhas. That suggested that
Minhas was in the United States. As an Awan associate, the first
place I thought to look for Minhas was prison. I was right. I also
figured he might talk, because being locked up in the Federal
Prison Center in Duluth, Minnesota, inmate number 43396-424
was safe from the Awan family.

Rashid Minhas is a criminal, so I took whatever he said with
a big grain of salt. But I recognized him as a man very much like
the Awans.

According to court documents, Minhas stole $1.1 million,
including $700,000 from American Muslims in a callous ploy
that used their faith against them. He set up purported travel
agencies that sold cheap tickets to the Hajj, the obligatory trip to
Mecca. Instead of providing the tickets, he sent buyers letters
saying Allah didn't want them to go, but that there would be no

refunds. "He blamed the whole thing on God, not on this thing that he did to us," one victim recounted in court. Prosecutors said, "Minhas did not just steal the victims' money; he stole their opportunity to satisfy an important religious obligation." As one victim said, "I don't know if we have another opportunity in our lifetime to…save that much money."

As a sentencing memo explains, Minhas used his knowledge of the travel industry's central computer system, the Airlines Reporting Corporation, to exploit a "loophole in ARC's electronic payment system for paper tickets to steal victims' money by selling paper tickets that he then voided."

"He is, as the victims will tell you, an exceptionally smooth salesman," prosecutors said. "When Minhas knew that his fraud had been discovered in March 2009, he fled the country for Pakistan," where he had transferred $300,000 of his ill-gotten gains. "To add insult to injury, when the victims found him in April 2009, Minhas required that the victims sign a release of liability. In most cases, even after signing the release, victims still were not repaid."

A week before his trial in August 2014, Minhas provided receipts indicating that Muhammad Aslam, the previous owner of the travel agency, and had stolen the money. "The receipts were fakes and were intended to frame Aslam," the government's sentencing memo says. In his rebuttal, Minhas noted that he was part of "the FBI Citizen's Academy working with the immigrant community."

I sent a letter to Minhas in prison. A few weeks later, I received a response: "The name you mention in letter, these are the DEVIL family from Pakistan. Awan brothers are professional liars, for money they can sell their own mother. He made fake robbery case on me and seventeen others, and they are waiting for him to back to Pakistan after losing JOB in U.S. government," it said. "Last time I seen Mr. Devil Awan in Pakistan 2010 about him and his father commit fraud with me and other landlords in Faisalabad, Pakistan...The way he used his resources through Congress to call U.S. Embassy in Islamabad and Pakistani officials, it was so bad."

Minhas became my pen pal, and he had much more to say.

Minhas wrote: "In 2007, Mr. Awan family showed me dirty blood in their body, and from 37 acres they only transfer 1000 sqft, oh yes, only 1000 sqft, on my name, and I was third thirty-four percent partner."

"On Funeral day in Faisalabad," after the car crash that killed Shabbir Ahmed and Imran's mother, "many peoples were telling me, [Muhammad] Awan transfer land on his name by FRAUD, just why GOD gave him punishment."

Imran had filed a police report in Pakistan saying Minhas had stolen $40,000 in cash and a laptop from him. When I asked Minhas about it, he didn't actually deny it, implying it was part of a war of retaliation against Imran. But he posed one question: how did Imran get so much cash to Pakistan? I had another: what was on the laptop—almost certainly a congressional one— that had wound up floating around a country that was, at that very moment, harboring Osama Bin Laden?

Minhas said that when Muhammad Awan was arrested for stealing land from the farmers, he screamed in the police station: "You don't know me, my SON (Imran) owns White House in

D.C., you will learn lesson forever...I am king maker and I can change prime minister."

When Imran arrived in Pakistan to bury his mother and extort and frame others, a U.S. Embassy official met him at the airport at 2 a.m. and escorted him into town to the hospital where his father was being treated. Imran wasted no time using this as a display of his influence. "Imran Awan said to me directly these words: 'See how I control White House on my fingertip, look [at] that guy (officer from U.S. Consulate was standing corner side in his father room in hospital). He was stand by inside airport waiting for me to welcome me in Pakistan.'" Imran bragged: "My boss called to Embassy."

What Minhas said next was shocking. His brother witnessed Muhammad give Rehman Malik, a former intelligence officer who went on to become Pakistan's interior minister, a USB of data. "After Imran father deliver USB to Rehman Malik, four Pakistani [intelligence] agents were with his father twenty-four hour on duty to protect him. Oh yes, some Pakistani [intel] agents were with him all the time, as per order of Rehman Malik (former interior minister). FBI can verify with my teacher SON in Lahore and other family members," Minhas said.

I wasn't confident in the truthfulness of this claim, but it provided an explanation for other stories I'd heard about Imran traveling with an entourage of Pakistani agents. Minhas said that, despite the ease with which I identified him as a person with knowledge of the Awan family's financial activities, the FBI had never contacted him as part of its investigation into the family.

I spent months weighing whether to publish Minhas' claims about the USB. It would be hard to either prove or disprove. One thing was clear: it was not as if the FBI had looked into this and found it to be false. It had no idea that this lead existed, just as it appeared blithely ignorant about so many others.

I thought about the strange course that led me here, an unwitting actor at the center of sensitive international events. Imran's M.O. for controlling Pakistani-Americans was, by now, a clear pattern: threatening violence against their loved ones in Pakistan.

"My three U.S. citizen children are in Pakistan," Minhas told me, and "Imran has corrupt police officer family members in Faisalabad." I confirmed he was telling the truth about that, and that Imran was paying one such officer.

If I published the story and the FBI still did nothing, Minhas' family could be in danger. If they asked around Pakistan *after* my story ran, if recent experience was any guide, witnesses would already have been silenced. How had this choice fallen to me?

I called the FBI and left a voicemail for the rookie FBI agent assigned to the Awan case, Brandon Merriman, but he never called me back. The Bureau never contacted Minhas.

You had the IT aide to Debbie Wasserman Schultz, who was busted funneling data off congressional servers, undeniably displaying massive unexplained political power in Pakistan, and even claiming the power to change the president. The FBI—by then under the purview of Trump's attorney general, Jeff Sessions—knew all of this, and refused to even look into it.

I ran the story. Witness intimidation simply couldn't be rewarded. The silence needed to end.

While the American press for the most part ignored the Awan happenings, the Pakistani media was all over it. In my dealings with Gilani, I met Wajid Ali Syed, the Washington correspondent for one of Pakistan's largest TV networks. A generous and gentle man, Wajid was politically savvy, but couldn't understand why Congress, the FBI, and the American media apparently had so little interest in the case. We decided to team up, and Wajid boarded a plane to Faisalabad to find out more. In Faisalabad, everyone from neighbors to shopkeepers told Wajid about the remarkable sight of Imran traveling with his entourage of armed government agents and his constant boasts of mysterious political sway.

Wajid discovered that the Awans' land fraud scheme had not stopped after the death of Muhammad's wife and the cutting out of his two partners. Amended incorporation documents Wajid obtained from the local courthouse revealed that Muhammad was now a seventy percent shareholder of the development company, while his second wife Gilani, his son Abid, and his daughter Adeela each owned ten percent.

They subdivided the land they held into residential lots and began work on constructing the infrastructure to accommodate an entire town—in Pakistan, it's called a "colony"—which would need water lines, electricity, and a school.

Among their buyers was one particularly large customer who would take an entire section of the town. Faisalabad Agricultural University trained thousands of students to set up the city's textile industry and fuel the city's growth as a hub for food processing and chemical production.

As the college expanded, it decided to build new housing for its faculty.

The Academic Staff Association in charge of constructing the residences was led by Dr. Zafar Iqbal. When Wajid found him at his colonial-style residence on campus, Dr. Iqbal trembled with rage at the mention of the name Awan. He gave Wajid a copy of a signed agreement to sell land to house one hundred teachers.[2] The faculty paid in full, and records show that in 2008, the deeds to half the land were turned over, but the rest were not. Just as the Awans never paid for the land when seizing it, now they had sold that same land without actually giving it over. Instead, they were trying to sell the same land again to others.

For years, the faculty never got their land. Finally, they managed to obtain a court order restricting the developers from selling any plots without first resolving the issue, Dr. Iqbal said. Essentially, this meant a large portion of Imran's assets in Pakistan were tied up. If he intended to flee to Pakistan to escape the investigation into his work in Congress, that made the plan untenable. In January 2017, the professors cornered Imran in Pakistan. Imran warned them of his "powerful political connections in Pakistan and in the U.S." Eventually, he promised the professors they would finally get their deeds, and he flew back to Washington.

Imran rounded up cash from the Capitol's credit union and wired money to Pakistan—but it didn't go to reimburse the professors for what they'd paid. Instead, some of it went to a cousin on the Faisalabad police force, Azhar Awan. On Facebook, Azhar posed with aviator sunglasses and a military-style uniform. When I asked Chris Gowen, Imran's attorney, about the payments to the police officer, he said, "You need to understand how land purchases work in Pakistan and I don't have time to explain it to you." But I had a pretty good idea, and Dr. Iqbal saw it with his own eyes. Somehow, after the payoff to the cop, the court order was no longer being enforced.

The rest of the funds went to Saif Ullah Awan, a cousin of Imran's. Putting assets in his name rather than the Al-Moeen company's name ensured Gilani would be cut out of the deal. In July 2017, deed records showed that the land was instead transferred to Saif, who Dr. Iqbal said "is Imran's front man here."

Wajid took pictures of billboards encouraging would-be land buyers to call Saif Awan. He was selling the land out from under the university.

THIRTEEN

BACK IN THE HOUSE

(EARLY 2017)

After I published Samina Gilani's allegations that Imran Awan had extorted her while using high-tech surveillance methods, the back-office bureaucracy of Congress got very nervous. Most of us manage to go through life without ever being accused of such behavior. What were the odds that the very people who were funneling data off the House network just happened to employ such tactics outside of work? It seemed a bit silly to say that they would prey on their own family, but wronging their high-profile employers would be the one red line they'd never cross. How could the Administration Committee have missed so much? Had they made a grave mistake with their lackadaisical response to the discovery of highly irregular logins to congressmen's computer accounts and major breaches of the House's IT rules?

Jamie Fleet, Nancy Pelosi's puppeteer, had an idea. He had previously told his Republican counterpart on the Administration

Committee, Sean Moran, that neither side should talk to the media. But now he told concerned House officials that *he* was the source for all those stories in the *Daily Caller*. He was so on top of the Awan incident that he had discovered all these frightening patterns and leaked the information to me because it deserved attention. Everything, in other words, was under control, and no one needed to do anything more.

It was a diabolical ruse. At that point, I had never spoken with Jamie.

This was only one front in an all-out war to suppress the investigation. With the Awans banned from the network, Representative Wasserman Schultz launched a crusade, such as had never been seen before, to defend a lowly IT aide.

In March 2017, three members of Congress—Wasserman Schultz of Florida, Gregory Meeks of New York, and Marcia Fudge of Ohio—set up a meeting with House Inspector General Theresa Grafenstine. Wasserman Schultz opened the meeting by saying of the Awans, "I told them to do all of it. They were authorized." Theresa responded that the congresswoman hadn't even heard what they were suspected of doing. When Theresa cracked open a massive binder of evidence and walked them through it, Representative Meeks slapped his thigh and laughed at her in the meanest possible way. "That's all you got? You need a new job." None of the members had a background in computer science, but for ninety minutes, they berated an inspector general who did.

In a speech to a cybersecurity trade group in late 2017, Theresa said, "When I go to these scary meetings and I've got this five-inch binder of papers outlining a potentially criminal case, I go in to tell a member of Congress, 'I think your staffer is violating the law,' and having that person tell me, 'I think you're out of your mind,' when I've got this five-inch binder, that's a very tough conversation which I have had. The level of imbalance of power, I can't even begin to tell you what that's like. There were a lot of threatening, intimidating people that were very difficult to work with…They were screaming, screaming, pushing back with irrational things."

Representative Meeks made comments similar to Representative Wasserman Schultz's to *Politico*, saying that he had authorized the Awans—even, apparently, relatives who weren't employed by him—to do things with his data. It was an odd defense to say that IT aides can violate House rules if directed by a congressman. It also contradicted what House officials had stated in a February 3, 2017 memo which asserted that members of Congress had been unaware of the suspicious activity and had not consented to it. This premise set the stage for the Capitol Police to make clear that members of Congress were not targets of the investigation.

Meeks told *Politico*, "I have seen no evidence that they [the Awans] were doing anything that was nefarious." Actually, he had seen investigative findings that used that very word, "nefarious."[1]

Meanwhile, Jamie was schmoozing the House's top bureaucrat, Chief Administrative Officer Phil Kiko, who signed members' paychecks and oversaw payroll and procurement. He even invited Kiko to his wedding in Gettysburg in April 2017.

Kiko is a stodgy career Republican with the looks and demeanor of a small-town cop. Speaker Ryan appointed him as the House's chief administrative officer in September 2016, after

Kiko had a disappointing run as staff director to Representative Trey Gowdy's Benghazi Committee. The CAO knew better than anyone that the Awans had committed fraud, because it was that office that uncovered the falsified $499 invoices.

Kiko vacillated about how to approach the investigation. It was above his pay grade to defy members, particularly those like Representative Wasserman Schultz who served on the subcommittee that controlled his budget. Yet, he was deeply concerned by what I had found, not least that the Awans' own stepmother had accused Imran of wiretapping and extorting her at a time when, if investigators had chosen a different course, he might already have been in jail. Still, as the weeks passed, he perceived no mandate and little direction from Republicans, and a crushing pressure from Democrats not to pursue the investigation.

Kiko had told multiple people that Wasserman Schultz put her finger to his chest and said, "You're a fucking Islamophobe," adding that she'd invited the entire Awan family to her daughter's bat mitzvah. "You will not so much as take away their parking spots," she told him. Some of them also recounted that Kiko said Representative Wasserman Schultz blurted out an unusual detail, perhaps to emphasize the extent to which she trusted Imran: "I helped him with a land deal."

It was part of Kiko's job to be even-handed, and in every aspect of his job, he strove to manage the concerns of members of both parties. Accusations of favoring his own ilk hurt, given how groundless they were, and he went out of his way to avoid them. But when it came to the Awan case, he always heard a lot more from the Democrats than the Republicans. Jamie often had more face time with the nonpartisan staff involved in the investigation than Sean did. While Jamie had made the handling of the Awan case a priority, Republicans on the committee derided Sean for routinely missing key meetings.

Representative Wasserman Schultz was a senior member of the Appropriations Committee's Subcommittee c the Legislative Branch, which controlled the budget for the Capitol Police, inspector general, and chief administrative officer. So, when it came to Democrats, she was better positioned than anyone to use the force of government to influence the investigation. But Republicans controlled Congress, so smart Democrats found pliable Republicans and used them. As a career Republican now serving in a nonpartisan position, Kiko was the perfect puppet. While Kiko had no power to order changes outside of the Office of the Chief Administrative Officer, he had the ear of the Republicans who did, and if initiatives were laundered through him, they'd be taken seriously.

Wasserman Schultz pointed out publicly that it was Kiko's office that was supposed to stop IT violations from happening in the first place. Such a long-running, and in retrospect, obvious, scheme having gone undetected for so long couldn't possibly look good for his office, which had dozens of non-political employees whose job was to ensure congressional operations ran smoothly.

Democrats had somehow found a way to turn a Democratic scandal into a failure of the Republican majority's congressional administration. More confident and media-savvy practitioners would have seen that this was a stretch. The public would certainly assign the vast majority of the blame to Democrats. But these Republicans weren't such practitioners, and there was more than a grain of truth to what people like Wasserman Schultz were saying.

I had begun to see that the Awan scandal had been going on for many years and occurred because of a breathtaking lack of oversight. It turned out that every one of the Awans' forty-four employers exempted the IT aides from background checks. The rules required them, but the CAO's office was so disorganized that no one noticed. They didn't even notice when Imran reported on his House financial disclosure forms that his wife did not have an income, when in fact she was on the payroll of the House itself—an obvious misstatement that could have led to scrutiny which would have uncovered additional issues.

A few years earlier, part-time employees had been caught in a similar procurement scheme. The official response was to have all such employees sign a form pledging not to violate the rules. But when nearly half, or forty-five percent, of the staffers didn't even bother to do that, the CAO didn't notice, or at least didn't do anything about it. Every year, the House IG's annual audits warned that "ineffective controls over property and equipment" was a "significant deficiency." And every year, it went unaddressed.

While other IT aides presumably weren't concealing Hezbollah-linked car dealerships, some simply never filed their House ethics disclosure forms. Some other systems administrators were simultaneously being paid as corporate contractors and direct employees; a brazen and unpermitted scheme that brought the contractor/employees lucrative federal benefits *and* extra pay.

Though the CAO had eventually detected the procurement scheme involving pretending everything cost $499 so it was treated as petty cash, the CAO's office had signed off on such vouchers for years. After it was discovered—though all assumed that the scale of the equipment scam was far greater than documented—they simply stopped counting after going back in time a short ways, largely because House administrators kept records in such an antiquated way that old records were difficult to review.

The missed warning signs were so blatant, and the whole situation so egregious, that everyone involved had egg on their faces. Americans who already looked on Congress with contempt would have a field day with it if they knew. If Democrats feared that not protecting the Awans from criminal charges could lead to the retaliatory release of emails they'd rather keep secret, Speaker Ryan's Republican officials came to believe that the Awan case would expose a different secret about the party in charge of the House: that they were morons.

A defensiveness emerged; one that seemed to lead Kiko to believe that advancing Democrats' desire to make the probe go away with as little trouble as possible was actually working in his own interest. Kiko pressed the Committee on House Administration to try to hire me away from the Daily Caller News Foundation. At the time, I took it to mean that he wanted an investigator on the inside who would actually get to the bottom of the Awan case. I am now certain that Kiko's attempt to put me on the House payroll was actually designed to stop the public airing of what had happened.

Kiko's deputy, John Clocker, went to the Appropriations Committee to say that if the CAO had the budget for more auditors—specifically, if the budget for five staffers was taken from the IG and given to the CAO—then maybe they would have caught this stuff. In April 2017, he went further, proposing to a House Appropriations Committee staffer an idea to save some money: abolish the Office of Inspector General outright, with its fifteen investigators and auditors. It was an ask only a desperate person would make. The appropriations staffer knew doing away with an entity whose sole mandate was to make sure Congress wasn't corrupt would be political suicide. "Are they high?" he said of the CAO.

It wasn't the last attempt to neuter the House IG. In July of 2017, the House Administration Committee sent a memo modifying the IG's auditing powers, signed by both the Republican and Democratic committee heads. It contained the kind of accounting jargon a layman would not have been able to grasp, and assuming Jamie brought it to his Republican counterpart Sean and requested his approval, Sean would have likely had to rely on his characterization of what it did. In the accounting world, the provisions were significant and severely curtailed Theresa's ability to do her job. If she had to stay on the payroll, they could pay her to sit in the corner and do little.

The problem was that the most recent House-wide audit had caught numerous unrelated problems with the House's finances, and the committee was at the time hoping the office would give them a chance to fix the problems before releasing the negative report. She refused to give the House a "clean audit" unless they restored her powers, and they did. But the situation was no different than any office worker who comes under the ire of one of her bosses. Sure, you might be able to hang on a little longer, but what was the point? The chain of command had no shortage of ways to make your life miserable if they wanted to. The writing was on the wall. Theresa was eligible for retirement and turned in her notice.

Her departure should have made Jamie happy, except that Theresa leaving on her own accord posed another problem. Once on the outside, they had no control of her. And with a reputation as sterling as hers, if any of the facts of the Awan matter ever came into dispute, her word would rise above those of partisans like himself. Something had to change. Jamie ordered her not to tell anyone she was retiring—not even her own staff. He had a "communications plan" for managing the announcement. He said, as if it could explain the bizarre request, he wanted to throw her a party.

What Jamie really seemed to want to do was make it appear that Theresa had been forced out of her job and left under a cloud. That would enable House officials to say, if it came down to it, that her work in the Awan case was compromised, and that she—rather than the culprits—should face the wrath of the House's ethics system. Ironically, the pretext he settled on stemmed from her status as such a distinguished expert. As international chairwoman of the cybersecurity experts' association, Theresa frequently gave speeches discussing the importance of ethics in government, best practices in technology security, and strategies for building these skills. Some of these addresses are online. A typical message is: "I want to be able to get out there as a woman and encourage children to enter STEM (Science, Technology, Engineering and Math) fields and really get out there and show that there are role models in the field who are women and minorities, to people who traditionally have not been drawn to this STEM field." Nancy Pelosi's operative seemed to take the position that this was dangerous stuff.[2]

In one case, Theresa travelled to Malaysia to speak at a cyber-security conference and sign a ceremonial statement attesting to the importance of ethics and IT security. The tab was picked up by that country's version of the National Institute of Standards and Technology (NIST), which House administrators knew because she properly disclosed it in compliance with House rules. After she announced her plans to quit, Jamie, the Democratic staffer, latched onto this with ferocity. In the hands of a skilled political operator, perhaps this could be twisted into something that could ride the current of the ongoing narrative about "foreign meddling" in American politics. "This is highly unusual," he said. "She's signing statements with foreign governments." Jamie said she could be accused of violating the Logan Act, a law created in 1799 that essentially dealt with treason and which, if the claim wasn't absurd, would make her the first person ever to be convicted under it.

The juxtaposition was breathtaking. After a full year of knowing about readily provable violations of critical House rules—the falsification of financial records and logging into servers without authorization—by Pakistani immigrants who had financial ties to foreign government officials, the House had done nothing even though it had the full ability to enforce these rules on its own. The Awans' lies year after year on their ethics disclosures—misstatements designed to hide troubling financial activity—were open-and-shut felony cases by themselves. Now more intensity was being put into punishing a speech about ethics paid for by a foreign government entity than was ever put into punishing Imran Awan for connecting to House devices from Pakistan or running a purported car dealership that took money from an Iranian fugitive.

A call was placed to the legal counsel for the cybersecurity experts' association, which possessed the contract for the speech that would be needed to pursue some sort of half-baked ethics charge against the House's own investigator. *We'll subpoena you for it if we have to,* the association was told. *There will be hearings on this. Do you want to be dragged before Congress? You're going to look really bad.* The cybersecurity expert's lawyer was no Michael Hadeed, and he wasn't intimidated. Rather, he found the whole thing absurd. *On what basis? What has she possibly done that you'd want to go through all this effort?* Called out on it, Jamie seemed to realize he'd gone too far, and that this attempting to make hay out of such a non-issue was not exactly subtle. It reeked of desperation. Maybe he wasn't thinking clearly.

Theresa retired from the House as scheduled.

But what remained were her subordinates, a whole staff of investigators, some of whom had in-depth knowledge of the Awan case. The Capitol Police sought to silence them from talking about it. "Consider this your 6-E," the police told them, invoking to the name of a form the FBI uses as a gag order in cases it is actively working. It was a ruse. There never was any FBI gag order; a sign that the Bureau wasn't all that interested.

In twenty years of documenting malfeasance in the halls of power, Theresa had never met a case so big that they'd rather get rid of her than have her findings see the light of day. This was that case.

FOURTEEN

LAPTOP IN A PHONE BOOTH

(CAPITOL HILL, MAY 2017)

The irony was that the Committee on House Administration top Democrat Bob Brady and his staffer Jamie Fleet didn't even like Representative Wasserman Schultz, who many Democrats blamed for their defeat in the 2016 presidential election. Even if crafty messaging obscured it, when people said Russia "hacked the election," that really meant one thing: Russia allegedly hacked the DNC's emails, which revealed that Representative Wasserman Schultz had rigged the primary election against Senator Bernie Sanders. She'd used the party committee to take sides instead of running a neutral primary, demolishing grassroots enthusiasm on the party's left flank and faith in the system among moderates. This sordid behavior took high ground away from Democrats and prevented Clinton—who cheated during a debate by receiving a question in advance from DNC honcho Donna Brazile—from invoking the sort of idealism at which Barack Obama excelled. For some Democrats, every time President

Trump did something that infuriated them, and that was almost every day, they couldn't help but think that if it weren't for Representative Wasserman Schultz, everything might be different.

Once, during a staged photo with Democratic lawmakers, Representative Brady was situated near Representative Wasserman Schultz. He pulled on an aide's sleeve and asked to be moved. When the aide asked why, Representative Brady motioned to Wasserman Schultz. "Because of that fucking bitch," he said, in full earshot of the congresswoman. Democrats knew that the Florida congresswoman pressured new lawmakers to put the Awans on their payroll and blamed her for putting their cybersecurity at risk *again*—at the DNC *and* in Congress. *Doesn't she ever learn,* they thought. What Jamie knew, but few others did, is that even after the police banned the IT aides from the computer network, Representative Wasserman Schultz had kept Imran on staff. The House tried to help the Awans' employers deal with the ban by providing free replacement IT workers, but Representative Wasserman Schultz refused to accept the money-saving service. She claimed Imran was now a "consultant" working on her "websites and printers," which anyone could see seemed to involve network access. As if to jab her finger in the eye of investigators, she added Imran's wife Hina to her staff as the probe was in full swing, even though she'd previously only needed one IT aide. When Hina moved to Pakistan soon thereafter, Representative Wasserman Schultz knew a suspect in an ongoing criminal cybersecurity investigation had left the country, seemingly for good, and removed her from her payroll. She kept paying Imran.

Democrats saw how abnormal this was. How could someone who had just lost her high-profile job as chair of the DNC following a hack go out of her way to harbor to a criminal hacking suspect weeks later? Representative Wasserman Schultz's recklessness was placing them and the investigation at risk. Her actions raised deeply troubling questions about how such an IT aide had her wrapped around his finger. If nothing else, her paying of Imran while he couldn't be providing any meaningful service, at least without violating the police order, only underscored the suspicions about how this all began: a "ghost employee" scheme where Awan family members were being paid for no-show work.

This was too much even for Jamie, who leaked the story to *Politico* that Representative Wasserman Schultz was still letting Imran work in the House. After all he had done to try to fix this mess, she was putting him in a position that he could and would not defend.

Behind the scenes, Democrats were deeply concerned, but they sent signals to the media that there was nothing going on. The media took it as gospel. For months, news coverage of the Awan scandal was extremely limited and there were no arrests. What were the police waiting for?

By May 2017, I was banging my head against the wall. In any other time, my stories about the Awan scandal would have been front page news, but the media was obsessed with Trump. The fact that that the topic overlapped with two of the most discussed explanations for Clinton's loss— cybersecurity and possibly foreign meddling—made the lack of pressure even more jarring. However, it was becoming clear that the media was not interested in pursuing facts wherever they might lead so much as working backwards from a single-minded focus on Russia; a conclusion in search of evidence.

With every rock I overturned, it only got worse, but there was only so much time and too many witnesses to talk to. The army of reporters that would have ordinarily fanned out on the network of clues was conscripted elsewhere. That month, I got an email from one of the *New York Times'* top political reporters complimenting me on my findings. "Keep it up," he said. "We just don't have the resources to do it right now because it's all about Russia over here... but we may wind up wishing we had."

Around midnight, as I sat awake wondering why this hadn't commanded a SWAT team caliber response from the government and how both Imran and Hina had apparently been allowed to leave the country after authorities had concluded that they'd hacked Congress, my phone rang. If it weren't for the late hour, I would have taken it for a telemarketer and hit "ignore." On the other end was a Capitol Police officer. I knew instantly that if he was coming to me, it was as a last resort and his investigation was being stonewalled. I was right, and from that point forward, thanks to a personal slight from Representative Wasserman Schultz, he'd be a major source for me. On that night, he had a story about something that happened a month before.

In early April 2017, the hallways of the House of Representatives might as well have been a representation of the post-election national mood. Desks and chairs were piled up precariously for janitors to come collect, the detritus of a chaotic transition of power. Many Democrats had been evicted and their replacements didn't want to so much sit in the same office chair, it seemed. Or perhaps the exiled lawmakers didn't want to give them the opportunity. But dwarfing the effects of Republicans' electoral sweep was a nonpartisan tradition, with incumbents of both parties stopping everything to move to office space higher on the pecking order based on their seniority—closer to the Capitol dome, bigger, or with more windows. During the daytime, the buzz of activity in the halls diminished the scale of the upturned furniture, but at night, it was all that was left. That's the scene that Imran Awan stepped into one night, two months after he'd been banned from the House network.

Though forty-three members of Congress had fired him, Wasserman Schultz hadn't, and that meant he still had the green badge that gave him twenty-four-hour access to the Capitol complex, which is how he found himself navigating the long passages of the Rayburn building at such a late hour.

The House buildings contain statues attesting to the nation's history, but they also contain more mundane nods to the past in the form of cubicles that once served as phone booths. Now they are dirty alcoves, containing only a ledge with a hole where the phone line used to come in. During a hectic day of committee markups, it's conceivable that a lobbyist might enter to use his cell phone out of earshot of rivals, though I'd never seen one do so. At night, there was no conceivable reason to; the vacant hallways afforded just as much privacy. It was one of these phone booths that Imran entered around midnight. He placed several objects on the ledge: a government laptop, a notebook that said "attorney-client privilege," a letter to the U.S. Attorney for the District of Columbia, papers from the Pakistani government, and Xeroxed copies of his driver's license and congressional ID.

Imran set them down, then walked away.

At 12:21 a.m., a janitor noticed the items and alerted the Capitol Police. According to a late-night police report, the prominently placed ID card copies served to make clear that this was not misplaced possessions they could helpfully return, but evidence in a criminal case. "Approximately three to four months ago, this officer was requested by [the sergeant at arms] as police presence of four individuals being interviewed," the cop wrote after recognizing the name on the ID as one of the suspects. "It is unknown to the officer whether he is still employed."

The officer lifted the MacBook Pro's lid and the screen lit up. In the center was a square icon with a username, and below it, the password field. The username: "RepDWS."

There seemed to be only two possibilities: Imran had stolen the congresswoman's laptop, or she had given him the laptop in order to circumvent (and violate) the police's prohibition on Imran touching the network, which blocked his own computer from connected to the network. If it was the latter, Imran hardly seemed inclined to repay the favor since it was difficult to imagine he could have *accidentally* left such sensitive items in a room in which they couldn't possibly have been out of sight. In fact, the phone booth was in a different building than the one that housed Wasserman Schultz's office.

His attorney, Chris Gowen, later said Imran was not in the building after hours that night; something that would be hard to justify for an otherwise unemployed "consultant" who wasn't allowed to touch computers. That would mean he left it there sometime before six o'clock, and at no point in the next seven hours realized he had misplaced a trove of the most sensitive items imaginable and returned to get them.

In court, Gowen also told the judge that Imran merely walked away from the items momentarily when the cops darted into the room and snatched them. That would mean Imran was skulking around House office buildings where he didn't work at midnight.

After finding it, the officer woke his supervisor at 3 a.m. and asked for guidance. He was told to file a report.

Word got back to Representative Wasserman Schultz, who my police source told me was "frantic" and "not normal" for the next month. She screamed at the police. She was seen at a T.J. Maxx that weekend snapping at her daughter. She went to the House's general counsel to get him to block police from looking at the laptop, but wasn't satisfied with his answer, so she used campaign funds to hire his predecessor, Bill Pittard. Pittard had built his career on blocking the executive branch from getting their hands on congressional material, and now was in private practice with the law firm Kaiser Dillon. It was a highly unusual step since the House's general counsel represents all members for free, and if he couldn't help, that suggested it was because there were no legitimate legal grounds for doing so.

Beginning six days after her laptop turned up in the phone booth, Wasserman Schultz's re-election campaign paid Kaiser Dillon $41,000 for its work on the matter.

This wasn't a casual engagement. Wasserman Schultz was prepared to wipe out the bulk of her life's savings to clean up the

Awan incident. She racked up $59,000 in Kaiser Dillon fees that were payable by her personally, as opposed to the campaign. The most recent approximation of Wasserman Schultz's net personal assets, according to ethics disclosures, places them at $106,000.[1] Curiously, Kaiser Dillon agreed not to collect the money. On her 2017 ethics disclosure, she recorded it as a $59,000 "gift."[2] This is extraordinary. Understandably, strict rules prohibit corporations from giving massive gifts, whether in kind services or cash, to sitting members of Congress. None of the other 435 members of Congress reported a gift anywhere close to this size that year. Receiving it would require special permission from the Ethics Committee.[3] Luckily for her, two of the members more tied up with the Awans than perhaps anyone but her—Ted Deutch and Yvette Clarke—were on the ten-person committee.

Deutch was the ranking member.

But her involvement didn't end there. A source told me the congresswoman "stormed" into the U.S. attorney's office. Her brother, Steve Wasserman, is a prosecutor in the Washington U.S. attorney's office, the office handling the case. Steve, a board member of the National Association of Assistant U.S. Attorneys, tweeted about the ongoing case under the handle "fedpros," dismissing it as the "non-case" against his sister.

Representative Wasserman Schultz hadn't fired Imran when presented with evidence of "unauthorized access," nor when he was banned from the network. She hadn't fired him when his wife fled the country. Now she *still* wasn't firing him despite that even in the most innocuous of circumstances, losing a member's personal laptop would be a firing offense for negligence alone.

And given the totality of it all, it was hard for a reasonable person to chalk this up to negligence. Imran doesn't make mistakes, he plans ahead. "He cannot forget this stuff. He is very cunning, he does everything on purpose," his second wife Sumaira told me. I took it as a warning shot: *you think I'm not crazy? You think I won't release your stuff if you don't find a way to get me out of this? Try me. Think about what I have access to.*

With none of this public, and given the way the media had treated this case, if I reported it citing a single anonymous source, it would be ignored.

Incredibly, there was a video. The officer pointed me to the video feed of a subcommittee hearing from earlier that week; one so obscure that it had only thirty-four views when I loaded it. After I reported on its context, the video would be on the nightly news. That's because the dynamic that I knew to be true was plainly visible on Representative Wasserman Schultz's face and audible in her voice, which seemed to be on the verge of cracking. You didn't need to have been following the story to see that she appeared genuinely afraid of the police seeing what was on that laptop. A counterintelligence agent and profiling expert told me her mannerisms screamed of being the victim of blackmail.[4]

It was a hearing of the eight-person appropriations subcommittee responsible for approving funding for Congress's own internal operations. The purpose of the meeting was to decide how much money would be allocated for the Capitol Police in the upcoming year. Weeks before the force would become national heroes for two of its officers taking gunshots to save Majority Whip Steve Scalise from a politically-motivated assassination attempt, Representative Wasserman Schultz was on a warpath, with the leverage clear: slashing the budget of the police force whose mission was to protect Congress. She excoriated the police force's plump and mustached chief, Matthew Verderosa, for tenuous grievances before concluding with her ultimate agenda. "I'd like to know how Capitol Police handle equipment that belongs to a member or staffer that's been lost in the Capitol complex and found or recovered by one of your officers. What happens?"

The chief responded: "You have to be able to positively identify the property and be able to establish ownership. If it's part of an ongoing case, then there are additional things that need to be done."

Representative Wasserman Schultz became increasingly hostile and said a member's equipment could only be taken if the member herself was the subject of an investigation. The chief hinted that he believed Representative Wasserman Schultz might be falsely claiming a staffer's laptop was actually hers.

The chief said "If it's subject to an ongoing investigation, there are additional things—"

Representative Wasserman Schultz cut him off: "Okay, but not an ongoing investigation related to that *member*. If the equipment belongs to the member, it has been lost, they say it's been lost, and it's been identified as that member's, then the Capitol Police are supposed to return it."

"It depends on the circumstances," the chief said.

She was daring him to reveal whether she was a potential subject of the criminal probe. "My understanding is that the Capitol Police is not able to confiscate members' equipment when…the…*member*," she said, drawing out the last word, "is not under investigation."

"We can't return the equipment," the chief replied.

"I think you're violating the rules when you conduct your business that way, and you should expect that there will be consequences," Representative Wasserman Schultz barked. Then she abruptly turned off her mic, ending the hearing.

A few months later, when the heat got to be too much, Representative Wasserman Schultz changed her tune. "This was not my laptop. I have never seen that laptop. I don't know what's on the laptop," she said.[5]

But hours after the exchange with the police chief Verderosa, she followed through on her threat and tried to unseat him from his own board. The appropriations panel reconvened to grill House Sergeant at Arms Paul Irving, who is the House of Representatives' top security official and a member of the board that oversees that police chief. Representative Wasserman Schultz told him it was inappropriate that the police chief had a vote at board meetings and underscored that Verderosa wasn't in charge. "I'd like to know, sergeant, if you think that we should be looking at restructuring the way the board makes decisions so that we can establish a more direct line of accountability…At the end of the day, [the chief] doesn't have a decision-making role."

The House and Senate sergeants at arms are joint supervisors of the police chief, with the Senate's sergeant at arms serving as chairman of the board in odd-numbered years, like 2017. Representative Wasserman Schultz objected to this, saying, "We have had jurisdictional issues and a challenging time conducting oversight because of the structure of the Capitol Police Board and there being an indirect line rather than a direct line to us in terms of being able to hold the board accountable." In essence, she suggested that the upper chamber should have no authority over the Capitol Police so that she could exert improper influence on individual cases by wielding the power of the purse. It was an extraordinary and irrational request made only days after Democrats were alleging that President Trump had obstructed justice by firing FBI Director James Comey.

Up next on the budget-approval gauntlet that afternoon were the chief administrative officer, inspector general, and a few other entities. Though members ordinarily only talk with top-level officials, Representative Wasserman Schultz asked the CAO, who oversees cybersecurity, to put the House's cybersecurity lead, John Ramsey, on the stand directly, and began grilling him for details about how much his office knew about her. "Are members monitored?" she asked. She had a follow-up: "If a member is using an application outside of the House infrastructure and the protection of the cybersecurity network, they're in violation of House policy? So, members are not supposed to be using Dropbox?"

"Not according to the policy," Ramsey replied.

Representative Wasserman Schultz, who knew more than any member of Congress in history about the perils of disregarding computer security warnings, defiantly boasted about violating House rules and blamed the House for not stopping her. "I am more than happy to admit that I use Dropbox. I have used it for years and years and years. It is not blocked. I am fully able to use it," she said. "So, there is a vulnerability in our network," she said. You need to "assure us that you take seriously protecting our network."

She asked how the CAO had made these rules known. Ramsey noted that his office had explained clearly to all House IT aides that they could not use unapproved programs that copied House data to third-party servers, including Dropbox. In an ordinary situation, a congresswoman might have been angry with her IT aide for failing to apprise her of that. But Wasserman Schultz was unwilling to question Imran's conduct, no matter the evidence. "Safe to say that you have not" adequately communicated the rules, she said. She dismissed official memorandums to the relevant point people as "just lobbing email into a tech person's inbox."

Chief Administrative Officer Phil Kiko interjected, apparently tired of the beating his lower-level employee was taking. "We do inform every IT person, IT administrator in every congressional office. If that's not enough..." he trailed off. His point was made.

The next time Representative Wasserman Schultz spoke, another witness was on the stand: a woman who hobbled to the microphone on crutches. The video feed's audio cut out during the ten-minute exchange. I asked the committee staff about that, and they responded by email that they'd had technical difficulties and would talk to the IT guy. I walked down the hall to my editor's office and asked him if I was going insane. Was it possible that the exchange was important and that someone within Congress' IT department was tampering with evidence; that it was not a coincidence that the audio for that exchange had cut out?

I quickly concluded that that the strange goings-on in this case were making me paranoid.

Months later, I discovered what was on the missing tape. The person being grilled was the inspector general, and the congresswoman was furiously attempting to pry information relevant to the Awan case. I tracked down someone who had been in the hearing room. That person still remembered the exchange. "I couldn't believe what she was saying. Then the audio disappeared."

FIFTEEN

MEDIA MALPRACTICE: SEE SOMETHING, SAY NOTHING

The Democrats' brazen public denial of the existence of any cyber breach was made possible by one thing: Republican leadership's bizarre silence. They had agreed to call it a "theft investigation," and didn't say a word about the case. Was it any wonder that this was largely being ignored by the media, who assume that if even Republicans aren't making hay of a Democrat scandal, there must be nothing to it?

The fact was the Democrats had their act together and Republicans didn't. Massive turnover among Republicans meant they had to rely on Democrats for institutional knowledge. The chairman of the Administration Committee, Representative Candice Miller, left office after 2016—at the peak of the Awan investigation—to become, of all things, a water authority commissioner in Michigan. At the same time, Speaker Ryan's internal affairs fixer, Kelly Craven, had left to work for the Indiana attorney general and was replaced by Jennifer Hemingway, who was coming in cold to the Awan case. Even Chief Administrative Officer Kiko assumed his post only in September 2016. All of this meant that if someone wanted a comprehensive overview of the Awan investigation, he was forced to turn to Representative Bob Brady, who had been the top Democrat on the Administration Committee for many years.

Replacing Representative Candice Miller was Gregg Harper, a Mississippi Republican who was elected more for his blandness than for Deep South, small government zeal. It was hard to dislike someone so harmless. The Committee on House Administration was perhaps the least prestigious panel in Congress, but one where a chairman could presumably avoid scandal and demonstrate his capacity for genial bipartisanship. It was perfect for him. Chairman Harper thought of himself as a "company man," that company being the institution of the House of Representatives. Chairman Harper was so risk-averse that the prospect of a fifty-year old man consuming high-end tobacco products might as well have amounted to shooting heroin at an orgy. When he agreed to retain the committee's top Republican staffer Sean Moran as staff director, Sean—who enjoys an afternoon cigar—took to hiding behind the bushes on the Capitol lawn, wearing gloves to keep the aroma off his hands lest he get in trouble.

Neither Representative Brady nor Jamie Fleet, his top staffer, were so timid. Though the committee's most interesting mandate is overseeing the integrity of federal elections, the FBI was investigating Representative Brady's own campaign for paying his opponent $90,000.[1] The opponent said he struck a deal with Representative Brady for a payoff in exchange for dropping out of the race. Two of Representative Brady's campaign consultants pleaded guilty to making false statements since the payment was disguised in campaign finance records. A lobbyist put out a murder hit on one of the consultants in an attempt to prevent him from turning state's witness to additional, unrelated political misconduct.[2] And Jamie—who got his start as campaign consultant to Representative Brady—continued to pull political strings.

During the summer of 2017, Chairman Harper's office got a call from a *Washington Post* reporter working on an article about the Awan affair. Chairman Harper could assume the reporter had the Democrats' spin, and now it was up to Chairman Harper whether to weigh in and shape the narrative. He was considering it until he got a message that made clear that this investigation was being controlled from on high. Tom Hungar, the Paul Ryan-appointed House general counsel who was the institutional lawyer for the House and represented it in cases against the executive branch, made it clear that Chairman Harper was not to speak to the media about the case.

Hungar filtered all evidence before it got to the FBI or prosecutors to check if constitutional privileges like the "speech and debate clause" applied. Hungar had not screened any evidence from the Awan case until they were banned from the House in February, meaning that for months after key evidence was discovered, no FBI agents or prosecutors had seen it.

While the House general counsel muzzled the Republican committee chair from speaking to the media, those rules did not seem to apply to the minority party, and Jamie Fleet, a mere staffer, spun freely to the media.

The resulting article in the *Washington Post* claimed, comically, that the data illicitly uploaded off of congressional servers was "homework and family photos." Readers were expected to believe that Imran Awan's friend, Rao Abbas, broke into the House Democratic Caucus server to upload thousands of Imran's eight-year-old daughter's digital homework assignments, and then all the relatives logged in five thousand times to download them. Who knew elementary school was so rigorous these days? In reality, the folders being funneled to a third-party server had names like "credentials." The IG report had even stated: "Based on the file names, some of the information is likely sensitive." Don't you think the inspector general would have reacted accordingly if the file names were all images and things like "Babysitters Club Book Report.docx"?

Of course, the whole point of Dropbox is to sync files. Delete or change files from home and they'll be modified or wiped from the remote computer too.

It didn't matter. Who knew whether Jamie had given the *Post* reporter, Shawn Boburg, the full IG report or only misleading excerpts. Either way, Boburg had been told a preposterous story, but it was the only story he had, so that's what he went with.

Boburg could not dispute the documented and consistent allegations by Imran's closest relatives of threats of violence, witness coercion, and wiretapping—certainly relevant to a case involving unauthorized access to political data—so he diminished them with a single sentence: "The Daily Caller has painted an unflattering family portrait." *That's one way to put it*, I thought.

Boburg interviewed Pat Sowers, one of the IT aides who had told me a number of sordid tales about the Awans, but chose to quote him saying, "It's possible that everything was done innocently."

Sowers was also clear, as was every House IT aide, that the Awans could easily read people's emails. But Boburg wrote: "The House network does contain lawmakers' email, but a senior House official said IT workers could not access it unless lawmakers provided their passwords." Even if this *were* true, one of the things the IG report found most suspicious is that the Awans were logging in as members of Congress themselves, making it obvious that they not only had direct access to members' personal files, but seemed to be seeking them out.

Running on the front page of the Sunday edition, the article included a posed glamour shot of Imran Awan dressed in his finest suit and staring meaningfully into the distance, taken by a *Post* photographer outside his lawyer's office.

One central element: the *Post* plucked a YouTube video-maker from obscurity and elevated him into a straw man. This nobody apparently speculated that Imran was a "spy" who was connected to Anthony Weiner and a web of other figures, yet there was "no evidence" of that, so therefore the entire Awan matter could be dismissed, the storyline went.

The *New York Times* printed an article following a similar outline, essentially dismissing the case as a "right-wing media" conspiracy theory. Since no Republican would pick up the phone, most of the column inches went to defense attorney Chris Gowen, who induced the *Times* to print outright falsehoods, including that the police had never so much as interviewed Imran. Gowen later acknowledged to me that this was a false assertion, but the *Times* refused to correct its piece.

It was beneath the *Washington Post* and the *New York Times* to write articles whose main thesis is "an unknown person on YouTube is wrong." Even this crude rhetorical crutch, used to piggyback on a narrative about conservative "fake news" was fundamentally flawed. The YouTuber was a Democrat whose admittedly overblown and factually flawed interest in the story stemmed from Representative Wasserman Schultz rigging the primary against his favored candidate, Bernie Sanders, to whom public records showed he donated money. But these flagship publications didn't care, calling him a "right-wing" troublemaker.

From then on, the media could dismiss the Awan case as a "conspiracy theory," or "discredited." That meant law enforcement and politicians would feel no pressure to act. Republicans' fear of the media blinds them to something Democrats know well: if you control the media, you control everything.

SIXTEEN

ARREST

(JULY 2017)

If you really want to know about someone, look at their trash.

It's a technique I've employed in past investigations, piecing together torn-up receipts like pieces of a maggot and diaper-themed puzzle; one that, assuming the trash cans are at the curb, is entirely legal. Samina Gilani told me that Imran was living in her old house in Springfield, and as the days passed with nothing but inaction from the authorities, I figured I had nothing to lose. Google Maps' street view captured the name of the company on his trash cans, and I called up the company and found out what day pickup was. One hot July night when I didn't need to be at work early the next day, I made the drive out to the house at 2 a.m. When I drove past, there was a yellow sports car idling in the driveway and a man who looked like Imran leaning into its driver's side.

I'd never been caught rummaging through trash before, and the prospect of it happening in this case, when the stakes were higher, made me nervous. I continued a block past his house, trying to go as slow as possible without activating the brake lights. There wasn't another soul in sight, except one man sitting in a dark sedan who caused me to draw in a sharp breath as I saw him out of the corner of my eye.

This was going to be a long night if I wanted to be certain Imran had gone to bed. Needing something to both kill ninety minutes and give me the energy to stay awake, I lit up a cigar. It was dead quiet. Lost in my thoughts about the case, billows of smoke met the humid air and drifted up until the white wisps got lost in the moon. It must have been twenty minutes later when it occurred to me that I never heard the car door close, indicating that the man in the car had never gotten out, as he would if he was a neighbor. I crept closer and confirmed he was still there. *Jesus,* I thought. *It's the FBI.*

I laughed to myself. At least if something went horribly wrong and one of the Awans tried to harm me, I'd be safe. Or would I? If the Bureau were serious about gathering evidence, it probably wouldn't take kindly to my walking brazenly up to a house it was surveilling and taking evidence from it. Then again, I hadn't seen any indication that the cops were performing anything more than a perfunctory investigation. This decision, which had to be made on the spot, came down to the question I'd been struggling with for months: were the authorities actually trying to get to the bottom of this case, or not? The fact that it was July 2017, and no one had been arrested for unauthorized access to congressional computers that had been fully documented in server logs for an entire year seemed to speak for itself. It seemed clear that the only purpose of the Capitol Police's ownership of the case was to keep it under the control of the legislative branch and keep it quiet.

Speaker Paul Ryan had told me the Capitol Police were getting "assistance" from law enforcement partners, and Andre Taggart, the marine who moved into Imran's hurriedly vacated house, had told me the FBI had showed up to collect the hard drives he found. Out of caution, I hadn't published in the Daily Caller what he'd told me months earlier because he didn't send me a copy of the FBI agent's business card as proof. But this, I figured, was as good as confirmation.

The FBI, I assumed, would be relatively free of the political pressures that might hinder the Capitol Police, and the FBI certainly had far more technical capability and expertise than the Capitol cops. If the FBI was truly in charge, maybe I was wrong, and it was being taken seriously after all. I ruminated on everything that had happened. The FBI never talked to Rashid Minhas, let Hina leave the country, did nothing for the Awans' stepmom Gilani, and hadn't talked to anyone in Congress that I was aware of. *Fuck it,* I thought. If the FBI wanted evidence, it would have had it by now. I drove around to the other side of the house, carefully lifted the trash can's lid, and hauled four large bags back to my car while a foul liquid dripped onto my baby's car seat.

When I got back to my apartment around 5 a.m., the sun was starting to come up and I sifted through the trash, separating scraps of paper from meat juice-lined plastic packaging that had been baking in the July sun. The papers included tax documents with a Hispanic man's name and a Social Security number on them, and legal documents with another guy's name on them.

After a shower, I decided to ignore these suspicious contents and published the story I'd begun work on months before about a lawyer threatening Taggart over electronics, including Blackberry phones and hard drives, that Imran had left at the house Taggart was renting. Now I was comfortable saying that the FBI was involved and in possession of that evidence.

That night, I received a phone call: Imran had just been arrested. After my story went online, he'd attempted to board the next flight to Pakistan.

Imran had purchased a flight on Qatar Airlines departing from Dulles International Airport to Doha, Qatar, at 8:45 p.m., and then to Lahore, Pakistan. He purchased a return flight for six months later in January 2018. The FBI and Capitol Police jointly arrested him at the airport, where he had $9,000 in cash in a briefcase, two wiped cell phones, and a laptop with only one file on it: a resume that listed his address as Queens, New York. While the FBI was examining one of the phones, it lit up with an encrypted WhatsApp message from his lawyer, who seemed to anticipate his client's arrest and was demanding to speak with him.

Awan was taken to the Capitol Police station for processing, and the police confiscated the $9,000. He was arraigned the same day in the U.S. District Court for the District of Columbia on one count of bank fraud. The charge was related to one of the most ancillary schemes I'd easily identified in the earliest days of my investigation: mortgage fraud. To me, it was a classic case of what cops call pretextual charges. When he bolted for Pakistan, the cops who were working on a long-term case had to scramble to stop him, and the open-and-shut bank fraud, however minor, was sufficient to hold him. He pleaded not guilty and was released without bail. The conditions were that he receive a GPS monitor, abide by a curfew of 10 p.m. to 6 a.m., and not leave a fifty-mile radius of his residence in Virginia. Imran was also ordered to turn over both his Pakistani and U.S. passports.

With an arrest, the media—however unwilling to do any investigating of their own—could no longer ignore the case, and after my 5 a.m. night and marathon writing session, I found myself all over national TV. Speaking from a small, dark booth in a "remote" studio in Washington, D.C., with a spotlight in my face, to TV network anchors in New York City, was a little disorienting. I was running on no sleep. But I looked straight into the camera and relayed what I'd been saying in vain for months: that the House had secretly caught the Awans hacking congressional servers a year ago, and there had been even more evidence of suspicious activity since. Surely Americans and fellow reporters must have seen that the FBI would not have been surveilling someone for committing mortgage fraud. It seemed like some of it might finally start to sink in.

The court case revealed the identity of the attorneys who had been pulling the strings for Imran behind the scenes for months: a team originally from Wasserman Schultz's Miami area consisting of Chris Gowen, a bearded, hobbit-like man with a perpetual smirk on his face, and Jesse Winograd, an espionage law special-ist. Gowen previously worked for the Clintons, serving both Bill and Hillary Clinton face to face as a personal aide and following them from Hillary's Senate office to her 2008 presidential cam-paign and the Clinton Foundation. He says he specialized in fetching them Diet Cokes.

He also had a track record of working on straight-out-of-Hollywood cases like this one. In the 1990s, a journalist-turned-lawyer named Steven Donziger played on liberal sentiment to conduct a multi-billion scam that the *Wall Street Journal* called the "legal fraud of the century."[1] The case involved an area of the Amazon rainforest where the oil company Texaco had drilled. As the *Journal* wrote, "Donziger sniffed the potential windfall of a media-ready environmental 'disaster' and sued the company for $113 billion. He enlisted all manner of celebrity helpers," speaking eloquently about the plight of poor indige-nous people and of polluted waters. The problem is that none of the rhetoric applied to the situation at hand. Texaco had cleaned up its oil pits after it was done drilling in that area, and even the experts hired by Donziger found no "scientific evidence that people in the...area are drinking water contaminated with petroleum." But Donziger sensed that a third world jury might be eager for a cash grab against a U.S. corporate giant, and that it had all the markers of a feel-good story. "All this bullshit about the law and facts, but in the end of the day, it is about brute force...This is not a legal case, this is a political battle that's being played out through a legal case," he said privately, adding that "the judges are really not very bright." He falsified evidence and bribed a judge in Ecuador to rule in his favor. A

U.S. court reviewing the judgment Ecuador awarded found that Donziger and his team "wrote the [Ecuadorian] court's judgment themselves and promised $500,000 to the Ecuadorian judge...The wrongful actions of Donziger and his Ecuadorian legal team would be offensive to the laws of any nation that aspires to the rule of law."

Gowen was just a child when the case in Ecuador began, but he served as the lawyer advocating for Donziger when a U.S. federal court reviewed the way the massive judgment was secured. And it's easy to see why. "Donziger is intelligent, resourceful, and a master of public and media relations. An extensive public relations and media campaign has been part of his strategy from early days, and it continues. Among its objects has been to shift the focus from the fraud" against Texaco to feel-good platitudes designed to play toward the emotions of environmentalists, the U.S. judge wrote. By all appearances, like Donziger, Gowen was as much a media fixer as a lawyer, preferring the microphone to the courtroom.

Gowen described Imran's arrest as "clearly a right-wing media-driven prosecution by a United States Attorney's Office that wants to prosecute people for working while Muslim." Keep in mind, the family was banned from the House computer network before I ever heard of them because of an investigation spurred by Democratic tips and pursued by a Democrat-selected inspector general. The acting U.S. attorney for D.C. was still an Obama holdover. And, of course, a huge portion of IT professionals are from India or Pakistan, which no one bats an eye at because most don't make "unauthorized access" to congressional servers or lie on seemingly every government form they've ever filled out. These are the kind of things any diligent judge would see if presented the facts.

But Gowen's strategy was to play to the Trump Derangement Syndrome that had taken over the media. The statement he released to the press following Imran's arrest was completely insane:

> The attacks on Mr. Awan and his family began as part of a frenzy of anti-Muslim bigotry in the literal heart of our democracy, the House of Representatives. For months we have had utterly unsupported, outlandish, and slanderous statements targeting Mr. Awan coming not just from the ultra-right-wing "pizzagate" media but from sitting members of Congress. Now we have the Justice Department showing up with a complaint about disclosures on a modest real estate matter. To an extent, the situation speaks for itself. Mr. Awan's family is presently staying with extended family in Pakistan because he and his wife were both abruptly and unjustly fired, leaving them without a reliable source of income to pay typical U.S. living expenses, and because extremist right-wing bloggers were beginning to harass them and their children—even going to their children's schools. Mr. Awan has stayed in the U.S. to earn some income to manage this situation as best as possible. He attempted to travel this week to see his family for the first time in months. The government had been informed he would travel and had stated no objection.

Gowen worked as a fact checker for Bill Clinton's memoir and taught a course on legal ethics at American University Washington College of Law.[2] Yet some of Gowen's statements appeared to be simply made up. If anything, the media was ignoring the story—certainly no reporters had gone to the children's schools. The basic witnesses I located had never been interviewed by any law enforcement, and prosecutors seemed unaware of almost everything until I reported it. Despite that, Gowen claimed the FBI "started this giant investigation that's probably the most thorough, exhaustive investigation in the history of this country."

Citing Gowen, the Associated Press said Imran's family was forced to live "in squalor" in Pakistan because of the investigation, making no mention of the fact that Imran and his wife had each earned $165,000 a year for a decade and owned at least four homes. Imran himself had told the Congressional Federal Credit Union bank clerk that he wired the money to Pakistan for a $300,000 funeral for his father, which a third attorney working with Gowen and Winograd, Aaron Page, doubled down on, explaining to reporters that it was an "elaborate funeral." Who would spend $300,000 on a funeral for a janitor-turned-con man, while living relatives resided in squalor? Worse, if the Awans were so destitute after the House paid them $7 million, to whom was all that money going?

Representative Wasserman Schultz fired Imran Awan only after the arrest. She claimed that she knew he was leaving the country and was OK with it, and that her chief of staff had filled out a form placing him on unpaid leave while he was gone. The truthfulness of this is dubious. Over the years, Imran had repeatedly gone to Pakistan for months without ever going on unpaid leave, including his recent trip from September to December of 2016. Why start withholding his pay while he was seven thousand miles away now?

While Gowen used the media to avoid accountability with an angle designed to play to the narrative about "fake news," Democrats hid behind identity politics. Representative Wasserman Schultz told her hometown paper "He's not my staffer. He no longer works for me. And when he was arrested, I terminated him. I kept him on the payroll during the time that he was not arrested and not charged with anything. And that was because, as I said, that I was concerned about the violation of his due process rights and also that there were racial and ethnic profiling concerns." Even after the arrest, she said Imran was being "persecuted."[3]

Gowen joined in with cartoonish rhetoric so overblown that it seemed astonishing that anyone could fail to see he was trying to divert attention from the facts. He said the only reason conservative media would be interested in an apparent government cyber breach was the following: "Whoa, we got Pakistan, we got female, we got Democrat. Let's roll.'"[4]

Even if journalists couldn't, the people closest to the case knew how cynical and Orwellian this was. *We got Pakistan?* Syed Ahmed, Samina's cousin, couldn't believe what he was hearing. "That's a completely insane statement. It has nothing to do with their being Muslim; they are bad people. What they have done to their mother, their father—they are not Muslims at all, if they prayed five times a day they would not do these things," he said. "If some Congress members are saying they are being picked on because they are Muslim, it's a joke."

Andre Taggart, who was threatened over the left behind Blackberries and computer equipment, said, "With respect to this situation, political affiliation is irrelevant. What people need to understand is this is real. It's not like right-wing wingnut-crazy making stuff up. This is coming from a black Democrat United States Marine that just wants to get these motherfuckers locked up and exposed, and the people that facilitated them should also be locked up as far as I'm concerned. He, his wife, his brother, they're all working down there—there's no way they could do this without help. If we can drag Trump and his wingnuts through the mud for the Russia influence that they are having, then it's only fair that we also expose this shit."

We got a woman, let's roll? While liberal feminist protesters gathered on the National Mall in pink "pussy hats," three Muslim women in Imran's life (you'll see who the third one is soon) said he had kept them "like a slave," held them "in captivity," or controlled them with death threats. A fourth, another mistress of Imran's, called the cops after he had apparently beaten her. Over in Pakistan, the widow of his father's business partner was similarly threatened. Could anyone genuinely believe that Republicans targeted Representative Wasserman Schultz and invented the Awan scandal because of her sex?

With sexual harassment charges and the "me too" movement rocking the nation, Nancy Pelosi said, "Predators have long counted on doubt and intimidation to stop survivors from coming forward. No more! Survivors, we stand with you." The evidence that Imran Awan abused women included at least five police reports, three restraining orders, and two lawsuits. I emailed every congresswoman who employed one of the Awans and sent them the official records documenting the abuse allegations leveled against Imran. I asked for a response. Only two bothered to reply.[5]

If identity politics had been rotting the brain cells of Americans for decades, this case might be the moment it finally jumped the shark. You had someone who evidence suggested hacked politicians, evaded taxes, abused women, preyed on the vulnerable and even commissioned police brutality—all signature Democratic issues—and Democrats were defending him? The "discrimination" soundbites got play, while public police reports and lawsuits showing objectively concerning conduct were ignored. With Americans' new Twitter-length attention spans, most people, including the pliable liberal media, never got that far. I wondered: If Watergate took place in this hyper-partisan, Twitter-addled, "fake news" era, how would it play out?

———

On August 24, 2017, the indictment was broadened to four felony counts, and added Imran's wife Hina as a defendant. Yet it was not the expanded indictment I anticipated; one that would focus on the misconduct the FBI had officially known about since December 2016. Instead, it just added a few more financial charges involving what obviously appeared to be the Awans' effort to flee that investigation. "Defendants AWAN and ALVI did unlawfully, willfully, and knowingly conspire, combine, confederate, and agree with each other to commit offenses against the United States," including bank fraud, false statements, and unlawful monetary transactions, the indictment said.

Even when it came to these money moves, it seemed to go out of its way to paint an incomplete portrait. Prosecutors hadn't even charged all the behavior laid out in the FBI affidavit upon which the arrest warrant relied. The affidavit spelled out how Hina pretended to have a medical emergency that required liquidating her House retirement account, and how Imran had impersonated his wife to take out a home equity loan that was to be used to renovate his house. It related how Imran told the bank employee the wire was for a $300,000 funeral, then instructed the employee to hold while he Googled another excuse they'd have to accept. It also spelled out how the pair evaded taxes on rental income and deceived the bank to hide it: they submitted a false lease saying Hina's mother lived there, when in fact, it was being rented to the couple whom I'd spoken to who said that Imran ordered them not to cooperate with police.

Anyone reading the indictment would have no idea that the proceeds of the alleged bank fraud were wired to Pakistan, that Hina snatched her kids out of school and flew to Pakistan with all her possessions and a suitcase of cash shortly afterwards, and that Imran was apprehended attempting to flee the country. To dance around these facts, the charges did not focus on the fact that the loan money wasn't used for its required purpose of home improvements. Instead, the charge focused on one minor matter: that the suspects said the home was their primary residence rather than an income property. If all someone knew was the facts presented in the indictment, it seemed like a pretty boring case. The U.S. Attorney's office didn't even send a press release. There was still no mention that this couple had been busted making unauthorized access to congressional servers, that police said key evidence disappeared afterwards, that a congresswoman's laptop turned up in a phone booth, or that a cache of missing House computer equipment was found in an elevator shaft.

But if Democrats had somehow managed to obscure the incredible facts at the heart of this case, something seemed to be on the horizon that would make that harder, and it involved the word *fugitive*. Hina was still in Pakistan when she was indicted. The FBI affidavit stated that the Bureau did not believe she would return to the United States:

> On March 5, 2017, your Affiant, along with agents from the FBI and US Capitol Police, approached Alvi at Dulles International Airport, in Dulles, Virginia. Alvi was about to board Qatar Airlines, Flight 708, to Doha, Qatar, on her way to Lahore, Pakistan. Alvi was with her three children, who your Affiant later learned were abruptly taken out of school without notifying the Fairfax County Public School System.
>
> Alvi had numerous pieces of luggage with her, including cardboard boxes. A secondary search of those items revealed that the boxes contained household goods, clothing, and food items. US Customs and Border Protection conducted a search of Alvi's bags immediately prior to boarding the plane and located a total of $12,400 in US cash inside. Alvi was permitted to board the flight to Qatar and she and her daughters have not returned to the United States. Alvi has a return flight booked for a date in September 2017. Based on your Affiant's observations at Dulles Airport,

and upon his experience and training, your Affiant does not believe that Alvi has any intention to return to the United States.

This was beyond bizarre; a smoking gun indicating that from the beginning, these defendants had been protected by the FBI. Agent Brandon Merriman had tailed her to the airport because of all the evidence against the Awans in the House of Representatives, found an illegal amount of hidden cash on her (which provided a pretext for an arrest as much as the mortgage fraud did), she'd refused to answer his questions (as prosecutors later revealed), and he *let her board the flight anyway, then filed paperwork saying he was sure she'd never return.* Why did Merriman bother chasing her to the airport if he had no intention of stopping her? It almost seemed as if the FBI was escorting her out of the country and into obscurity rather than pursuing a criminal case.

But if Representative Wasserman Schultz's systems administrator, which Hina Alvi had been, became a fugitive in Pakistan, her protestations about how the Awans had been targeted by Islamophobes—meaning presumably the Capitol Police, the inspector general, and federal prosecutors—would be a tough sell to the public.

Hina retained a separate Washington attorney from Imran, hiring a small-time criminal defense lawyer in a two-person practice. That raised the possibility that her legal defense might be pitted against his.

The arraignment for the expanded charges was set for September 1, 2017: the Friday before Labor Day weekend, when many reporters would be off work and Americans would be too busy enjoying the holiday to pay attention. But Hina was not present at the arraignment.

Imran had not even been held on bail, but Gowen requested that the GPS monitor on his client be removed. As for the 50-mile restriction on his movements, Gowen said Imran had been driving for Uber and "the 50-mile radius makes that hard... if he rejects a call he will lose his job." In the compact D.C. region, a 50-mile Uber ride would be rare, so that seemed to make little sense.

Assistant U.S. Attorney Michael Marando, a career prosecutor with gray hair and mopey eyes, warned the judge that Imran was a severe flight risk. "From day one there was a pattern of flight. It began September 2016... a pattern of transfers to Pakistan, hundreds of thousands of dollars," he said. As for his wife Hina, "She gave every impression to the government that she was leaving the country with no intention to return," Marando said. "Imran had what the government would characterize as a one-way ticket to Pakistan," he added, noting that his date of supposed return on his roundtrip ticket didn't match with his wife's.

By September 13, 2017, the prospect of Hina's return seemed to become even more unlikely. Even as Representative Wasserman Schultz painted Imran as a choir boy, his own wife and fellow congressional aide said otherwise. Hina turned against her husband, filing a lawsuit against him in Pakistan alleging fraud and an attempt to control her by threatening her loved ones in Pakistan with "dire consequences." By now, Imran's *modus operandi* of controlling people with the threat of violence against their loved ones overseas was familiar, right down to the wording that might as well have been Imran's catch phrase: "dire consequences."

"My husband Imran Awan, son of Muhammad Ashraf Awan, committed fraud along with offence of polygamy," Hina said in the lawsuit. It named Imran's secret, second wife, Sumaira Siddique. The fraud to which she objected was not what occurred in the U.S. House of Representatives, or even that Imran had a second wife, but that he had falsified marriage paperwork and lied about it. "A few months ago I got apprised of the fact that my husband has contracted second marriage secretly, fraudulently and without my consent with Mst. Sumaira Shehzadi alias Sumaira Siddique, Daughter of Muhammad Akram r/o Township Lahore. The second marriage of my husband is illegal, unlawful and without justification," it said.

I learned about this soon after it happened in a way that any competent investigator could have matched: I got a Google Alert notification that Pakistan's ARY news site had obtained and reported on the filing. Following standard journalism protocol, I emailed the link to Gowen and asked for a comment. Gowen denied the undeniable without bothering to explain, writing: "totally false.... You are a liar, a trump pawn and a very bad person."

Was he just trying to get me to print a statement that would signal to liberal-leaning journalists and readers that they should disregard my reporting? Or was he claiming ARY had fabricated the document? To cover all our bases, Wajid, the Pakistani correspondent I was working with, set out to obtain the lawsuit from Hina's Pakistani lawyer, who promptly answered the phone and promised to send the document in full in a few days. But he never followed up, and when Wajid approached him again, something had changed, and he seemed disinclined to cooperate. Wajid had a colleague go to the Lahore courthouse and take pictures of the full filing, which contained allegations of violent threats that weren't included in the ARY article. In the court filing, Hina's Pakistani lawyer wrote:

> Respondent has contracted a second marriage on 17-08-2015 with one Mst. Sumaira Shehzadi alias Sumaira Siddique... without obtaining prior permission. Rather he mentioned himself as bachelor in... marriage certificate, he falsely declared that he has no wife or biological children at the time of contracting second marriage. This act of the respondent was shocking for the complainant and she asked the respondent about his second marriage on which he became furious while admitting the same and said he has no need to obtain permission from the complainant....
>
> He further said furiously that the complainant has no right or power to restrain him from second and even third marriage. Furthermore, the respondent threatened the complainant of dire consequences. He also threatened to harm the lives of family of the complainant if she intervenes into the affairs of the respondent.

When Hina's arraignment rolled around, the question was whether she would be there—and if she was, whether prosecutors would induce her to turn witness against her husband.

When Hina's arraignment rolled around, the question was whether she would be there—and if she was, whether prosecutors would induce her to turn witness against her husband.

The next court date was the day before the Columbus Day weekend in October 2017, another date selected to ensure minimal media attention. But the E. Barrett Prettyman federal courthouse is only three blocks from the Capitol, and all the major networks were staking out the lobby. A lone CNN producer, like a sheep accidentally separated from the herd, approached Gowen outside the courthouse, asking a clumsy question about the Awan case. The rest of the media, it turned out, was hoping to confirm vaporous, and false, rumors about the seating of a grand jury to investigate connections between Russia and Trump associates. Imran walked right by the press, unnoticed.

In the second-floor hallway, I spied Hina's attorney, Nikki Lotze, who'd ignored my many emails about how Imran "furiously" threatened to "harm the lives" of Hina's loved ones if she "intervenes into [Imran's] affairs." She was alone with no sign of her client. I asked her about Hina's allegations against her husband regarding fraud and violent threats and she stared at me blankly. I said Gowen indicated there never was such a lawsuit and asked her if that was true. She launched into a halfhearted screed about Islamophobia, but what she was saying made no sense, and she seemed to know it. She simply wasn't as good at this as Gowen. I sighed. "Look, are you saying your client didn't say that her own husband controlled her with death threats?"

"I don't see how that's newsworthy," Lotze finally said.

As I took my seat in a windowless courtroom on the second floor, other than myself and one television producer, there were no media in the courtroom. Imran was there, and at the last minute, the double doors opened and Hina appeared.

She and her husband avoided eye contact and did not speak to each other, but Imran handed her an envelope, which she put in her bag. The two indicted congressional aides were seated directly across from each other at the defense table. They looked down, to the left, or to the right—anywhere but at each other.

The joint appearance was the opening to what would assuredly be a long and dramatic sequence of court battles. I never would have imagined it would be one of the last times they'd appear in court.

The court case had been assigned to Judge Tanya Chutkan, a Jamaican-born justice nominated to the bench by Barack Obama in 2013. Around the time she received the Awan case, Chutkan was also assigned the Fusion GPS case involving the opposition research firm hired by the DNC to create the "dossier" tying, on the flimsiest evidence, Trump to Russia. Fusion put the wife of top DOJ official Bruce Ohr on its payroll and used the husband to feed the information to the FBI. Fusion GPS then used that to convince newspaper reporters that there were newsworthy government actions supporting connections between Russia and Trump. Chutkan recused herself from the Fusion GPS case because of ties between the firm and her previous legal work.[6]

After Hina pleaded not guilty, Judge Chutkan asked her to turn over her passports, and Lotze handed over a U.S. passport. Prosecutors asked if she had a Pakistani one, as Imran did. Hina shook her head "no." Lotze leaned in and then spoke. "She does have one, your honor, but it's not here." Hina had returned from Pakistan for the express purpose of turning herself in, the claim went, but hadn't brought one of her passports because it was "expired." Prosecutors knew that both she and Imran would only have to go to the Pakistani embassy to obtain replacement foreign passports and leave the country. Judge Chutkan wasn't bothered. "Try to make arrangements to have it sent to the government," she said. Hina was released with no bail—not even an ankle bracelet monitor. With Hina's arraignment complete, Gowen wasted no time getting to the point: Hina's return meant that Imran, too, should get his GPS removed. He was a family man, his attorney argued, and wouldn't try to flee because he loved living with his wife.

I was starting to see that there were a few reasons why Hina would return. First, Imran might have forced her to come, because having a fugitive as a co-conspirator didn't help his case, nor the Congress members' political futures. Second, prosecutors could have given her immunity to testify against others. Third, Hina had reason to be confident that despite all the evidence gathered in the House, she'd never see the inside of a jail cell.

Even as Gowen told the judge that Hina's presence was enough to keep his client in the country, he acknowledged that the pair were currently staying apart "in a one-bedroom apartment and then also a house." He asked the judge for permission to let the couple sleep separately or together. The Pakistani lawsuit showed that even in Pakistan, the couple stayed in separate towns. But prosecutors never told the judge about that weeks-old Pakistani filing, which indicated that Imran's codefendant could be in danger and operating under duress, as well as that Hina was a prime candidate to be a government witness. Instead, prosecutor Marando conceded that Imran was not a danger to the community.

"Why should I keep him on the GPS monitor?" Judge Chutkan asked.

Marando explained that Imran was taking elaborate measures to cover his tracks. "I cannot say what goes on in the mind of an industrious person who wants to leave the country," he said. "But he's traveled to Pakistan numerous times and made numerous wires of significant amounts of money for the purchase of property, potentially to set up a life there. He had on him two cell phones [and a] laptop. One cell phone was wiped two hours before we arrested him. He was taking active measures to [evade] our investigation."

He continued: "There wasn't much on the laptop, but there was a resume with an alias in Jackson Heights, Queens."

Even when the prosecutor acted like a prosecutor, his argument belied a complete unfamiliarity with the evidence. The presence of a resume with a Queens address was notable. Representatives Meeks and Clarke were from nearby, as was a relative to whom Imran had sent money, Saif Rao; and Jackson Heights, Queens, harbored a notorious false identity market for immigrants. But the so-called alias was simply "Alex Awan," the innocuous American nickname any witness could have told Marando Imran often went by. With this kind of grasp on the facts, it was impossible for Marando to identify problems with the defense's logic.

With the hearing about to adjourn, Gowen jumped up out of the blue to address the judge with what seemed to be his main objective: "We do expect there being an attorney-client privilege issue in this case.... What occurred is a backpack from my client was found... there was a note that said 'attorney-client privilege' and a hard drive. We feel very strongly about this." He asked to approach the bench, and static white noise blasted out of speakers hidden behind ornate wooden clocks that had no hands.

Anyone who had read my reporting would realize that this was Representative Wasserman Schultz's laptop. The facts tracked exactly with the text of the police report I'd published months earlier, but which had gone entirely dismissed by the media, as if they thought I'd made it up. I thought: *did they really think I made it up, or did they just prefer to ignore it?*

Now, assuming the judge bought the argument, it would be up to Imran to decide whether prosecutors would see what was on Representative Wasserman Schultz's laptop. The privilege argument was ludicrous, akin to claiming a killer could place a Post-It note that says "attorney-client privilege" on a gun before firing it and then claim prosecutors couldn't use it as evidence. For months, the court case would be postponed, with prosecutors saying they were haggling about whether prosecutors could look at the laptop.

Of course, to the judge, this was just some case about bank fraud. And if I hadn't spent months prying facts loose, no one would have known that a congresswoman's laptop was placed in a phone booth by a hacking suspect, or even that there was any cybersecurity issue in the House.

With that, the defendants left the building—separately. If a tree falls in a forest and no one is there to hear, does it make a sound?

SEVENTEEN

INSIDER THREATS

There was an elephant in the room that every House official who discussed "procurement irregularities by IT support staff" went to great lengths to avoid: support staff didn't have the power to do anything with congressional funds; bosses signed off on all expenditures. The nature of many of the procurement schemes tended to implicate chiefs of staff and possibly congressmen. The role of a tech person was merely to place an order for equipment at the request of a chief of staff, and then, when it was received, have the chief sign a form acknowledging receipt and authorizing payment. The point was inadvertently driven home by Democrats who sought to downplay the Awans' stature, as members such as Ted Lieu of California had done, falsely claiming that the Awans were corporate contractors or were not really on their staff, or—more accurately— referring to them as unimportant support staff. Clearly such people don't have the authority to spend taxpayer money. Only the members and the chiefs of staff could do that.

That meant, in the offices where the Awans had purchased unusual amounts of equipment, the chiefs of staff must have known they were signing off on things the office didn't need. The Awans had accumulated massive stockpiles of high-end equipment, which investigators had photographed sitting unopened in boxes and which the February sergeant at arms memo said was "being stored at unknown locations for long periods." In some cases, it was delivered straight "to the homes of some of the employees." There was little doubt that this equipment was disappearing. Before he knew any details of what the House had found, Abid's acquaintance Syed Ahmed told me Abid was sending iPhones to Pakistan. Even though they'd have no reason to know some of it went abroad, why did managers of these budget-strapped offices think they were purchasing so much equipment that they had no immediate need for and that they never saw?

Even if the equipment itself seemed prosaic enough, chiefs of staff were signing off on forms that said things that clearly made no sense, describing high-end computers as costing only $499, or iPhone warranties as costing as much as the phone itself. At best, these offices were being run by incompetent and fiscally illiterate managers. Alternatively, it suggested that there were kickback schemes going on between several members or chiefs of staff, beyond the one that Representative Clarke's chief of staff Wendy Anderson suspected had taken place in that office.

Any autopsy of what had occurred could not avoid the conclusion that the Awans' forty-four Democratic employers—including some of the most vocal Russia hawks who screamed about Russian hacking of DNC computers—had acted, at best, with extreme negligence when it came to their own IT. They put a twenty-year-old and a McDonald's employee on their payrolls as their sole systems administrators, knowingly allowed people who were not on their payroll to access all their data, and exempted these sensitive positions from standard background checks that would have caught major red flags.

After the arrest, the Awans' lawyers made it abundantly clear that no trial could proceed in court without these issues being laid out in detail.

Abid Awan's attorney, Jim Bacon, told the *Washington Post*: "In a fluid situation, you do what you're ordered to do." Any missing equipment, Bacon said, "disappeared after it was brought to the folks who were demanding it....It sounds to me like there's a lot of scapegoating here."[1] The *Post* printed this as if that made the whole thing a non-story instead of what it was: the remarkable assertion that members of Congress "ordered" staff to commit fraud, and that their top staff were making off with equipment. One of Imran's lawyers, Aaron Page, told me on the topic of falsifying invoices: "This is what experienced members of Congress expect: to expedite things, they adjust the pricing." He couldn't explain how it "expedited" things, rather than simply made it easier for equipment to disappear. Nonetheless, he expressed confidence that his client wouldn't be charged with procurement fraud despite the existence of manipulated vouchers. "It will be proven false if we have to prove it false," he said. "And I don't expect we'll have to." Why would someone caught falsifying government documents be so confident that he wouldn't have to prove his innocence? Because these veiled threats worked. It was another warning shot at these "experienced" members of Congress not to break from the lockstep protection of the Awans. And the rhetoric worked because there was truth behind it.

When it came to the cybersecurity anomalies, Gowen blamed members, pointing to Congress' "inefficient and decentralized IT system," or what Bacon called a "shocking lack of IT and hardware security on Capitol Hill."[2] Would intelligence committee member Joaquin Castro really be willing to take the stand in a courtroom and admit that he'd never bothered to run a background check on his IT staffer? Would Representative Wasserman Schultz say under oath that she imagined her computers were being safely administered when Imran was in Pakistan for months on end? Would Representative Andre Carson dare testify about his response to the secret email account linked to his intelligence staffer? Did Representative Ted Deutch realize that a judge would not permit his "no comment" routine when asked if he had ever seen his purported IT aide who worked at McDonald's?

If this case didn't have undertones of extortion before, it did now, as the Awans' lawyers could call one in five House Democrats as witnesses and expose their negligence, if not their acting as co-conspirators in a theft scheme. It would be the trial of the century, and under no circumstances could it be allowed to take place.

After these warnings directed at Democrats, something changed. Imran, who had previously cried himself to sleep next to Sumaira, now seemed to have no fear at all. While the investigation, however ambivalent and slow-paced, obviously once had enough mandate behind it to trigger a dramatic airport arrest, in the weeks after, it suddenly reversed course, with the prosecutors seeming to become part of the same team as the defense.

The DOJ seemed willing to do the Democrats' bidding. Instead of seizing evidence through warrants and interviews with witnesses, prosecutors seemed to simply leave it to Gowen to provide much of the information and explanations they'd use to form their conclusion. "We are trying to be as helpful as possible to law enforcement to provide them any information or access they need," Gowen told Fox News.

The focus on Dropbox and, to some extent, even the House's network logs were somewhat of a red herring. Imran had direct physical access to these machines and could have copied their contents onto a USB or hard disk at any time without leaving any auditable trail—for nefarious purposes or even regularly as a rudimentary backup system. There was no way to rule out that Imran didn't have copies of everything, and the only way to attempt to prove it might involve searching every property he was associated with for every disk, USB, and hard drive, as well as every server he connected to from home. Of course, they did none of this. If prosecutors wanted to say they found nothing, such passive measures would be a good way to do it. They were dealing with someone who was actively hiding his actions and had enough IT skills to know how to thwart such a casual review. "He was always very discreet in these matters," Sumaira told me. "He said, 'I work very carefully on my laptop because they watch the IP,'" Sumaira said. "He never used his regular phone number to direct call, he always used WhatsApp because it's untraceable."

Defense lawyers, meanwhile, could turn to harassing truth-tellers.

Hours after I published the story quoting former tenant Andre Taggart saying he'd turned damaged hard drives over to the FBI, Gowen's law firm sent him a letter demanding $15,000 in damages related to the home, all of which Taggart said were made up.[3] Typical of the list was supposedly killing a tree in the front yard by not watering it in the few months Taggart lived in the home. They even charged Taggart for buying his own washer and dryer and gifting them to the home, calling it debris that was left behind. He had moved out months ago and never heard anything from Imran or his lawyer in all that time. Taggart knew why they were crawling out of the woodwork now: retaliation.

"It went back to the interview I'd conducted two days prior, which he'd undoubtedly seen, and I don't know if it was an intimidation factor, but it had the complete opposite effect," Taggart said in response. "Look, these people took advantage of us, and when I moved in I found government-issued equipment and I went through the proper channels and turned it in. I served in the marine corps for fourteen years, and if I downloaded files to an offsite server, I'm going to prison for a lot of years," he said. "These guys are fucking crooks. They'd do *anything* for money. It's ridiculous that he's only being investigated for bank fraud. He's a con artist. Let's say he gets a slap on the wrist, he goes home happily ever after with the millions of dollars he's siphoned from this country."

Gowen likely hated Taggart because he was a black marine whose Facebook page was full of anti-Republican screeds, which made him kryptonite to Gowen's tribalism and identity politics ploy. "Andre Taggart is a criminal. He stole all of Imran's stuff. There's not one single agent in the FBI that will deny that. Marine. Taggart. Criminal... All of you think Donald Trump is a hero and the guy that's going to get us out of this," he ranted.

"That whole story has gotten the FBI and U.S. attorneys FURIOUS at all of these little twerp reporters, that have been writing that, because what it was, was an old BMW radio that was in there that was damaged from a car accident. That was the only thing that was found."[4]

It was a stunning response. Taggart wasn't an idiot; he knew the difference between a bunch of Blackberry phones and an old car radio. He knew what he handed over to the cops, and he did it with no knowledge of any congressional investigation. He only did it because Gowen's law firm and Imran raised his suspicions by being so adamant about getting the items back. It took chutz-pah—or more likely, a reliance on the fact that most listeners didn't know these details—to even say such a nonsensical thing.

Not only that, but what was Gowen doing hanging out with FBI agents and U.S. attorneys, talking shit about witnesses and the media together? What kind of conversations were going on that Gowen was so sure that FBI agents believed the witness was the real criminal? If what Gowen said had any basis in truth—if the FBI really did allow themselves to be sicced on a witness instead of the suspect, and if they would really claim that the cache of electronics Taggart turned over consisted of only one car radio implausibly smashed in a car accident—then I could reach only one conclusion: the police had lost, removed, or refused to record the rest of the items.

I never thought I'd entertain such a notion in the United States of America, but if that's all the police contend they found in Taggart's house, I am certain of it. Taggart is one of the most level-headed, clean-cut people I've ever met, who rose from a rough neighborhood of Rochester, New York, and had rigor, discipline, and ethics instilled in him through the U.S. Marines. Now his love for country had him simultaneously protesting against the Trump administration and against what he saw as an obvious security threat. A slew of Blackberries, an industrial-sized box of printer toner, wireless routers, and smashed hard drives turning into a single car radio through alchemy? Give me a break. Taggart had no incentive to make any of this up. People in power had reason to make it go away.

Then there were the legal threats Gowen directed at me, a lone reporter with limited resources who seemed to be able to find more information than prosecutors could—or wanted to. He constantly threatened to sue me. But when asked on what basis, his claims were laughably false. He implied that I Photoshopped the Fairfax County police reports documenting abuse of multiple women, which are easily verifiable public records. He claimed that I was paying witnesses to talk. He had one fixation above all else: finding out who my sources were. He tried to do a deal with me where I would turn over all my notes to him.

But strangest of all was the evidence that the government was turning over to Imran.

At Imran's second court appearance in October 2017, prosecutor Marando said, "Earlier this week, there was the inadvertent disclosure of law enforcement materials to defense counsel. There may be a motion on that." In other words, law enforcement had improperly given a trove of evidence to Gowen.

Imran's second wife Sumaira told me that when it happened, Imran came home joyous and gloating about it. As he recounted it to her, "The cop came to Chris Gowen's office with a stack of papers....Then he came back and said, 'I thought you guys were the other party.' He was very, very angry. But Gowen made copies." In Sumaira's mind, things were starting to add up. This could explain how Imran seemed to know exactly what she'd told the FBI, causing her to believe providing more evidence to the Bureau would only trigger more retaliation.

I emailed Bill Miller, a former *Washington Post* reporter who is now the spokesman for the U.S. Attorney's office in Washington, and sent him a detailed outline of what I was writing: that the government had improperly handed over evidence to the defense. Instead of getting a response from Miller designed to ameliorate my concerns, three hours later, I got a response from Gowen. "I hear you are writing another article about me—I assume you don't want to fact check it?" Gowen wrote. "From what I hear, you have it totally wrong as usual." I had not told a soul but Miller about any upcoming story involving Gowen.

I followed up with Miller to ask if prosecutors had provided information about my upcoming story to Gowen. "I'm not going to get into what we do internally," Miller said. "I communicate with the prosecutors regularly when I get media inquiries."

I asked Gowen how he got the information. "I have been told by my source on the Hill," he said. If true, this would imply that prosecutors were leaking to Democrats, who were providing information about an ongoing criminal case to the attorney of a hacking suspect.

If this happened because Awan was working members to get him off the hook, it was a crime. Any former senior congressional staffer who "within one year after the termination of that employment," communicates with his former office to seek "action by a member, officer, or employee" can be jailed for a year.

Gowen claimed the evidence inadvertently disclosed was a copy of a laptop belonging to Imran's former tenant, Laurel Everly, who voluntarily turned it in to the Capitol Police in hopes of seeing whether she'd been hacked. Everly had previously told me that she found Imran to be an "extortionist" and possibly an identity thief, and as she'd heard more about what happened on Capitol Hill, she believed Imran was a national security threat. She felt that on a case this important, investigators surely wanted every scrap of evidence they could gather, however small. But she also said she worried that Imran would somehow wind up with even more information about her; she knew he was the type of person to retaliate. In the end, she decided to trust prosecutors for the good of the country. I rolled my eyes when she turned it in because it was almost certainly peripheral to the investigation—Imran had little reason to be interested in the data of an ordinary person like her, and any years-old hacking was unlikely to be detectable anyway—but Everly knew little about computers and I didn't blame her for being scared or for assuming prosecutors were collecting massive quantities of evidence.

Gowen told me: "I was told there was nothing on it and was a giant waste of time, and the laptop was returned." He said the

Capitol Police officer who agreed to take it from Everly was disciplined, "poor guy."

There seemed to be only two explanations for giving the laptop to Gowen: either the government was incredibly incompetent, or it wasn't an accident at all. Unaffiliated lawyers I spoke with said the police should never deliver anything to the defense. As Chris Farrell of Judicial Watch said, it was the latest indication that the Capitol Police's continued involvement in the case seemed to be for one purpose: "to bury, constrain and minimize the Awan case." He said the disclosures, both from the police to the defense and from the prosecutors to the defense or House Democrats, were "disgraceful and amateurish."

"What were the consequences for this misconduct? Who was disciplined or fired?" he asked. What is needed, he said, is "a legitimate, full investigation by a competent law enforcement agency."

If Gowen was telling the truth that the "inadvertent disclosure" was Everly's laptop, then prosecutors seemed to care little that they'd given all of an innocent person's personal data straight to a person who'd been indicted after an investigation into behavior that could involve using people's digital files against them. The government hadn't told Everly about any mistake. Miller, the prosecutor's spokesman, wouldn't tell me whether government policy obligated it to inform people who were harmed by such accidental disclosures. He also wouldn't say whether the disclosure was actually the tenant's laptop, or something more.

If it was her laptop, Everly didn't realize how bad the disclosure was. When she called prosecutors to find out if what I'd reported was true, they simply ignored her, leaving no recourse but to call Gowen's office. When she dialed the law firm's number, a voice from her past came rushing back to her: Imran himself answered the office's phone. Gowen, the former Hillary aide, had put the suspected House hacker on his law firm's payroll while he awaited trial, meaning Imran would have direct access to all the evidence.

A lawyer doesn't pay a client, the client pays the lawyer. This only raised a question that had been obvious from the beginning: how did the notoriously cheap Imran wind up with a well-connected Clinton lawyer? As acquaintances watched the glacial pace at which the case against Imran was moving, they often asked me if I thought prosecutors were giving him harbor because he had agreed to implicate congressmen in a theft scheme or in other misconduct he'd discovered through their emails. I always knew this was unlikely. Imran had never met a business partner he wouldn't double-cross, but Gowen's connections to Wasserman Schultz, the Clintons, and the Democratic establishment were as deep as they come, and his presence aligned Imran's interests with their own. Sumaira told me how Imran wound up being represented by Gowen. "He told me, 'The people who are supporting me, they hired Gowen. I want to get my case done no matter what and the people who are supporting me hired him for me.'... What he told me is Gowen has very good connections on the inside, they're having two-to three-hour meetings sorting it out." Sumaira was aware of Imran paying Gowen only $20,000 out of his own pocket, and with Gowen placing him on his payroll, that money would be recouped. The payroll maneuver was also a way around the judge's order that the $9,000 in cash confiscated from Imran at the airport could not be returned to him for personal use but could be used to pay his legal expenses.

But Everly's laptop was just the tip of a much more concerning iceberg. Prosecutors filed papers saying they'd rned over a copy of the laptop left in the phone booth to the defense; the one with the username RepDWS and which Representative Wasserman Schultz said was "a member's." So, Imran was banned from the House computer network because, as the House's chief administrative officer wrote, he was an "ongoing and serious risk to the House of Representatives, possibly threatening the integrity of our information systems." Then after that, he was in possession of a congresswoman's computer and left it in the most suspicious possible circumstances. Representative Wasserman Schultz's desperate measures made clear that whatever was on it, she did *not* want it being made public, including by suggesting it had privileged legislative information on it. Now prosecutors were delivering a copy of the laptop's hard drive directly to him?

It turned out that prosecutors were giving Gowen *everything* they had in the House investigation, even though Imran had only been charged with bank fraud. Under the legal process of discovery, defendants are entitled to evidence they need to defend themselves against specific crimes with which they've been charged. Former prosecutors I spoke with said this additional, voluntary disclosure was astonishing, outrageous, and unheard of. Kendra Arnold, a lawyer with the Foundation for Accountability & Civic Trust, had an observation: "If he was Joe Smith from Idaho, this is not how the prosecution would be proceeding."

What was occurring seemed obvious. The FBI and the DOJ were getting massive political pressure from Democrats not to bring the case to trial. On the other side, Republicans were exerting no pressure at all since most of them didn't even know what had occurred. The DOJ didn't necessarily want to drop the whole thing, but the only way to pursue the case without revealing the true facts in open court was to negotiate behind the scenes, turning over all the evidence outside of formal channels and figuring it would be enough to strong-arm the defense into a plea deal. The problem is that if Gowen sensed their desire to avoid public courtrooms, all the leverage was in his hands: he didn't need to accept a thing.

Prosecutors seemed to freeze in their tracks. They couldn't make the case go away because server logs, invoices, and other documents left no doubt that crimes had occurred on and off Capitol Hill. But they also could not close the case because Democrats on Capitol Hill were using its "ongoing investigation" status to avoid talking about it. They postponed court dates eight times.

EIGHTEEN

INSURANCE

The retaliation against would-be witnesses rained down hardest on the Awans' stepmother, Samina Gilani.

The deposition in the civil court case about possible life insurance fraud took place on October 4, 2017—two days before Imran and Hina were scheduled to appear in federal court. It was conducted in the office of Jim Bacon, the Awans' money-laundering specialist lawyer, with the assistance of a translator. It turned out that the Awans' plan was to use the lawsuit for the same purpose that I'd wanted to: to force "discovery" to learn more about the criminal case on Capitol Hill.

Bacon did so in a more aggressive and overt manner than I ever imagined possible, openly attempting to force Gilani to reveal details of the probe on Capitol Hill and badgering her in ways that, to a non-lawyer like myself, seemed like witness intimidation and tampering with an ongoing investigation. There wasn't the slightest bit of effort to mask what he was doing.

And when it was Gilani's turn, her attorney, the beta-male felon Michael Hadeed, didn't ask Abid a single question.

It was a stunning gauntlet. For hours, Bacon hammered Gilani about the congressional criminal investigation, again and again. "Come clean. That's the best," Bacon—whose very named seemed designed to offend the Halal-observant widow—advised her. "Have you ever told anybody that Mr. Imran Awan committed any crime? Have you ever told anybody that Hina Alvi committed any crime? You understand me, don't you?"[1]

It is a basic tenet of our criminal justice system that grand juries are shrouded in secrecy, but Bacon didn't care. He obviously wanted to know whether a grand jury was mulling a new indictment that would go far beyond bank fraud. "Did you ever testify anywhere about any of the Awan brothers?" he demanded. "Did you ever file any... declarations, or solemn statements, or affidavits for the FBI or anybody?"

"Did the FBI or any Capitol Police or any government official ever ask you to sign any papers?"

"Do you know what a grand jury is?"

"Did you ever testify in court about the Awan brothers anywhere?"

If members of Congress claimed what happened was no big deal, they should have asked Bacon, who was concerned the investigation might involve a nexus with terrorism. "Have you ever told the police, when you called the police about your husband, or the FBI, or the Capitol Police, or anybody that Mr. Awan was involved in any radical Islam or radical Islamic activities?" Bacon asked.

"No, never," Gilani responded, adding that they'd never asked.

The typical antidote to abuse of the deposition process is simple: the opposing lawyer will object. Hadeed periodically tried, meekly. "I'm going to object on this irrelevant questioning," he said.

But Bacon ignored him. "It's very relevant to her—"

"The only relevance in this case —it's just simple, man. It's just interpretation of a contract," Hadeed said. He entreated with one of the most fearsome legal arguments of our time, one passed down from ancient Greek tribunals to the English common law system upon which United States civil torts are based: "C'mon." He gave up without even waiting for a response. "Anyway, go ahead."

"What did you talk about with the FBI when they came to your house?"

Hadeed tried again: "I'm just going to object based on relevance."

Gilani had figured out by this point that there was no stopping Bacon. "They wanted to know about the money, where did they send that. And I told them I don't know about that."

I knew from my reporting that Hina had long been sending people money in suspicious ways. Bacon wanted to know if the FBI had discovered that. "Now, did they ask if Hina was sending any money or was it just Imran that they were asking about sending money?" This lawsuit involved only Abid and life insurance, and there wasn't a legitimate reason as to why trying to find out whether the FBI had caught on to his sister-in-law's money trail would relate. Like every other aspect of the Awan affair, this kind of shocking conduct could occur only because one side was so motivated to make what happened go away that they'd do anything, and the side that was supposed to keep them in check was weak and anemic.

Hadeed interjected: "Listen. I have a right to say this because it makes the case simpler.... This case is based solely on the January 16 date of death and the January 17 attempt to change the beneficiary."

Bacon barked: "We'll be here another couple of days. So what time do you have to leave tonight? I'm not leaving until I get everything I need out of you."

Hadeed said: "Well, just ask questions that relate to the case and maybe we can get on faster."

Bacon ordered Hadeed: "You're testifying now. Don't do it again."

Hadeed pleaded: "Don't trick her."

Bacon repeated: "Don't do it again. Don't do that again."

Hadeed said: "I can object on attorney-client privilege."

Bacon ordered: "No, you can't."

It only got more surreal from there, as Bacon pressed Gilani for more information about the investigators and other witnesses. "Did they explain to you what they were specifically investigating?" he asked.

"Did they tell you anybody else they spoke with?"

Again, a single-minded desire by the Awans' lawyers to find out who witnesses were. I'd seen how that ends.

"Were there any other questions that were asked about any other family members?"

If Gilani's answers were to be believed, the FBI investigator didn't want to find out about the Awans at all. The Bureau was checking off a box. That was obvious enough from who it sent to speak with Gilani: Brandon Merriman, a first-year agent from a sleepy Virginia office. He wasn't exactly the FBI's varsity team.

"Did they ask you to get them any information or find out anything for them?" Bacon asked.

Bacon tried to convert Gilani into a mole who would leak sensitive information from the investigation to her victimizers. "If they want to speak to you again, will you ask them what's going on with their investigation?"

Bacon forced her to reveal her Social Security number and other sensitive details. When Bacon asked Gilani for the name and phone number of the people who were financially support-ing her— which would give away where she was staying—she said, "I don't want to give you a name."

"I'm sorry, but you have to," Bacon replied.

"No, I don't want to tell you."

"Counsel?" Bacon asked. "She can't refuse or I'm going to go to court and ask the judge to order a response. I hope you explained to her she has to answer the questions."

Hadeed said, "I'm going to object to the relevance of the question. It has nothing to do with the issues in the case, but…"

"You have to give me the name."

Bacon pressed for other information, important to the Awans, but irrelevant to this case. "Now, did you ever tell any police officers or government officials that the Awan brothers were paying the police officers? And that they had a cousin whose name was Police Officer Azhar Awan?"

Finally, when Gilani couldn't avoid answering questions she didn't want to answer, she lied. She said that she had never spo-ken to me and that she didn't even have an email address.

It was a brilliant move on Bacon's part. He had set up a situation where no matter what, the Awans won. If Gilani told the truth, they had info that would give them an upper hand in the criminal case. If she lied, they could use the dishonesty to cast doubt on any testimony she might give at an eventual felony trial.

And if she played dumb, they could use her claims of knowing nothing to contradict more forthcoming testimony at a criminal trial. "Do you know anything about Imran's financial affairs?" Bacon asked.

"No, I don't," she replied.

When Bacon gleaned that there was more congressional oversight into the case than he knew, he had a conniption. "I've asked you whether you had a conversation with anybody about the Awan brothers. And anybody means anybody at any time up to today. Who did you speak with yesterday, ma'am?"

"The people from Capitol Hill."

By this time, Hadeed seemed to have abandoned his client. "Alright. I want the record to reflect that I am now learning about this myself for the first time, too. So, examine her. I'm sorry. I don't know."

"I think this is important," Bacon said.

Gilani pleaded: "But I told you I didn't tell anything about them."

Bacon wasn't done interrogating her about the investigation in Congress, and why she agreed to cooperate. "Correct me if I'm wrong, they did not just show up out of the clear blue at two or three o'clock last week. They contacted you to set up a time and come see you, didn't they?"

"Yes. They told me they will come."

"Did they call your land line or your cell phone?"

"Cell phone. On my cell phone."

Bacon tried to make her reveal the identity of the congressional investigators. "If you pull up your phone, will you be able to see the phone number that called you?"

"No."

"What about the Awan brothers did they ask you?"

Hadeed had completely thrown her under the bus. "Just tell them everything. Don't worry. You have to. Just answer. It's okay. Tell them whatever—whatever they ask. I mean, unless you're under oath to tell a grand jury."

Bacon: "Did they give you any papers and ask you to go somewhere like a subpoena?"

"No."

"Okay. When they asked you to tell them some things and they said they could help you, did they explain what kind of help they were willing to give you that they wanted to help you with?"

"They didn't say anything about help."

Bacon was getting at whether the government was willing to put Gilani in the witness protection program. Something that, based on what she'd told me, was entirely reasonable and probably necessary. "Did they ever indicate what the possibilities or the kind of help they could give you; whether they could take care of you, whether they can put you somewhere else, so you can get away from them or anything like that?"

No, they'd never bothered.

It was hours into the grueling session when Bacon made his big reveal: he knew the exact dates that Gilani had corresponded with the FBI over email, as if he could see her email account.

Imran had warned her not to talk to the police, and Bacon wasn't happy.

"You're a liar, aren't you?" he lashed out. "[redacted] is your email address, isn't it? And you send emails from that address including two emails to the FBI, didn't you?"

"Yes, a long time ago."

"Ma'am, you lied to me, didn't you? You lied to me, didn't you? You're a liar, aren't you?"

"I forgot about that. It was not in my mind."

"Ah," Bacon roared. "I think we need to take a break before I explode."

The deposition ended with an ominous warning. Bacon told the widow not to "dig a hole deeper and deeper to the point where you can't get out."

————

Bacon would not tell me how he knew about Gilani's email correspondence with the FBI. But given that she said Imran had stolen two laptops from her and placed devices behind her computer, one possibility was obvious. To test whether the Awans were hacking Gilani's email while the criminal case was proceeding, I sent emails to her with a tracker—an embedded one-pixel white image that caused a server ping that reported back to me when, where, and on what type of device the email was opened. The emails were opened in London, Pakistan, and Texas. Gilani's sister, who lives in Pakistan, said she helped manage Gilani's email since Gilani does not speak English, but said there is no reason emails should have been opened in the other locations.

I emailed Gilani to let her know her email account might be compromised, but it was likely deleted before it ever got to her. That email was opened in London and Kansas, but never in Virginia or Pakistan.

The Awans weren't done following through with the retaliation they had promised would come to Gilani for speaking to the police. Two weeks after the deposition, on October 19, 2017, a bank account Gilani controlled was drained of $5,952, its entire balance, through a transfer to Abid Awan. Bank of America later credited the amount back to the account as an unauthorized transfer. "He used the online method" to make the transfer, Gilani told me. "It is another fraud of Abid Awan."

But she was too afraid to press criminal charges. "Abid Awan is threatening me," she explained in an email. "They can hurt my relatives in Pakistan." A figure in a criminal congressional cybersecurity breach case had told me in writing she was being violently threatened to keep quiet, and the prosecutors handling the case were completely uninterested. It was obvious she knew more about money flowing from Capitol Hill to Pakistan than she was willing to say, and if her cousin Syed knew about iPhones and iPads going to Pakistani officials, she did too. But there was no offer of witness protection.

The brothers, it seemed to me, were covering up a likely case of hacking and extortion on Capitol Hill with more hacking and extortion—and it was working. In fact, Gilani testified under oath in the deposition that the Awan brothers—who prosecutors knew were improperly funneling data off the House network— were inclined to use their high-tech skills to engage in hostile surveillance. "He has connected my phone, my house phone,

with his own phone," she testified. "Whenever I talked to someone in Pakistan, [Imran] told me later on that you told this, you
said this." This statement was being delivered to prosecutors on
a silver platter in the form of a sworn legal document. But prosecutors didn't want to know what she had to say. I know that
because when I asked Hadeed for the transcript of the deposition,
the court recorder had to type it up from her audio tape, since no
one else ever ordered it.

———

A few months later on March 7, 2018, the parties were back
in civil court for the judge's decision on who would get the life
insurance money. The shaved-headed Bacon was slamming the
widow even before she arrived.

Gilani was two minutes late. "Is your client lost? Does she
own a watch?" he said. Sitting in the pew-like seats, which were
otherwise empty except for Wajid and a TV reporter named
Neil, I thought to myself: *maybe your client is holding her in
captivity again.*

Bacon couldn't stand that reporters were there to witness the
ugly scene. He threatened Hadeed for giving me a copy of the
video that showed the Awan brothers preemptively building a
body of evidence for the inevitable fraud allegations by having
their father sign the insurance paperwork. "Are you going to
share any more info with them? I hope not. I hope you learned
that lesson," he said, glaring at us.

As Representative Wasserman Schultz publicly painted the
Awans to the media as innocent victims of Islamophobia, Bacon

mocked the elderly, burka-clad widow relentlessly: "She's a wacko lunatic, what are you going to do?" he said. "Is it like talking to a wall?" he asked Hadeed. When Gilani arrived and the court-appointed translator began doing his job, Bacon tried to make him shut up. "I can't hear myself think," he said. The judge told him Gilani was entitled to know what was going on in her own court proceeding.

The immediate facts of the life insurance couldn't be more suspicious. Jamal had filed a death certificate to the government that falsely claimed his father was divorced, and Abid used that certificate to remove Gilani from the life insurance policy—after her husband's death. When Hadeed tried to bring up the lie on the death certificate, Bacon acted like he was crazy. "Why is that even relevant?"

Hadeed didn't bother to explain, nor did he introduce any evidence to the judge about a pattern of fraud by Abid. For example, the witness who signed the life insurance paperwork was Abid's wife Nataliia, from whom, he previously swore under oath in order to perpetrate obvious bankruptcy fraud, he was separated. Hadeed didn't point out the timing of the move as it related to the federal criminal case—that Abid's brother Imran committed bank fraud the very next day after the life insurance move, wired the money to Pakistan, and got arrested by the FBI—which would have established a motive for Abid. He didn't question the mental capacity of the dying, heavily medicated man—who visitors to the hospital room told me was very out of it—to understand paperwork.

In fact, Hadeed withdrew earlier allegations of fraud entirely and asked the judge to try the case based solely on interpretation of the contract language. "It's simple," he told me. "The other stuff wasn't necessary."

Hadeed said three different signatures from Abid on financial documents did not match and put Abid on the witness stand. It would be the only time any of the six House hacking suspects ever faced questioning in court, where any lawyer worth his salt could confront them with their many lies. Though Hadeed only kept him up there for a few minutes, Abid was cocky and evasive. I was sure that if the Awans ever had to answer for their conduct in a real prosecution, it would be a spectacle indeed.

"Why do your signatures look different?" Hadeed asked.

"My signatures are not very consistent, I'm just a human being," Abid said.

"You were aware you were changing beneficiary from your father's spouse to yourself?"

"That was my father's request," Abid testified.

"You're not answering the question," Hadeed said.

After a couple rounds like that, the judge got fed up. "I don't understand why the witness is having such trouble with the question. Your job is to answer the question."

"I'm not very smart, so it takes a while sometimes," Abid said with a smirk.

No one was surprised that based on Hadeed's limited legal argument about the life insurance contract's language, the judge ruled that "the son as the owner of the policy has the absolute right to change the beneficiary." The court awarded Abid the $50,000 life insurance payout.

"You should have taken the settlement. Now she's not getting a penny," Bacon taunted. "You're not getting anything."

After the verdict, I huddled with the other two reporters in the room. Neil, the TV reporter, said of Bacon: "I knew he was taking advantage of this poor woman, but it was such a sight, you almost couldn't help but root for him. He was like Mike Tyson just pulverizing them while they're already down. He wouldn't stop. A display of sheer power. And Michael Hadeed's just there like *babababababa*," he said, running his fingers over his lips.

Wajid, the Pakistani news correspondent, had a theory: "It seemed like he threw the case." Wajid said that was a common occurrence in Pakistan, and Gilani reached the same conclusion, wondering if the relatives who referred her to Hadeed had set her up. But Hadeed had a different explanation, one that seemed to illuminate Bacon's threat about "learning a lesson." When Neil asked Hadeed some questions outside of court, he seemed uneasy. He said Bacon threatened to sue him for defamation for conducting basic advocacy for his client. "I don't want to subject myself to that. I don't want to get myself in a lawsuit over this," he said.

NINETEEN

HELL HATH NO FURY LIKE A SHARIA WIFE SCORNED

Chris Gowen, the Clinton aide-turned-defense attorney, couldn't stop himself from uttering over-the-top falsehoods. Appearing on Sharyl Attkisson's TV program, he said "There's never been an accusation that he or anybody in his group did anything to...break a rule in Congress or anything like that."[1] It was absurd; the entire family had been banned from Congress for violating nearly every IT rule, and the violations were indisputably memorialized in server logs.

Attkisson asked about the lawsuit filed in Pakistan by Imran's own wife and fellow congressional aide, Hina, alleging that her husband threatened her with "dire consequences."

"Did he threaten his wife?" he asked.

"No, absolutely not," Gowen said. A response that could only amount to accusing Imran's wife of being a liar.

Then Attkisson asked about his other Sharia-law wife, Sumaira. "Was he married to two people?"

"No," Gowen replied.

For Sumaira, this was the last straw. Gowen knew that Imran was married to a second woman under Pakistani law. In fact, he was furious with his client for his polygamy, which made it hard to paint him as an all-American family man. Gowen demanded that Imran tell him everything, and that he grant Sumaira the divorce she was begging for. Imran refused. Sumaira had gone so far as to show up at Gowen's office and ask him to secure the divorce, which Gowen had said he would do.

Imran had a different tactic. He caused the copy of the marriage certificate in the Pakistani courthouse to disappear. Sumaira found out because she used to work in the courthouse, and the clerk who agreed to do it was her neighbor's brother. Still, both she and Imran had copies of their marriage license, and he adamantly insisted that she remain his wife, refusing to grant a divorce.

One factor had allowed Democratic members of Congress to weather this whole scandal without turning on each other or the Awans: they hid in the anonymity of a crowd of forty-four and attempted to portray it as an institutional scandal; ideally one for which the Republicans whose job it was to police the House were responsible. Without a face, the whole thing becomes easier to deal with. And sometimes, dozens of faces are almost as good as none.

But these lies diminishing Sumaira's very existence were getting personal. She made the hardest decision of her life to turn against her own husband and pick up the phone and call me. Now, not only did Imran have two wives, but both had identified him as someone who controls people with threats.

Sumaira's motivation was bigger than personal insult. As it became clearer that Imran had the entire Congress wrapped around his finger and was going to get away with it, he developed a cocky confidence. It was frightening to think what someone as prone to retaliation as Imran might do. "He's going to get out of the situation with clean hands and put the victims in the bad situation," Sumaira said.

Imran told her he had offers from three members of Congress to come back and work in the House, even as his felony trial loomed. "I am sure he will do the same again," she said. She realized how extraordinary it would be for Democrats to put a cybersecurity violator back on their payroll. "If you don't have a deep leverage with the people you are working with, you are not able to do that." She summed up Democrats' irrational refusal to condemn Imran as well as anyone could: "They're not protecting him, they're protecting themselves."

As prosecutors continued to stall without charges, she began to see that Imran's confidence was not unfounded. "They are prosecutors and the defense in one, there is no one on the other side. He's the biggest vagabond in Pakistan. This is amazing, I don't even have words. It seems like the whole case is upside down."

Sumaira told me that after she called the Virginia police in June 2016—around the time the House investigation was heating up—to say she was being kept "like a slave," she was so frightened of Imran that she retreated to the home of her father in Pakistan, where the family was so wealthy they had a servant who slept in the garage. When she returned to Virginia, Imran had stopped paying her rent and she became homeless. She couldn't ask her family for help because the Sumaira they knew wouldn't allow herself to be treated so poorly by a man, and based on the way they saw Imran speak in Pakistan, they believed she was married to an elite legislator. She wound up in the Patrick Henry shelter house, a home for abused women a few blocks from my apartment. Hina came by the homeless shelter to taunt her, saying "Bitch, I will never let you have a roof over your head."

At the shelter, social workers quickly spotted her legal acumen and good character, paid for her to enroll in law school in the U.S., and placed her in county-supported transitional housing. It was a shining success story for the social services facility.

But Sumaira had one weakness: love. When Hina fled the country, Imran said she wasn't coming back, and Sumaira hoped things would be different. She fell back into old patterns, with Imran staying most nights with her. But she began to realize she'd made a grave mistake. When I complimented her on her articulate and intelligent nature, she said, "If I were actually smart, I would have seen him for who he is a long time ago. I made a mistake. I mourn on my wisdom." Imran installed hidden cameras in her apartment and began blackmailing her with videos of them having sex; videos she hadn't known were being filmed, but which would cause her family in Pakistan to disown her if released.

"When Hina came back, I was with my kids and Imran at Popeye's Halal Chicken in Sterling, and she showed up like she was coming to beat me, and I said to Imran, 'I'm gonna call the police.'" Imran couldn't allow that to happen. "He grabbed my phone... it was a huge scene, people were recording it."

Sumaira was originally attracted to Imran's outgoing personality and confidence, but eventually concluded that he was a master manipulator who cared only about money. Not long after the Popeye's incident, Sumaira was in a minor fender bender. She was completely unharmed, but Imran became enraged, telling her that if she had any sense, she'd feign a back injury and file a claim against the other driver's insurance. "You'll get $30,000," he said. When Sumaira told him that would be wrong, Imran went to her son. "Your mom doesn't love you," he said. "I want you to have presents and she doesn't."

In mid-2018, while prosecutors appeared to be treating Awan with kid gloves and negotiating a plea deal, he escalated his efforts to hide money. He asked Sumaira to create an LLC to stash assets for him, and even asked her and another relative to buy kilogram bricks of gold, worth $40,000 each, for him in New York. She said he was sending large sums of money to Saif Ullah Awan, a relative in Pakistan, and Saif Rao, a jeweler and import-export businessman in Queens, New York. Numerous other relatives told me the exact same thing.

If the FBI wanted to know where the money was going, Saif Rao was part of the answer. Saif Rao splits his time between New York and Pakistan, where his family owns a jewelry business. On Facebook, he posted pictured of gold bars between messages like: "To believers Allah blessed with Zum Zum and to the disbelievers, Urine of cow." According to public records, Saif Rao also goes by the alias "Saif Iqbal," and previously lived in California. In markers of possible money laundering, public records showed him associating himself with a bankrupt Christian church in Texas and a painting business in California, whose owner said he'd never heard of him. He had a federal tax lien placed against him for $1.1 million.

For years, Imran transferred money to Saif Rao. Sometimes to evade detection, it would go from an account in Hina's name to one in Saif Rao's brother's name. In 2015, Sumaira was with Imran when he got a call from a bank that had flagged one of the transfers as suspicious. On Facebook, Saif Rao is friends with Haseeb Rana, the former IT aide whose father told me Imran had him doing the work of others. Rana is Indian and lived in Virginia, hours from Saif Rao's New York home, so there is little reason for them to know each other except that Imran was controlling the money earned by his proxies on Capitol Hill, letting them keep a cut of their paychecks and directing some of the remainder to Saif Rao.

Sumaira also shed light on something else that I had suspected must have been true given how many nights Imran spent with her. When his other wife, Hina, filed the lawsuit against Imran in Pakistan just before returning to the U.S. to face indictment, her claim that she had been blindsided by his polygamy was a ruse. Hina had known about Imran's other women for years. "He used to tell her everything regarding my bedroom and show her my videos. They are perfect for each other. Both care only about money," Sumaira said. The Pakistani lawsuit appeared to be one more manipulation that would allow Hina to establish herself as a victim if it came to it, or perhaps to file for divorce and gain access to the Pakistani assets herself.

TWENTY

JEFF SESSIONS IS MR. MAGOO

It wasn't just the media who Speaker Paul Ryan and Chairman Gregg Harper never told what happened. Rank-and-file Republicans—who would have demanded justice, ensured a thorough investigation, and made it a campaign issue—had no clue what had occurred.

Police told Chairman Harper's Committee on House Administration in June 2017 that they had no plans to conduct further interviews even though many people with knowledge of wrongdoing had never been approached. Despite that, Chairman Harper continued to defer to prosecutors, telling me as late as April 2018 that it was "in the hands of the Department of Justice." Chairman Harper knew as well as anyone the extent of the wrongdoing that had occurred. Didn't he suspect something might have gone awry? What did he think prosecutors had been *doing* for the last year? If they were done gathering evidence, then why didn't they either close out the case as unfounded, or go ahead and finally charge someone?

Apparently to Chairman Harper—a former prosecutor—the "ongoing" status of the investigation meant that his fellow Republicans couldn't be informed of even the barest outlines of what had occurred. This was akin to claiming you couldn't tell a murder victim's loved ones that the person was dead until a conviction was secured in the killing. The notion that congressmen couldn't opine on a case until it had wound its way through the courts plainly didn't apply to his Democratic colleagues, who were constantly talking about purported collusion between Trump and Russia. And certainly, the chairman's fellow Republicans had seen enough instances of politicized conduct by the FBI in the 2016 election to make clear that oversight was often appropriate and necessary.

When I met with the vice chair of the committee, Representative Rodney Davis, the genial young Illinois legislator and former congressional staffer was quick to project a top-secret, 007 vibe, as if the invocation of secrecy made him feel important. "I just can't talk about it, because it's an ongoing investigation," he said. But as I rattled through some facts of the case, basic elements seemed to both trip him up and pique his interest. "The House Democratic Caucus? What do they have to do with this?"

I paused. "Sir, it sounds like you can't not talk about it because you're not allowed to. You can't talk about it because you don't know a thing about it."

He laughed. "I guess you're right. This is really troubling stuff, and I wish I had been informed of it. Can I get a copy of that IG report?" Even the second-in-command on the committee with direct oversight of the House's IT scandal didn't have the slightest clue what this was all about. That made it impossible to realize the perversity of the response. Representative Davis was interested to know more and wanted to help. But it was not his place to cross the chairman.

Scrutiny might have come from other bodies like the Intelligence Committee, led by the tough investigator Representative Devin Nunes of California, except that the executive branch has no shortage of ways to neuter congressional oversight. The FBI told the Intelligence Committee that the Awans had no connections to foreign government officials despite running a car dealership that took money from an Iraqi government minister, wiring money to a Pakistani cop, sending devices to Pakistani government officials, convincing Pakistanis that he was a White House employee, and receiving protection from armed Pakistani government agents. By making that assertion, the Bureau left Nunes no choice but to consider the case outside of his jurisdiction.

The inbred nature of Congress also meant that when it came to a scandal in their own backyard, ordinarily tough investigators had personal conflicts. Trey Gowdy, the chairman of the oversight committee, was out of the question because of his close relationship with Chief Administrative Officer Kiko, and Representative Gowdy visibly recoiled when I asked him about the case.

That left the House Freedom Caucus, a rowdy coalition of Republicans often described as the most conservative in the House, but who in reality are defined by a more nuanced trait: an independence that makes them more willing than any members of either party to pursue their convictions instead of bowing to the House Speaker or minority leader. If anything, you could say that these members were *less* "Republican" than their colleagues. They did what they felt was right, and if Speaker Ryan didn't like it, well, he didn't elect them. They were often joined by other members like Representatives Thomas Massie and Matt Gaetz, who harbored libertarian-leaning views that overlapped with liberal positions at times. What bonded them together was, more than anything, the notion that being one of the 435 House members should mean more than just falling into line behind Paul Ryan or Nancy Pelosi.

These Republican congressmen were not happy that their leadership hadn't told them about the frightening events in their own chamber. Some of them, such as Representative Ron DeSantis of Florida and Representative Jim Jordan of Ohio—a darkhorse candidate for Speaker of the House himself—demanded that the House conduct oversight hearings on the House's IT scandal. But Speaker Ryan's leadership team intervened to block them.[1] Fearing for the integrity of the legislative body, the members resorted to hijacking the Oversight Committee's room for a rogue, unsanctioned hearing. They smuggled in cameras at the last minute, fearing a typical audiovisual request would alert leadership that something was going on. I testified as the main witness, shocking members of Congress with events that had occurred beneath their noses.[2] My information came largely from official House documents that their fellow Republicans had refused to share with them. The rest came from fairly straightforward investigative follow-up that no one else seemed to have done.

Being sought out by congressmen who wanted to pick my brain was an odd reversal for a reporter accustomed to chasing *them* down hallways to ask for information. But they deserved to know. I began briefing a group of a dozen congressmen, led by Representatives Louie Gohmert of Texas and Scott Perry of Pennsylvania, sometimes over Texas barbeque. These congressmen were different from the others I'd encountered. They didn't care if the truth made the House, Democrats, or Republicans look bad. They only cared about getting the facts, and they took the extraordinary obstruction as a sign that they were onto something big, not that they should back off. Most important, unlike members of Congress who seemed to want to pass the buck to others wherever possible and then take credit later if it became advantageous, these congressmen were willing to put in the effort to find the truth. Unlike members like Chairman Harper, these congressmen often did the work themselves rather than ceding large portions of their responsibilities to staff.

Both Representatives Gohmert and Perry came from military backgrounds. Representative Gohmert was a judge and is an active member of the Judiciary Committee. Physically, he is unimposing: a balding sixty-four-year-old with a slow Texas drawl. But it didn't take long to see that his power came from his mind, which had an uncanny ability to file away every fact, date, and claim he heard, stored in an internal database constantly being mined for discrepancies and problems. When it came to government corruption, if you were on the wrong side of one of these facts, Representative Gohmert's questioning came like a roaring M-16 in the Iraq desert.

Representative Perry was a member of the committees on foreign affairs and homeland security. He has a work ethic that rivaled Imran Awan's superhuman industriousness, having been working since the age of thirteen, and put himself through college while holding a full-time job. But unlike worn-down veterans of Congress, the tall, skinny Perry somehow managed to reach his fifties with a wry smile and impossible youthfulness about him. He was always eager to take on Washington dysfunction, even if it meant losing again and again. While Sergeant at Arms Paul Irving, Samina Gilani, and the many House staffers who told me they knew what was going on but that there was no point coming forward, had stopped fighting because it was clear the fix was in, what made Representatives Gohmert and Perry different is that they felt such battles were still worth fighting—for the principle of it, and in the off chance that maybe, someday, the Swamp could be overcome.

House leadership was not providing answers to their questions about the Awan case. But while Representatives Gohmert and Perry knew that hiding the facts from Congress' rank-and-file helped facilitate a DOJ cover-up, at the end of the day, congressional oversight wasn't what was needed. This was a serious criminal matter and it needed less politics, not more. This needed to be handled by someone with the power to jail people, and quickly. On March 1, 2018, the pair met with Attorney General Jeff Sessions, Assistant Director of the FBI's Criminal Division Stephen Richardson, and a few other FBI and DOJ aides about the case, demanding to know how clear-cut evidence of crimes on Capitol Hill was not resulting in prosecution. Sessions promised to get to the bottom of it but was fed blatantly untrue answers by the FBI. Most of Sessions' staff seemed to accept those answers at face value.

At the meeting, in front of Sessions, Representative Gohmert gave the FBI a binder of documentation including a list of sources who had critical information. This included information about claims by Stephen Taylor, the fellow Democratic IT aide who said he had firsthand knowledge of Imran selling access to congressional offices. His testimony could support an attempted bribery charge. Most attention-grabbing to the average person, he also saw Imran going into the DNC headquarters on a regular basis as if he were secretly working there.

The media constantly claimed that my reporting on the Awan matter was aimed at somehow disputing the DNC narrative, something they could not have thought if they had actually read any of my sixty articles, which clearly focused on the House Democratic Caucus and House servers, not the DNC. They would be shocked to know that I did have credible information about the DNC and deliberately decided *not* to report it, figuring if I stayed away from this controversial topic, surely they'd acknowledge the events in the House that I was documenting, events that in my mind were just as serious. I was getting played.

But as it became more obvious how Imran and his family inappropriately blurred the lines between various offices in the House, under-the-table DNC moonlighting would fit the pattern. That's not to say that Imran took the DNC emails, but if he was working there while on the taxpayer clock to save the bankrupt DNC some money, it could be illegal, and it seemingly should have come up in any thorough investigation into the DNC hack. By this time, President Trump's campaign was being sued by the

DNC, which alleged that it worked with Russia to hack the political group. "Just heard the Campaign was sued by the Obstructionist Democrats. This can be good news in that we will now counter for the DNC Server that they refused to give to the FBI, the Debbie Wasserman Schultz Servers and Documents held by the Pakistani mystery man and Clinton Emails," Trump tweeted, giving Imran one of his signature nicknames.[3] What Trump didn't know is that Sessions' FBI had information that might expose misconduct at the DNC and be advantageous to Trump, but never pursued the lead.

In the meeting, the FBI called the Awans "the Family," like the mafia. The congressmen were told teams from three different divisions of the FBI were working the case, probing public corruption and national security as well as bank fraud. One of those teams was the counter-intelligence unit—the same unit led by Peter Strzok, who made key decisions on the Clinton emails and Trump-Russia cases and promised to "stop" Trump from becoming president. Now the unit's failure to talk to even basic witnesses was starting to make sense.

When it came to the procurement scheme, the FBI said it "knows" that multiple staffers, in addition to the "Family," were involved. But most Democrats were refusing to cooperate, the FBI said—an admission that was obvious enough given how the case had been treated in the House, but which contradicted statements by Democrats and House officials. The point was that the "victims" weren't clamoring for a prosecution. For many cops, that's enough not to bother.

Imran was not exactly cooperating either. The FBI was providing him a "proffer"—a process generally used to allow a suspect to provide information about others in exchange for a plea deal— but his defense attorney was rejecting the offers. Through eight such meetings, the government kept giving him more and more chances, presumably settling for less and less. The $7 million-dollar question was: if Imran was refusing to plea, why didn't they simply bring charges in court?

Representative Gohmert pointed out that prosecutors had never talked to the former inspector general, Theresa Grafenstine, even though she'd done the foundational work on the probe. Theresa was no longer part of the legislative branch and thus not subject to the "speech and debate clause" that could limit prosecutors' ability to gather information. She could be a way around the obstruction.

"We can subpoena her tomorrow," an FBI official said to Sessions. "We've got a grand jury running." There was, in fact, no grand jury currently hearing evidence to support charges in the Awan house case, even though an FBI memo dated December 6, 2016, talked of "fraud against the U.S. government" and referenced banking records showing that Abid was hiding money through car dealerships. But admitting that they had never even brought these facts before a grand jury, which undoubtedly would have returned indictments, would have raised more than a few questions from the attorney general.

The congressmen told me Sessions seemed taken aback—he had never heard of any of this. The systematic fraud in the House of Representatives, massive violations of cybersecurity, disappearing computer equipment, and a congressional laptop popping up in a phone booth had not been brought to the attorney general's attention by the FBI. He seemed genuinely interested in getting the truth, but he was utterly dependent on the FBI to report it to him. *You'll get your answers*, Sessions told the Congressman. *I want all these things looked into*, Sessions told Stephen Richardson of the FBI Criminal Division.

Representative Gohmert had seen how the FBI chose to pursue some investigations with all the fire and fury it had, while others it phoned in. In its efforts to find criminal charges against former Trump campaign chairman Paul Manafort, prosecutors sought out an Associated Press reporter who'd broken news on the topic, milked him for information, and used it to build a case.[4] When it came to the Awans, even though it was clear that my reporting was the only thing advancing the investigation and that I had more information than I had published, the FBI and prosecutors were uninterested in receiving information from me, and weren't even contacting sources whose names I'd printed, like Rashid Minhas. When it came to investigations against Trump, they raided the office of his lawyer, Michael Cohen. When it came to Representative Debbie Wasserman Schultz's laptop in a phone booth, prosecutors entertained a preposterous attorney-client privilege argument, apparently based on the presence of a hand-scribbled note that read "attorney client privilege" nearby. Richardson confirmed that the laptop was the former DNC chair's, and assured Sessions that they were "close to resolving that issue" without explaining why they hadn't simply fought the attorney-client canard from the beginning. Trump was right. Whatever was on that laptop, Representative Wasserman Schultz desperately wanted to keep it out of prosecutors' hands, which should have made them all the more eager to look at it.

When it came to these Democratic members of Congress and their employees, it seemed the FBI was being exceedingly credulous, naïve even, in accepting any implausible explanation at face value. The FBI's "investigation" seemed to consist of simply asking Gowen for an excuse, then scoffing at any suggestion that it might not be true.

To test this, Representative Gohmert asked about the electronic devices the marine, Andre Taggart, had turned in. They were non-government and there was nothing on them, an FBI official in the meeting said. As with everything else, he didn't explain. I thought: Was he really contending that Imran was the first person in the modern era to prefer a Blackberry over an iPhone for personal use, and that he'd bought many for himself? That he collected industrial-sized quantities of printer toner on his own dime? How did they conclude that the items didn't belong to the House when the inventory lists had been gamed by Imran himself? Or was Richardson claiming even more bizarrely, as Imran's lawyer did, that Taggart had never found anything but a car radio?

As another way around Congress invoking privilege and Democrats refusing to cooperate, the questioners mentioned the involvement of the multi-billion-dollar company CDW-G. It was a private company whom the DOJ could subpoena whether the House liked it or not, and the company (or its employee) systematically falsified financial documents, apparently at Imran's request. The company had publicly acknowledged that prosecutors had already subpoenaed it, while also saying prosecutors told it—for reasons that were unclear—the company wasn't a target.

The FBI officials in the meeting said they were not aware that invoices from the company CDW-G had been subpoenaed and suggested that the U.S. Attorney's Office must have handled that part of the investigation. Those records were a basic part of the procurement fraud. How could the FBI claim to be investigating procurement fraud without knowing the first thing about how it happened?

One problem, a common technique to hamstringing congressional oversight, was that Richardson and the others answering questions in the meeting were too high up. It's a misconception that higher-ranking officials know more; in almost every case, they know less than the rank-and-file working directly with the evidence. Representatives Gohmert and Perry needed to meet with agents working on the case. The officials agreed to schedule such a meeting. It would give lawmakers an opportunity to share evidence with the agents, and perhaps reveal whether the FBI was pursuing the investigation aggressively or just going through the motions. The DOJ said the briefing would have to be held in a Sensitive Compartmented Information Facility, or SCIF. But DOJ dragged its feet on setting up the meeting until it was clear it wasn't going to happen until *after* the March 8 court date, by which time a plea deal might already be inked.

Three days before the court date, the court appearance was postponed by two months until May 3. The SCIF meeting was scheduled for March 20, but at 9:45 p.m. the night before, the DOJ canceled it over email. The agent handling the briefing had retired, the DOJ said. Had he abruptly retired without notice just that day? Was only one FBI agent to attend the briefing? And if he was an important member of the investigative team, how would the investigation proceed without him? The SCIF meeting was rescheduled for May 18—restoring it to a pointless position after the court date.

Prosecutors never subpoenaed Theresa Grafenstine—not "tomorrow," or ever. But in late April 2018, prosecutor Michael Marando asked her to meet at a coffee shop. It was two years to the day since she began an investigation in which she was the most knowledgeable official, and it was the first time prosecutors ever attempted to talk with her. At the table were Marando, a Capitol Police officer, and Spencer Brooks, an FBI agent who previously worked an aggressive case against former representative Steve Stockman, a Texas Republican who was charged with wire fraud, violating election law, and filing a false tax return.[5]

For two hours, Theresa walked the group through the whole story: what she had found, how it was clear House leaders wanted an investigation that was designed to find nothing, and how the Capitol Police had gladly acquiesced. She looked straight at the Capitol Police officer and told him his boss was a moron. "You have these people who are not cyber guys leading a cyber investigation, and that's a way to kind of kill it." She told them how months into the probe, the Capitol Police had said, "Well, maybe one day we'll do a search warrant. We don't think we're there yet."

Marando then made a remarkable claim. "I told them to say that," he said. "We know it made them look dumb. We were doing stuff behind the scenes that we couldn't tell anyone about so it wouldn't get back to the members." The implication was that they actually *did* get a search warrant on the Awans' homes, but the language was evasive. When she asked point-blank if he had executed search warrants on their homes after all, he wouldn't say yes.

Not even after the missing server? The Capitol Police officer responded with a stunning backtrack: "It never went missing." First of all, that didn't answer anything. It was indisputable that the police *believed* it to be missing at the time, and nevertheless left the Awans on the network and let Imran leave the country. The inaction of the Capitol Police left no doubt that they didn't *want* there to be a problem, so it was a little too convenient that the missing server had now apparently gone un-missing. Second, the officer said it with scorn, even though if the server really never went missing, that meant it was an egregiously embarrassing error on the part of his own police force. Yet another misstep that spoke volumes about why the Capitol Police should not have been handling this to begin with.

"So, Jamie Fleet and Phil Kiko made it up? Why would they do that?" Theresa asked. Both men had talked with great concern about how the server was missing, and Kiko had written an official memo stating that it was "missing." Why would Nancy Pelosi operative Jamie, who had gone out of his way to hinder this investigation, concoct a smoking gun that made the Awans' conduct seem *worse*?

"I looked at the serial number myself last week," the officer said. "It's in the evidence room."

Marando tried a contradictory tact. "This is bigger than you know, and we don't want anyone to accidentally interfere. There's a lot here that we're working on." She should sleep easy knowing that the apparent inaction was precisely because it was being conducted at the highest levels, like a national security operation. He looked at her, his pleading eyes feigning empathy, and said, "We're on your side."

But Theresa wasn't so sure. "You know what, time will tell. Everything you said to me is pandering and humoring just to hear me out. If you wanted to know what happened in this case, you wouldn't have blocked me from investigating it a year ago," she said.

Marando asked, "How do you know the Capitol Police blocked your investigation?" It was as if he wanted her assistance in preparing a defense for the criticism. Then they talked about Tom Hungar, the House's general counsel.

"Tom Hungar is withholding evidence from you," Theresa said.

"No, he's not. He's fully cooperative," Marando said.

Theresa replied: "I was in several meetings where he specifically said he was going to go through and scrub everything for speech and debate."

"He's been completely cooperative," Marando repeated.

"Sean Moran and Jamie Fleet, we suspect them of leaking." he added, referring to the Republican and Democratic lead staffers on the House Administration Committee.

Theresa laughed. Jamie had made no secret that he was a source for *Politico*'s reporting on the scandal. Marando seemed more concerned with who knew what than with prosecuting the suspects.

Then they talked about me. "Are you talking to that reporter, Luke? Every time he writes a story, we have to expend energy putting out a fire. He's beating a dead horse. We just want to wrap this up."

That raised the question: was there a predetermined conclusion? In the FBI's investigation into Hillary Clinton's emails, almost every major player was given immunity, and a statement clearing the candidate was drafted before the investigation was complete. I couldn't help but wonder if something similar was happening here.

———

After the amped-up pronouncements to the attorney general about three teams of the FBI's finest agents being all over the case—notwithstanding the FBI affidavit in which a first-year agent followed Hina to the airport, found $12,000 in undeclared cash in a cardboard box, and was refused an interview, then let her board the flight anyway while recording that she'd likely never return to the United States—the FBI began sending a different message to the AG's office, one impossible to argue with because it was so blithe: "there's nothing there." It was obvious that Sessions was not getting the full picture from the FBI, and that Sessions needed an independent assessment. If anything, this case was turning more interesting, implicating the FBI in misconduct.

Representative Gohmert's office arranged with the DOJ for former Inspector General Theresa Grafenstine to meet with Rachael Tucker, who had worked for Sessions since he was a senator and now served as a top political appointee for the attorney general. In January 2018, they met at a cafe down the street from the Justice Department; an arrangement that kept Theresa's name off the visitor logs in case rogue elements of the FBI were looking over Sessions' shoulder. Theresa gave her a copy of her presentation as well as a timeline outlining her efforts to brief Ryan and other members of Congress. But a few days later, Tucker seemed to lack a grasp on the basics. "What is CDW-G?" she asked.

If Sessions' staff was willing to put the time in to study the facts, they would quickly see that the FBI's assertions that there was "nothing there" were plainly false. But if they lacked the rigor or dedication to sort through materials and identify issues and discrepancies—the kind of nuance required to do real over-sight work that cuts through spin—they'd be left simply relying on the FBI's word because it was the easy way out. And that's what appeared to be occurring. "I just don't have time to deal with this much more," Tucker said.

Theresa pointed out that she'd already spoken with the FBI with troubling results, so it would be more helpful to meet with someone who could oversee the FBI's handling of the case, such as a Sessions staffer or the U.S. attorney that supervised prosecutor Marando.

Tucker was defensive. "Listen," she said, "None of that is my fault. I understand you all are frustrated but I'm trying to make it right and dwelling on things like, 'they're not actually interested,' isn't helpful."

Tucker was more concerned with political risk to Sessions—as if the Democrats would ever warm up to the man they'd incessantly called a racist—than to catching the FBI in lies, even if it was now clear that the FBI's conduct in the case didn't mesh with the facts. "My job is to protect my boss. I can't be seen as influencing an investigation," she said. "It looks weird and is not good for my boss. I'm not contacting the U.S. [attorney] or prosecutor on this."

She reflexively defended the meager resources the FBI had dedicated to the case, deploying first-year agent Brandon Merriman, failing to talk to basic witnesses, and declining to search the suspects' homes. "What I will say is that these are people with very limited amounts of time. They don't have time to hear it," Tucker said. The FBI had plenty of time to spy on Trump's campaign aides and conduct a pre-dawn raid on his campaign manager, and on any given day they were handling any number of relatively mundane cases. But when it came to systematic fraud in the House, disappearing equipment, data flying off of the House network, and a vanishing House Democratic Caucus server, there simply weren't resources.

Theresa had a choice: talk again with the FBI, or Sessions' office would move onto other issues. Theresa mulled it over and agreed to talk with the FBI a second time. But Sessions' aide never relayed the message, instead claiming Theresa had refused.

———

On May 10, Representative Gohmert and the other members of Congress, many of them part of both the Freedom Caucus and the Judiciary Committee, decided they needed to speak with the former IG themselves. Theresa refused, both because she feared an appearance of partisanship and because she felt she'd already done her part and then some. She was tired.

With the repeated delays in court, the DOJ appeared to be gauging whether they could get away with brushing the entire

Awan affair under the rug—thereby avoiding the ire of more than forty irate Democrats—or whether doing so would damage the Bureau's reputation. That depended on what witnesses knew and what they would say publicly.

If I published everything I knew, it would be hard for the FBI to claim it was all some misunderstanding. But there was only so much time. One story I'd sat on, until then, was about the government "inadvertently" giving evidence to the defense and prosecutors leaking what I was working on to Democrats. When Theresa read the story, it dissolved her concerns about meeting with Republicans. It was obvious that Republican bias wasn't the issue in this case; Democratic partisanship was.

Theresa agreed to meet with Representative Gohmert and his fellow lawmakers on May 16, one day before they were to meet with the FBI in the SCIF. The FBI was likely expecting ill-formed, vague questions that they could easily wave away. Instead, the meeting with Theresa would help the congressmen to prepare questions that were targeted like lasers. Representative Gohmert and Theresa both knew what every good prosecutor knows: the best questions are the ones to which you already know the answer.

Representative Gohmert sent a few questions to the FBI in advance. But the biggest ones were saved for in person. The FBI seemed to suspect that Theresa was talking to Representative Gohmert, and prosecutor Marando asked to meet with her again at the exact same time she was supposed to be on Capitol Hill.

This time, the agent who summoned her had one incredible request: do *not* bring any evidence to the meeting. We *don't* want any documents.

When she got to the room with Special Agent Spencer Brooks, Marando, and the Capitol Police, the questions were direct: Are you talking to members of Congress? What work materials do you have at your home? It seemed like a trap. Lying to the FBI is a crime, and while Theresa had no nondisclosure agreement and was free to say what happened, she knew there were risks. Her words could be twisted, they could make an issue out of notes she retained, or they could find some other issue.

At the meeting, Marando lifted a folder, pulled a document from it, and brandished it like a cop revealing a *gotcha* to a suspect. The folder contained information Theresa had given to Jeff Session's aide, Rachael Tucker, and that she had apparently simply handed over to the FBI. Of all the documents in the stack, Marando was interested in only one: the timeline showing that Pelosi's and Ryan's offices had been amply warned of the findings. He pulled it out and slid it across the table as if to say *well how do you explain this, tootsie?* "Who wrote this?" he asked.

"Why do you want to know?" Theresa said. "I wrote it. It's based on my calendar."

"Why did you give it to the AG's office?"

She didn't understand the problem. "What would you have had me do?" she said. "Don't you work for him?" It was clear the dynamic of the meeting had changed. The room went silent.

"We figure you're an ally, someone we could bounce things off," Marando said, even though they had told her almost nothing about what they had found, making it impossible for her to provide guidance. "But you don't have to be here."

"Exactly," Theresa said. "If you're working this case, why am I talking to you instead of a grand jury?"

Stunningly, Marando seemed to imply that if Theresa, the sterling-credentialed key investigator in the case, went before a grand jury, it would be as a target. "We would have called you to the grand jury, but we didn't want to put you on the spot and make you have to get counsel. Do you have a lawyer? They can be expensive. We thought it would be better to have you as a friendly."

"Why would I get counsel? Are you accusing me of something?" Theresa responded. "I sat on the other side of the table where you're sitting for twenty-five years, and that stunt where you whipped out the folder two hours in? That's my move. And that's why I wanted those people's emails. So I would have answers and could whip out my folder on them."

"If you're thinking of making me a scapegoat on this or suggesting I don't have integrity..." she said. Just as Imran framed his victims in Pakistan, the DOJ might be intending to blame the only investigator who actually pursued this case in order to explain their own inaction.

Meanwhile, Speaker Ryan's office was alerted to the members' request for the SCIF briefing. The Republican speaker's team wanted Democrats present at the briefing, which would likely eat up all the limited time they had with antagonistic obstruction. Speaker Ryan also alerted Chairman Gregg Harper, who'd been telling me he was on top of the case. Harper, whose position as head of the Administration Committee necessitated his attendance more than anyone else, didn't bother to attend.

The FBI's assertion that the briefing could only be held in a SCIF signaled that highly classified information was about to be shared. In other words, that the FBI had found something concerning national security. That was enough to garner interest from more members, including Judiciary Chairman Bob Goodlatte and Intelligence Committee Chairman Devin Nunes. Whatever was learned in that meeting is unknown to me because members are prohibited from sharing what they learn in classified settings.

Before the door closed, members were instructed that no notes could be taken. It's customary to disallow cell phones and electronics into the SCIF, but they were told that no paper, no writing implements, nothing to make any record would be allowed, which was not customary. Members of Congress would not be allowed to review notes of what they were told—a valuable record should the FBI change its story—and they had to discard the carefully considered questions they had prepared. Five FBI-affiliated personnel were present. Members were not allowed to record their names or what their involvement was with the case.

If the FBI had evidence that necessitated a secure setting, it wasn't reflected in the prosecutors' charges. It seemed the whole point of holding the meeting in a SCIF was to appease members with an explanation they couldn't cross-reference with people who could poke holes in it; people like me, Theresa, or one of the Awans' relatives.

The Awan court date was postponed a seventh time to June 7. For once, it didn't seem to be scheduled for a date when it would go unnoticed, like a holiday weekend. But a few days before, I saw otherwise. The DOJ revealed that its long-awaited inspector general's report on the FBI's handling of the investigation into Hillary Clinton's emails would be released just before the Awans' court date. It was brilliant: the very same people who were interested in the Awan case—mainly conservatives who saw the Department of Justice as being infected with pro-Democrat bias—would be having a field day diving into the three hundred-page report. It would be the perfect time to let Imran off the hook.

Nonetheless, Representatives Gohmert and Perry asked for another meeting with Sessions, but the only time it could be scheduled was a day before the court date. Sessions would listen, but it sure seemed to me at this point like it was for no reason but to make the congressmen feel heard.

Before the meeting, it was announced that the DOJ IG report on Clinton's emails would be delayed. The Awans' court date was also postponed to the day before the Fourth of July holiday. Whereas before, the postponements had talked about "voluminous discovery" and negotiating over attorney-client privilege issues, the court papers recording this delay implied that a deal was in the works.

On June 13, Representatives Gohmert and Perry spoke with Sessions on the phone. They asked Sessions to have a trusted personal advisor review the facts with Theresa. The AG needed to see the facts without the FBI's filter. Then, if the AG still believed there was no case, and that the FBI had presented the facts accurately, they would be satisfied because they knew Jeff Sessions to be a man of honor. The AG agreed to their simple request. "I'm not afraid to take them on. If laws were broken, they must be prosecuted," Sessions said.

But I wondered: why would Theresa trust Sessions' people any more than she trusted the FBI, given what happened when she talked to Rachael Tucker?

The question, it turned out, was moot, as the opportunity was never presented to Theresa. Sessions had again tasked none other than Tucker with the follow-through since she had been listening in on the call, and his staff defied his order. No one from Sessions' staff would be going over the facts to see how they meshed with the spin the FBI was feeding the attorney general. Tucker claimed to Representative Gohmert's staff that there never was any such promise, and said she merely asked the FBI about the case one more time and was told there was no case other than bank fraud. Sessions was being poorly served not only by the FBI, but even by his innermost staff.

Tucker had caught the disease. It was a den of revolving-door nepotism where no one wanted to ask hard questions or confront people with uncomfortable truths, people they intended to work in close quarters with. Tucker felt like she had to remain on good terms with the FBI, and she didn't want to go up against its officials.

TWENTY-ONE

COVER-UP

By May 2018, there was no doubt that Paul Ryan's earlier statements on the case didn't hold water. His spokeswoman, AshLee Strong's, emails to me dodged the issue of why the House preordained it a "theft" investigation before investigators could possibly have ruled out a hack; prior to having looked at the data flying off the House network, or even at the copy of the House Democratic Caucus server they'd made before it went missing. Strong refused to say there even *was* any cybersecurity investigation, reiterating that it was a theft probe. At first, I took this as a bold-faced lie. But by now I realized she was telling the truth, which was even worse. It came down to semantics. Her description of it as a theft probe didn't deny that cybersecurity violations *occurred*, only that they weren't being *investigated*. Anyone who'd witnessed the bumbling actions of the FBI and Capitol Police could see this was true. No problem has ever been solved when people refuse to acknowledge that it exists, so even though

server logs and official documents showed cybersecurity violations, obviously the House wasn't taking corrective action.

But that wasn't the end of the insanity out of the Speaker's
office. Strong claimed that the reason the suspects were left on
the network for seven months after problems were known was
because the police were conducting a sting. Intentionally letting
a hack continue during the height of an election was like police
saying they'd let a killer rack up a few more bodies to make the
prosecution easier. But since she was refusing to acknowledge any
cybersecurity rule violations, I'll assume she meant a sting to
catch theft and fraud. That wasn't any better. At the end of the
sting, the entire family was banned from Congress, obviously
suggesting they had found something. So then where were the
theft charges?

If they *hadn't* found anything during this lengthy sting—one
that conveniently delayed action until the most politically convenient time—then it was no wonder. The premise of a sting is that
the suspects don't know they're being watched, and House
authorities couldn't possibly have thought that was true. Even the
Democratic staffer of the Administration Committee, Eddie
Flaherty, was telling people during that time period that the
suspects were coming by to speak with his boss about how they
were under investigation. Abid had even been fired by Representative Clarke's office. Representative Xavier Becerra had ordered
Abid to stop logging into his computers.

Though Democrats said months into the probe that Awans
couldn't be interviewed because the investigation was so top
secret that even the congressmen couldn't know, those members
seemed to know about it from the moment it began. Records

show that as soon as the probe was initiated in April 2016, House members began paying CDW-G hundreds of thousands of dollars in invoices that were more than a year overdue, indicating that they were seeking to clean it up. Mark Takano of California paid $28,000 of delinquent invoices, some dating as far back as 2014. The figures for Katherine Clark of Massachusetts and Jackie Speier of California were nearly as bad. It was obvious from the way they'd treated Imran since—particularly Representatives Wasserman Schultz, Clarke, and Meeks—that if Imran didn't already know about the investigation, one or more of these members would have tipped him off. Even prosecutors said that when Hina and Imran wired $300,000 to Pakistan, the pair "likely knew they were under investigation at that time."

Speaker Ryan's office knew this was a significant issue. My emails to Strong were opened two hundred times in numerous locations. She responded: "I needed to track a few more things down on this. I'll send response tomorrow." But whatever information she found seemed to change her mind about responding.

A few days later, Speaker Ryan had scheduled a press conference on the topic of cybersecurity in politics alongside FBI Director Christopher Wray. I intended to ask about Imran, but the event was cancelled at the last minute, so I attended Ryan's weekly press conference instead. The press conference's first discussion focused on the fact that the special counsel's Russia probe turned one year old that day, leading Republicans to say that it needed to make its findings and wrap up. The Awan investigation had been going on for twice as long, with House officials hiding behind the "ongoing" nature of it to completely avoid talking about it.

I planned my question to circumvent that trap, focusing on choices made by House officials before the criminal investigation. As soon as I said my name, Speaker Ryan inhaled sharply. "In the House, there was this issue of Imran Awan, the Democratic IT aide," I said. "I've come learn that the House IG was briefing you guys in the House from July onwards." The police weren't brought in until October, and "he was left on the network until shortly after the election. Can you address why?"

"That's a question you would ask the people who made those decisions," he responded.

I did a double take. *That was you*, I thought. "But I'm asking on why you guys waited in the House—the Administration Committee and your office—to involve the police."

"I'm not going to comment on an ongoing police investigation," he said. Speaker Ryan was smart enough to know that this was circular logic, but so few people understood the situation that no other reporter in the room was going to call him on it. I brought with me to the press conference a colleague from the Daily Caller News Foundation to increase the odds that one or both of us would get to ask a question. After I asked mine, Strong came around the side of the podium and took a picture of my colleague, as if to flag that he shouldn't be called on. He wasn't.

The establishment forces were getting desperate. They knew that if they acknowledged the facts of this astonishing case, a plea deal simply couldn't be justified. The basics of this simply didn't take much investigating. The House financial records that were systematically falsified plainly constituted false statements on government documents. The server logs clearly showed unauthorized access. If people realized that these things had occurred without consequences, well, if there are sanctuary cities, Paul Ryan was running a sanctuary Congress.

Chief Administrative Officer Phil Kiko's press secretary, Dan Weiser, had for a year now refused to let me speak with the House official, saying the office was prohibited from releasing statements of any kind dealing with an ongoing investigation or internal affairs. I was tired of it. I saw how lazy the rest of the media were, and how satisfied they were to merely write down official statements and leave it at that. Plainly, this was no ordinary investigation, and ordinary reporting techniques were getting nowhere.

At 6:30 p.m. just after Memorial Day 2018, I told my wife I'd either be back in ten minutes or several hours. I hopped in my car to make the mile-long drive to Phil Kiko's house. I was wearing a T-shirt and shorts and let the humid summer air rush through the open windows as I made my way to what can only be described as a run-down shack on the side of a highway where Kiko, who grossed $170,000 a year, lived with his wife Colleen, who made a similar government salary. In the gravel driveway, which formed the entirety of the front yard, were cars with bumper stickers for a Republican candidate running in Maryland. Also in the front yard of the Arlington, Virginia, home was a black SUV with D.C. tags—the kind VIPs drive. Kiko is close to several congressmen, and I worried he might be entertaining one. If so, this was about to go very poorly.

But I also knew that in September 2017, the Senate had confirmed his wife Colleen to a high-level appointment as chair of the Federal Labor Relations Authority in a unanimous vote.

While struggling to understand Kiko's exceptional failures in the Awan case, it briefly crossed my mind that perhaps he feared that if he didn't bend over backwards for Democrats in the Awan case, they'd block his wife's confirmation, which would only require one objection. It was only speculation, but because of it, I took the gamble that the SUV belonged to Colleen and not a visitor, and that she was at home cooking up some dinner. It was just what I had hoped.

Sure enough, Colleen opened the door and smiled pleasantly: "Hi." I smiled back. "I'm Luke Rosiak. I know Phil from work."

"Oh, nice to meet you!" she said. "I was just about to serve up dinner. Would you like to come in?"

I sniffed the air. "Mmm," I said. "Smells delicious. I'd love to join you."

She led me to the dining room table. "Honey, Luke's here!"

"Nooooooooooo," Phil howled.

Colleen was afraid she'd made a grave mistake, as if I were an ax murderer. Her eyes flashed. "Get out!" she said. I backed out the door and she slammed it behind me.

But a few seconds later, I heard the door unlock, and out stepped Phil. For forty minutes while enduring a dozen mosquito bites, we stood by the side of the highway. "I figured you'd come by eventually," he said.

"It's a big deal, and someone's got to look into it."

"I know it is. I don't blame you."

I told him what I knew. "They're saying you made it up, that there never was any missing server."

"I don't know what they're doing. They don't tell us anything. It's in the hands of the police," he said.

"But you know what you saw," I replied. It was ridiculous. Kiko was the one who wrote a letter saying the server was missing. There was no way it went un-missing without him being consulted. If he really was just hearing this for the first time, he should have been more bothered than he was.

"I just want you to know, I'm a good investigator," he said sadly.

But when I told him other specifics I'd learned, he stared blankly.

"Look, the Democrats are going to blame this whole thing on you," I said. "They're saying you failed to enforce the rules, to keep tabs on what's going on, and now they're saying you framed these guys, planted evidence. Don't you see this is going to backfire on you?"

"We'll see what happens," he said.

"I just needed to warn you that after this story goes up, you're probably going to be threatened by Wasserman Schultz again."

A few days later, I published the story about what multiple people heard firsthand from Kiko: that in the early days of the investigation, Representative Wasserman Schultz had put her finger to his chest, demanded that he drop the probe, and called him an "Islamophobe."

By the time I got to the office that morning, I had five missed calls from Kiko's spokesman; the one who was previously unable to speak. If I didn't remove the story from the internet, they were going to put out a statement calling me a liar, he said.

Kiko hadn't denied it in person. I'd also run the allegations by the spokesman repeatedly before publishing and he said it was not possible for him to discuss it no matter what. The most charitable explanation for Kiko's meek conduct in this investigation was his sense of propriety and bureaucratic caution. What had changed now that meant he could violate his own "no discussing an ongoing investigation or internal matters" policy? It seemed obvious: he'd been threatened again.

But I figured there was no way he'd actually release a statement. He'd have to be extraordinarily scared in order to do so, and here's why: Kiko must have assumed one of the sources for my story to be Sean Moran, the top Republican staffer on the Administration Committee, who essentially amounted to Kiko's supervisor. That would mean the CAO in a Republican-led Congress would be violating his own rules for the purpose of publicly calling his own Republican boss a liar, all to protect the reputation of a Democrat who had repeatedly bullied him to try to affect his handling of a misconduct case.

But he did it.

"At no point was I threatened or accused of any prejudice, whatsoever, by any individual over the CAO's corrective actions in response to the activities of five shared employees subject to a pending investigation. Any assertion that I was called an 'Islamophobe' is false. Furthermore, I was never informed of any 'land deal' involving any of the individuals under investigation as falsely reported," Weiser blasted out in a statement attributed to Kiko.

Multiple people who had heard the story from Kiko himself independently repeated it to me word for word. It happened. But even if you didn't have that knowledge, this hyperbolic statement was absurd.

Representative Wasserman Schultz had been all over the media saying this was a partisan witch-hunt fueled by religious bias. And Kiko was the Republican who'd played a key role, writing the letter that kicked them off the network. She'd excoriated Kiko's subordinate in a videotaped hearing. She'd even threatened a cop on video. Who could possibly believe that Representative Wasserman Schultz had never said privately what she implied publicly?

Well, some people could. Suddenly, Shawn Boburg of the *Washington Post*, who had ignored the story as I reported on new developments, was interested again. "The administrative office for Congress rarely puts out public statements but did so today challenging a Daily Caller @lukerosiak story about Debbie Wasserman Schultz," he tweeted. But even he had to admit something smelled suspicious here. "CAO Phil Kiko did not comment before publication but now calls key anecdotes in story 'false,'" he added.

I asked Kiko's spokesman Weiser to comment on why he could give a statement in this instance but not others. He did not respond. Then I sent him a list of questions calling Kiko's own conduct into question, including his attempt to abolish the inspector general's office. Weiser said he could not comment. It was incredible that Kiko was willing to go further to protect Representative Wasserman Schultz than he was to defend himself. He was prepared to be the sacrificial lamb.

Hours after Kiko's statement, the DOJ filed paperwork on the Awan case saying a plea deal was set to be entered on July 3.

Representatives Gohmert and Perry's fatal error had been going to Jeff Sessions instead of President Trump. That night, I appeared on Lou Dobbs' TV show on Fox News and decided to use the opportunity to send a message directly to Trump, who is known to watch the show. I pointed out how this case rendered everything the Democrats had been saying for the last two years about hacking as hypocritical: that Democrats couldn't claim to abhor what had happened at the DNC while lying about and covering up a massive cyber breach in their own ranks. Democrats chose to allow a hack of unknown severity to continue for seven months, until after the election, sacrificing national security in an attempt to win an election. It bordered on treason.

And there was little doubt that the FBI's "investigation" into the case was blatantly rigged.

Trump was watching. Soon after, he tweeted: "Our Justice Department must not let Awan & Debbie Wasserman Schultz off the hook. The Democrat I.T. scandal is a key to much of the corruption we see today. They want to make a 'plea deal' to hide what is on their Server. Where is Server? Really bad!"

It was a reasonable statement to say that the DOJ shouldn't let a cybersecurity violator plead guilty to minor bank fraud charges as part of a plea bargain. But Imran's attorney called President Trump "that idiot" and told CNN: "It's a major concern that the plea agreement could be off the table in the wake of the President's tweets."

He should have known that Sessions would not listen to his boss.

TWENTY-TWO

THE PROSECUTION SLEEPS

With Imran's exoneration virtually in place, law enforcement suddenly kicked into high gear. "The FBI wants to interview me," Pat Sowers, a Republican IT aide I'd mentioned in a few of my earliest stories, told me. "Tom Hungar, the House general counsel, said the FBI wanted me to submit to a voluntary interview because they believed I might have information relevant to House IT matters."

Sowers thought the Awans had committed the cardinal sin of his profession and brought a bad name to their fellow shared employees. "Ray Charles can see that these guys broke the law. We all knew there was something not right. We knew they were committing fraud with the way that they were employed." The problem was the congressmen who employed them knew, too, he said. He believed the security of the nation might be at risk, and that the pattern of facts was so extraordinary that it demanded attention. "Why was that laptop left in that phone booth? Who was supposed to collect it?" He was willing to do anything he could to help bring justice and order to the House and tell everything he knew.

That's why he declined the interview.

"My lawyer said they should subpoena me if they want to talk," he said. Only then could the interview be fully candid. "If the FBI interviews a staff member, someone has to be present" from Congress, like a hall monitor. In the case of Democratic IT aides, that could be someone from a member's office who'd been protecting Imran for a decade. Who in their right mind would think that was a legitimate interview? On the other hand, "if they subpoena me and give me a list of questions, I'll answer them," he said. "I'm willing to say anything I'm legally allowed to, and there's no reason for Tom Hungar to be involved. He said his role was to make sure they didn't ask anything privileged. This seemed to contradict statements by Ryan's office and the prosecutors that nothing was being withheld under the speech and debate clause. If nothing else, a monitor's very presence might change what was said.

Sowers had seen the news articles saying a plea deal was already inked. It was clear the agents weren't interested in building a case against the Awans, and given the evidence they'd obviously gone out of their way to ignore, what possible upside was there for him? "I don't want to implicate myself if they decide to go after me, even though I did nothing wrong," he said. It should have sounded crazy, but it didn't.

It wasn't that Sowers didn't want to talk. "If they actually wanted to talk to me, they'd subpoena me," he said. If not, the whole thing was some sort of joke. The subpoena never came, and the handling of the whole thing soured Sowers on Congress for good. The next day, he called the members he worked for and resigned. "I said I'm done. I'm calling it quits."

Theresa, the former inspector general, was in a similar position. On June 29, five days before the plea deal, she got a voicemail from Special Agent Spencer Brooks. "We need to talk to you right away. It will just be a quick phone call," he said. Theresa didn't immediately return the call. If the government actually wanted to know what she had to say, they'd postpone the court date a ninth time in order to speak to her. They didn't.

It was starting to seem like they might be planning something terrible for Theresa. After all, she'd already spoken with the FBI for five hours and the DOJ had decided to let Imran walk. So why this eleventh-hour call? I had a theory. Representative Gohmert had raised the specter of a DOJ IG review of the handling of the case, and the FBI must have been nervous about what it might find. The Computer Fraud and Abuse Act statute plainly stated that "unauthorized access" to government computers was a felony, and the server logs proved that had occurred. How could they explain their failure to file these criminal charges? They needed a fall guy. I believed that this was one final Machiavellian trick: they called Theresa knowing she'd refuse to talk to them again. Then, when someone inquired, they could say that the House's inspector general, a key figure, had refused to cooperate; so, their hands were tied. Of course, they wouldn't mention that she'd already spent five hours with them. In fact, this might be why they had wanted to interview her in a coffee shop instead of a government office building: the avoidance of paper trail wasn't designed to protect her, it was designed to protect them.

On July 2, the day before the court date, Representative Gohmert's chief of staff, an indefatigable woman by the name of Connie Hair, got a call from Sessions' staffer, Tucker. She confirmed the deal would be accepted by all parties the following day. Connie warned that Imran was telling people he already had three job offers back on Capitol Hill, and members feared their data was at risk. Tucker said it wasn't up to her to make rules about who Congress can hire. But Connie knew that Congress would just say they were never convicted of anything related to their jobs. Everyone was passing the buck.

Connie then became another person to get a last-minute visit from investigators handling a case whose outcome had already been decided. The Capitol Police showed up at Gohmert's office. When I stopped by later, Connie told me what happened. "They asked me what documents I had. To me it seemed like they wanted to know if I had anything that was going to contradict their narrative."

"We asked [the police] if nothing else, why [the Awans] weren't being charged on the obvious problems with ethics disclosure forms: the non-disclosure of income, strange LLCs, homes they owned," Connie said. "Senior staff all have to fill out these forms, and there were gross contradictions between public bankruptcy filings and incorporation records and their ethics disclosures, year after year. Why weren't they being charged? We would be. They said, 'no reasonable prosecutor would bring those charges.'"

Connie had heard those words before. "It was the same ridiculous thing James Comey said when he let Hillary Clinton off the hook."

"They said that it would be up to the Ethics Committee to make a referral. I said what about Corrine Brown," the Florida ex-congresswoman who was in prison in part for lying on those forms? "The Awans are not employees anymore, why would it be up to the Ethics Committee to prosecute?"

There was, of course, an equally plausible explanation for why the Capitol Police were not going after the Awans: the Awans had compromising emails from a sizable portion of the Democrats in Congress.

Connie asked them to go through other examples of indisputable evidence and illuminate how they concluded that they were not crimes, but they refused. "They just said, 'We looked into it and there's nothing there.' But then they said more information will come out in court tomorrow, that there's going to be some interesting stuff."

"They said, 'We've talked to a lot of people in the last two weeks.'" That last part, at least, was true.

While those witnesses wondered why the FBI would bother talking to them when a plea deal was already set, Imran feared his Sharia-law wife, Sumaira, could blow up the deal at the last minute. A week before the final court date, Imran and Sumaira had an argument over the phone. Imran talked badly of Sumaira's kids, and Sumaira lost her cool, saying she'd hunt him down. He asked how she was going to find him—he'd be in Pakistan. Sumaira told him she was going to come forward, both to me and to prosecutors.

"And he said, 'If you do this with evidence, I will do this, this, this to your family. I will do it in Pakistan and you will never catch me,'" Sumaira recounted.

At 9 a.m. on July 3, two hours before the plea deal was set to go down, I was about to hail a taxi to the courthouse when Sumaira called me. When she woke up, there were two FBI agents outside her door, she said; Spencer Brooks and Nathan Frank. They told her they were investigating her for threats at the behest of Imran Awan. Above all else, they said, they were there to make sure she didn't try to go to the court date, as if they feared that she would stand up and tell the judge the truth about her husband.

In addition to outfitting her apartment with hidden cameras, Imran had been recording his calls with her, and it seemed that he'd isolated audio from her side of the arguments and told the FBI that Sumaira should be pursued for violent threats. It was hard to see how this fell within the jurisdiction of the FBI or warranted the time of two agents, and Sumaira couldn't believe what she was hearing. She reminded the agents that Imran had tried to have her killed in Pakistan. "Yeah, she told us that before," Brooks nodded to Frank. Let me get this straight, she thought. The FBI had taken no action when Imran made repeated "unauthorized access" of a congressional server. The FBI had not even bothered to interview a relative who attested that House electronics were being shipped to Pakistani officials. And now they didn't find it notable that a criminal suspect who was potentially wiretapping congressmen and using their information as leverage was trying to get out of it by wiretapping someone else and using *that* as leverage? No, the FBI's finest would simply take the information as a tip and and knock on the door of a 110-pound woman in a burka for the crime of being rude to Imran Awan.

She showed them text messages which made clear that—though Imran was always very careful what he put into writing—it was he who was badgering her. She then retreated back into her apartment. She didn't know what else to do, so she called me looking for advice. Ordinarily, I wouldn't think it was my place to give it, but by now, I couldn't help but feel like an ambassador for the America I thought I knew. Of the things she'd told me over the past months, there were certain things I felt that the FBI would not ignore.

At 9:45 a.m., she called me back to say that she had done the deed. She'd called Special Agent Brooks and told him clearly about every one of the items we'd just gone over. That Imran made death threats against her and was blackmailing her with a sex tape. That she believed these were criminal actions and wanted to pursue charges. That Imran told her he was a "mole" in Congress and bragged about how he'd get away with it because he "knew too much." And finally, that he'd asked Sumaira to buy gold bars and establish an LLC for him, which she understood to be an attempt at money laundering to hide assets from the FBI. Special Agent Brooks said he didn't know all of that and thanked her for the information.

Now there was no denying it. The FBI had shocking information straight from the person who slept next to him, and a clear request to press charges from a victim. There was still enough time for Brooks to call prosecutors and wave them off of offering the plea deal to Imran. As my taxi neared the courthouse, I figured if the Department of Justice prosecutors had any integrity, they would postpone resolving the case while they sorted out these major new revelations. They'd already delayed the court date eight times, what's a ninth? But as I passed through the metal detectors and made my way into the courtroom, Brooks and Frank were nowhere to be seen. Apparently, preventing a key witness from going to court was more important than attending it themselves. Not only that, but prosecutor Michael Marando, the only government attorney who actually knew the facts of the case, wasn't there either. He would never be seen again in connection with the Imran Awan case.

Hours before the court date, court records showed that a new prosecutor was added: J.P. Cooney. Cooney didn't look anything like what you might imagine a fearsome federal prosecutor to be. He was skinny, with a pock-marked face, a protruding Adam's apple, and an awkward posture. Cooney had been the prosecutor in a recent high-profile political case: he led the prosecution of Democratic Senator Bob Menendez for corruption. It resulted in a hung jury and the DOJ didn't bother to try again.

Needless to say, this last-minute swap meant the two sides were as uneven as Jamie and Sean, or Hadeed and Bacon. The defense would never send in a newbie one day before the big day after two years of work by someone else; why would the government? One thought came to mind: Marando's knowledge of the case meant he had a legal obligation to identify discrepancies and push back against any false statements made by the defense. This new guy was a clean slate. It was clear he'd been assigned to the case at the last minute for one purpose: to make it go away.

More than a year before, on the first court date, I'd followed Marando, flanked by a phalange of assistant prosecutors and FBI agents, through the courthouse hallway until they were diverted to a back elevator, into which the whole crew could barely fit. A dark-suited man emerged to tell me it was a restricted area and I could go no further. I overheard one of the agents: "Wow. I've done quadruple murders and they've never taken me up the special elevator."

But today, Cooney's slight frame sitting solita   at the prosecutor's table told you everything you needed to know about the case. The court clerk was surprised. "Anyone else coming with you?" he asked.

"Nope, just me," Cooney replied.

With FBI agents Brooks and Frank absent, sitting in the back row of the spectator's area was their junior varsity counterpart, Brandon Merriman—a stocky, tan man who looked like a washed-up jock. And for once, there were a lot of reporters in attendance; more interested in prosecutors announcing there was not a case than in investigating the evidence of fraud, and worse, on Capitol Hill.

The judge got right to the point. Contrary to what the Capitol Police had told Connie, there would be no interesting information emerging today. The purpose was simple: to make this go away for good—and just in time for the 2018 midterm elections. "Mr. Awan, have you ever pleaded guilty before?" the judge asked.

"No, I have not, your honor."

"I have to ask you a series of questions under oath... if you do not give truthful answers, you can be prosecuted for perjury," she said. She carefully asked him a series of questions. There was only one problem: she had no idea what this case was about. "The facts are laid out in the Statement of Offense... I actually don't have a copy," she said.

"We left a copy here," Cooney gestured.

"I've heard very little facts in this case. This statement is saying this is what you did in this case. Did you falsely represent to the Congressional Federal Credit Union...?" She described the minor transgression.

"Do you understand you could receive a maximum of thirty years imprisonment? Sentencing guidelines call for two to five years. The maximum fine is $1 million." But in this case, the government would ensure the penalties were small.

"The parties have submitted a written letter that outlines the plea agreement in this case. It is eleven pages long. One count of making a false statement on a loan application. In return, the government will not pursue any other charges. The government has agreed not to oppose a probation-only sentence and will not seek a fine or restitution." Oh, and the charges would be dropped against Hina, who falsely claimed a medical emergency to liquidate her federal retirement account before moving to Pakistan with a cardboard box full of undeclared cash.

"It also includes a paragraph that says public allegations that Mr. Awan stole congressional computers, that the government conducted a thorough investigation and found no basis." It was an almost unheard-of inclusion, prosecutors going out of their way to say that Imran had not done things.

> The Government agrees that the public allegations that your client stole US House of Representatives ("House") equipment and engaged in unauthorized or illegal conduct involving House computer systems do not form the basis of any conduct relevant to the determination of

the sentence in this case. The Government conducted a thorough investigation of those allegations, including interviewing approximately 40 witnesses; taking custody of the House Democratic Caucus server, along with other computers, hard drives, and electronic devices; examining those devices, including inspecting their physical condition and analyzing log-in and usage data; reviewing electronic communications between pertinent House employees; consulting with the House Office of General Counsel and House information technology personnel to access and/or collect evidence; and questioning your client during numerous voluntary interviews. The Government has uncovered no evidence that your client violated federal law with respect to the House computer systems. Particularly, the Government has found no evidence that your client illegally removed House data from the House network or from House Members' offices, stole the House Democratic Caucus Server, stole or destroyed House information technology equipment, or improperly accessed or transferred government information, including classified or sensitive information.

The judge continued that Imran was receiving partial immunity. "It specifies that he will not be charged with any non-violent offense for which the District of Columbia was made aware." She had one final question: "Has anyone made any promises to you in connection with your plea deal other than what's in the plea agreement?"

"No," Imran responded.

"Mr. Awan is now judged guilty for the offense." The *Washington Post* reporter stood up and left the hearing halfway through, causing the judge to pause.

Gowen seized the opportunity to speak up, and yet again, the prosecutors and the defense attorneys appeared to be working together. "Both parties are in agreement to ask for an expedited sentencing."

Like the prosecutors, the judge seemed to believe that asking a criminal defendant's attorney was an accurate way to gauge the truth. "I know very little about you. I'm going to be looking to the material that your lawyer provides so I can know more about you."

Gowen then took it upon himself to speak for the prosecutors. "I don't believe the government objects to this: he's had the GPS on, he's cooperated with the government through eight meetings with the government," he said. If Marando had been there instead of Cooney, he perhaps could have evaluated whether refusing proffers constituted "cooperating."

"With respect to the 50-mile radius and the GPS..." The judge complimented Imran for fulfilling his meager check-in responsibilities. "He's done so well," she said.

Cooney replied: "Under the circumstances, we do not oppose the request to remove the GPS, but not the 50-mile radius."

"What's the reason for fifty?" the judge said. *Let me guess,* I thought. *It has something to do with Saif Rao in New York.*

"He has some friends and relatives in New York," Gowen said. "Can in-person check-in be changed to phone?"

Cooney was beginning to realize that Gowen had little gratitude. "It's the first step down, so I'm reluctant to do it all at
once," the prosecutor said.

The judge sided with Gowen. After all, this was just a bank
fraud case, and with no prison or fine on the table, what reason did
he have to flee? "I'll change it to twice a week by phone. You can
come downstairs to pretrial services to have the device removed."

Now it was Hina's turn to jump on the precedent. Lotze, her
lawyer, spoke up for the first time. "Hina askes to waive the once
a week check-in."

The judge let out a loud sigh. "It's a phone call."

When court let out, a citizen journalist bolted down to pretrial services, where Imran would have his ankle monitor
removed, and U.S. Marshals protected Imran from *him*. Imran
disappeared through back hallways. A loading dock gate opened,
and a car with blacked out windows backed into the dock, where
U.S. Marshals could be seen.

I had nothing to ask Imran or Gowen. I didn't blame a
defense attorney for trying as hard as he could to get his client
off the hook. My questions were for the FBI and the DOJ.
Cooney simply ignored my questions as he walked down the
hallway. Someone patted Merriman on the back and said, "good
job." The DOJ's spokesman said he'd send me a statement. But
when I got outside, it seemed all the reporters who hadn't followed the case at all already had it, and the *Washington Post*
and *Politico* were already up with stories.

Imran, it turned out, had given an in-person interview to the
Washington Post before the hearing. The defense, of course,

knew exactly what was going to occur. "Awan told *The Washington Post* in an interview before Tuesday's hearing that he questions whether the case would have been pursued if he did not have a Pakistani name. He said he came to the United States as a teenager, put himself through college, became a US citizen and built a career on Capitol Hill—what he portrayed as the fulfillment of a dream."

His quotes were cartoonish. "This has cost me my reputation, my livelihood, my family," he said. "I can't believe this." He added, "The president used me to advance his political agenda." The *Washington Post* didn't seem to feel the need to inquire about how Donald Trump could have cost Imran his family. They say Republicans like to put government in the bedroom, but something told me this might have had more to do with the fact that his family members said he enslaved, threatened, and extorted them.

Gowen released a flamboyant statement that said Imran had been cooperating with the government for nineteen months, since November 2016. If this were true, it completely disproved Speaker Ryan's claim that he left them on the network until February 2017 in order to conduct a sting. Then again, the statement also claimed that the media and Republicans had been trying to frame Imran since before they even knew what had occurred. The statement read:

> For the past 19 months my client, Imran Awan has been the target of a coordinated effort by House Republicans, the President, and right-wing "media" in an effort to destroy the reputation of a dedicated

public servant for political purposes. Today's plea deal resolves, in black and white, that all of the coordinated allegations were not true. My client is not a "spy," nor part of a "spy ring." There has never been any missing server, smashed hard drives, blackmailed members of Congress, or breach of classified information. This was all made up, for purposes of clickbait, Fox News stories, and political opportunism....

A small army of federal investigators and prosecutors have chased down every wild accusation and found them all to be ridiculous distortions or often wholesale inventions. Imran cooperated with the investigation for 19 months, he answered every single question law enforcement had, and turned over every document requested.

Then, he used prosecutors' words in his own press release, printing the paragraph from the plea agreement about how investigators had talked to forty people and concluded that he'd done nothing wrong in the House.

The *Washington Post*'s headline read: "Ex-congressional IT staffer reaches plea deal that debunks conspiracy theories about illegal information access." CNN went with: "Ex-House staffer, subject of conspiracy theories, pleads guilty to bank fraud charge."[1]

"While Awan's year-long court case revolved solely around bank fraud charges pertaining to an application for a home equity loan, conspiracy theorists have speculated wildly about the case," the story read. For months, I'd begged reporters to obtain the February 3, 2017, memo from the sergeant at arms that plainly said the server was "missing" and that the Awans made unauthorized access to House computers. But no one had bothered, and without exception, their articles attributed these government-documented facts to "claims by conservative media."

The *New York Times* again essentially let Gowen write their story. "Mr. Gowen said his client falsely listed the property as a primary residence in an effort to quickly transfer money to his father, who was gravely ill and living in Pakistan," the paper of record explained. Imran, after all, was simply a big-hearted family man. The *Times* belatedly acknowledged that it had been misled. "Correction: An earlier version of this article, using information from Mr. Awan's lawyer, referred incorrectly to a transfer of money by Mr. Awan. According to his lawyer, he sent money to Pakistan to help his father; he did not send it directly to his father. And his father had been living in Virginia, not Pakistan, before his death." But it simply changed the sentence to read that he wired the money to Pakistan to "help" his father in Virginia—something that obviously failed to explain the actual purpose of the transfer.[2]

As proof of the thoroughness of its investigation, the DOJ said that it had interviewed forty people over the course of a two years. I'd interviewed more than that in the first month. Hell, the Awans had more than forty employers. The suspects themselves numbered seven. This left no room to talk to even the congressmen who employed them, to say nothing of chiefs of staff, their peers in House IT, and others who knew them inside and outside of the House. And now I knew why the agents came out of the woodwork to talk to witnesses after it was already too late to make a difference: to run up this count. It may be that before the final week, only fifteen people were interviewed over two years.

Trump's own attorney general, the narrative went, had embarrassed Trump by debunking a case the president had followed. But the DOJ's sole public statement didn't "debunk" anything. Instead, it simply contradicted all available primary evidence without explanation. No matter; the media had their anti-Trump narrative and they weren't going to question it.

The truth is, you had to believe in conspiracy theories to believe the prosecutors' apparent position that various people over the last decade—who for the most part didn't know each other— had somehow all created remarkably consistent but totally false claims.

Or there was the eminently more logical explanation: Imran had a long history of extortion-like tendencies, allegedly threatening witnesses, turning victims into culprits, and lying and then getting out of it with more lies, all backed by an unexplained political influence that reeked of blackmail. He had done it again.

———

Both parties asked for an expedited sentencing, and Gowen came prepared with a lengthy letter that purported to tell Imran's story. The prosecutors didn't dispute a single thing in it, even though much of it was readily disprovable with Pakistani and U.S. records. The truth was that since Imran had been convicted of nothing but a single count of bank fraud, the missive was scarcely necessary. This wasn't a plea for a lenient sentence, it was a brazen middle finger to anyone who thought that facts mattered and that the Department of Justice would enforce the law.

Imran, the shocking new story went, never did anything wrong in the House. Instead, he was a philanthropist who only wanted to set up a charity in Pakistan. Of course, he lacked the funds to do so, but also was in a "panic" that he had to create a generous charity that instant, so he committed bank fraud in the United States to finance it.[3] For months, Gowen had successfully courted the media's sympathy by saying Imran didn't "have a pot to piss in" and his family was "living in squalor." Now, the same media were eating up a story that he was simultaneously a charity magnate building a shelter for battered women. In his sister's telling, Imran's charity project extended to "a school for orphans, a mosque for the village to pray in, and a maternity clinic." How many pots of piss would that cost?

It was a bizarre tale, one that any clear-thinking observer could see made no sense. This charity endeavor, the court accepted, was doubly motivated by Imran's love for his family. The shelter would be to "secure his father's legacy." Imran loved his father so much that he abandoned him in Virginia during his final months on earth to go to Pakistan? The only use Imran might have for a battered-women's shelter, I thought, was to fill it up with all the women who alleged that he had personally abused them. Not five feet from him, as the judge heard this comical tale, was Hina Alvi, who said in a lawsuit months before that Imran threatened her with "dire consequences," pledging to "harm the lives of family of [Hina] if she intervenes."

But few people in Washington were thinking clearly in 2018, and Gowen took advantage of the city's epidemic of

Trump Derangement Syndrome. Facing an Obama-appointed judge, Gowen made a showboating speech which concluded that Imran should not go to jail because Trump and other Republicans are "deranged," "pathetic," and "without a shred of decency."

He said the Awans' "employers had no interest in letting them go and were forced to let them go because of a politicized investigation."

Gowen said that Imran had provided investigators "access to his phone, computer, and cloud," but did not add that rather than issue a search warrant, prosecutors had relied on Imran voluntarily handing over his devices, giving him ample time to modify their contents.

When Imran entered court, he smirked at me, then approached the judge and choked back tears. He never once had to testify or face cross-examination, but now he gave a sob speech to the court.

Imran played the part of a kind, godly family man. "We want to thank the prosecution, the FBI, and the Capitol Police," Imran said. "Those people who wrote these stories about me, I forgive them because I am seeking your forgiveness." He added, "Allow me to walk out of this courtroom and be with my family. I stand here with God in my heart. My heart is a sail, and the wind is blowing."

This contradicted Gowen, who casted doubt that Hina and Imran would stay together—not surprising after Hina's lawsuit —saying, "By the end of this today, you will allow Hina to build her family wherever she chooses and allow Imran to visit his father's grave and secure his legacy."

No matter. It was now Judge Chutkan's turn to come to his defense. "Mr. Awan and his family are immigrants, they came here legally. He excelled when working in Congress, and his support for his family has remained strong despite the unbelievable amount of scurrilous media attention."

She continued: "There have been numerous baseless conspiracy theories lobbed at him from the highest levels of government, all of them fully investigated by the U.S. attorney. Based on the material submitted by the defense, the harassment of threats will probably continue for some time." She then slowly and dramatically read the paragraph that prosecutors had so unusually inserted into Imran's plea agreement; the one that claimed he had done nothing wrong in the House. "The government included that extraordinary paragraph in its plea deal and I commend the government for that."

Gowen offered to pay a fine, but Judge Chutkan turned down the offer. "In this court's opinion, he has suffered enough. You are hereby sentenced to time served and three months supervised release. ... Good luck to you Mr. Awan, and have a good Eid." Imran hugged Gowen.

Democratic chiefs of staff, many from offices most suspiciously linked to Imran, were now so confident that the media whitewash was complete that they went on the record to defend someone who violated every cybersecurity tenet in the House and made unauthorized access to their servers. The cognitive dissonance with Democrats' public statement about cybersecurity didn't even matter. Joshua A. Rogin, the chief of staff to Representative Ted Deutch of Florida who implausibly had nearly the entire Awan group on his payroll despite also having another IT aide, wrote a letter of support saying Imran has "paid his debt to society one million times over."[4]

Others coming forward to defend Imran were Jameel Aalim-Johnson, the former chief of staff to the notoriously corrupt Congressman Gregory Meeks;[5] Patrice Willoughby, the onetime executive director of the Congressional Black Caucus who said Imran had been the victim of "racist" attacks; and Eva Dominguez, the former chief of staff for Representative Robert Wexler who claimed that Imran's alleged charity extended to sending "money every month to the widow and children" of the driver who was killed in the car crash in Pakistan that wounded his father. Pakistani media told another story: that Imran had extorted the widow, Bushra Bibi, threatened her, and framed her family members for crimes.

Just as I warned him the Democrats would, Dominguez singled out rubber-spine Chief Administrative Officer Phil Kiko, who had bent over backwards to accommodate Democrats in the investigation. Dominguez rewarded him by calling him a "Speaker Ryan-appointed...right-wing extremist."

Outside the doors of the courthouse after these sentencing pleas were heard, I gave a television interview to One America News, the only network in attendance. As the cameras rolled, a court security guard emerged. Badge on his chest, he walked into the shot and said "OAN is not a real network. They're not fair." It was a surreal and fitting symbol of the partisans embedded in the justice system from the highest to the lowest levels.

The same day Imran Awan was sentenced to three months of probation for bank fraud, Trump's former campaign manager, Paul Manafort, was convicted of eight crimes in an investigation by Special Counsel Robert Mueller that was supposed to find collusion with Russia, but instead found bank fraud, tax fraud, and failing to report foreign assets—all of which the Awan family had also done. Manafort faced up to 240 years in prison. On the same day, Trump's longtime personal attorney, Michael Cohen, pleaded guilty to eight crimes, largely involving making a false statement to a financial institution and tax fraud. Again, things the Awans had also done. The plea deal came with three to five years in prison, and Cohen took it under threat of a much longer term.[6]

It was a "nightmare news day" for Trump, Vox reported.

Trump highlighted two tiers of justice, lamenting: "Somebody made a better deal: Awan, the IT guy for Congresswoman Shultz. He had all the info on Democrats, all the info on everyone. He went to jail holding the hands of the Justice Department and the FBI, they sat there together smiling and laughing, and he got nothing. And he stole money. And he had more information on corruption of the Democrats than anyone, and they don't even have his computers and his servers. They gave him nothing."

"Double standard!? I mean, he was worse than anybody, in my opinion. The reason he got nothing is because the Dems are very strong in the Justice Department. I put in an attorney general that never took control of the Justice Department — Jeff Sessions — and it's kind of an incredible thing."

Sessions responded: "While I am Attorney General, the actions of the Department of Justice will not be improperly influenced by political considerations. I demand the highest standards, and where they are not met, I take action."[7]

But Trump seemed to see what Sessions could not: "Jeff Sessions said he wouldn't allow politics to influence him only because he doesn't understand what is happening underneath his command position."[8]

A justice system not influenced by politics is what we all want, but this day showed it as clear as could be: that's not the one we have.

TWENTY-THREE

AFTERMATH

So that's how I wound up here, talking and mourning with Sumaira on this Fourth of July. Tonight, the fireworks' climax didn't seem so spectacular. The truth is, I didn't even recognize it as the grand finale until what stood out to me was the silence and the crickets. Maybe I was just jaded. After what I'd seen, it'd take a lot to surprise me.

People whose job it was to take swift action had turned out to be cowards. People who could have looked the other way showed unfathomable courage while facing retaliation or threats. Confronting the swamp means stepping into quicksand: the more you fight, the deeper it drags you down.

I am fatigued, like everyone else. This swamp was too deep to drain. Theresa, who had been fighting this battle longer than I had, was hiring a lawyer. Samina Gilani was homeless. Sumaira was praying for safety and a fresh start. People like Sean Moran were still phoning it in.

The brothers' plan to get Gilani out of the way and seize the assets hidden in their father's name was not deterred in the slightest by the Fairfax County judge's ruling that Abid and Jamal submitted a death certificate that falsely claimed their father was not married to Gilani. Abid simply ignored the ruling and repeated the lie on public probate documents even as prosecutors drafted the exoneration statement for the family. In May of 2018, Abid attested to Fairfax County that his father was unmarried, that he had no will, that no one else was seeking his assets, and that his estate was worth exactly zero dollars. He was appointed as administrator. Hina also went back to Fairfax County court, in her case to change her name, making it more difficult to tie her to these activities. She now goes by Tina Alvi.

Sumaira finally secured a divorce from Imran in exchange for the unemployed single mother giving her car to the supposed international charity magnate. It signified the return of her dowry.

Imran claims he has job offers to return to Capitol Hill. Congressional chiefs of staff like Shelley Davis of Yvette Clarke's office have not been charged with procurement fraud. Members of Congress who seemed to know of problems before authorities did but didn't step up, like Kyrsten Sinema of Arizona and Michelle Lujan Grisham of New Mexico, were poised to ascend to the Senate and the governor's mansion, respectively. Xavier Becerra was now attorney general of California and a potential future presidential candidate. Another Awan employer, Hakeem Jeffries, would go on to be elected chairman of the House Democratic Caucus, and Pelosi, of course, would assume the speakership.

The House's penchant for protecting current members of both parties paid off for Representative Yvette Clarke during the 2018 primary election in Brooklyn, when she narrowly escaped losing to a more progressive young outsider from the Bernie Sanders wing of the party, just as Alexandria Ocasio-Cortez defeated the congressman in the neighboring district. Representative Clarke won by a mere one thousand votes. If it weren't for the House's extraordinary secrecy about ten percent of Clarke's budget disappearing under the most suspicious possible circumstances, her Democratic opponent could almost certainly have moved the needle enough to defeat her. Instead, the Uniparty of entrenched incumbents remains intact.

I return home and kiss my daughter goodnight. Now walking and with a personality of her own, she wasn't even born when this began. I think of the future. Where do I go from here? What can be done to get politics out of our justice system? Will America, in her lifetime, ever become a place—perhaps the first in history—where the connected elite are beholden to the same set of rules as the rest of us?

Some people say things have to get worse before they can get better. The DOJ's handling of this case makes clear that the bias displayed in the 2016 Clinton and Trump investigations is not an aberration, but a plague, and Jeff Sessions was not the man to cure it. Speaker Ryan is on his way out, he says to spend more time with his family in Wisconsin, though it remains to be seen whether his next job will have a Washington address or not. His willingness to capitulate to Democrats in this case, even if it meant handing the presidency to Hillary Clinton, casts a permanent shadow on his legacy and bolsters the sense—widespread among Trump supporters—that establishment Republicans can't be trusted.

Other people say that this problem is behind us, that Imran Awan and his clan are off the House network, and none of this matters. These are the same people who were never going to tell you that any of these extraordinary events occurred at all. But as I lie awake at night, I think about all I've learned, and how what I've told you isn't even the half of it.

Do they even know that the Awan group's relatives and associates continue to occupy sensitive IT roles in the federal government, including one who got a top-secret intelligence contract with the Obama White House despite the fact that his previous position was operating a car dealership? That another associate won a multimillion-dollar Department of Defense contract (in fact, he got preference for it by invoking his status as an ethnic minority)? That a former roommate runs IT for the Department of Homeland Security's Customs and Border Protection?

Do they want to know?

This is the story of a cover-up, manipulation, and the subversion of justice, and it is a true one in a world where true stories often don't have happy endings. But one conclusion seems clear: the DOJ, Democrats, and some establishment Republicans are all on the same team. One where insiders go along to get along.

If I've learned one thing, it's that the so-called "Deep State" isn't about Democrats versus Republicans, it's about entrenched insiders and the lengths they'll go to keep their hold on power.

EPILOGUE

Nothing has changed. Two years after the Committee on House Administration was informed of the systematic falsification of invoices, it held its first-ever hearing related to the incident.

Holding the gavel was Gregg Harper, who was set to leave Congress in January 2018 without ever publicly saying the name "Awan." Chairman Harper deferred generously throughout the hearing to ranking member Bob Brady, who likewise never said "Awan" publicly. Representative Brady did not run for re-election in 2018 after becoming the target of an FBI probe involving allegedly paying his opponent to drop out of his 2016 race.

These are the same men who oversaw the House's sexual harassment settlement slush fund— designed to silence victims— and then took credit for abolishing it. But as of this writing, it has not been eliminated at all. Representative Ron DeSantis proposed an aggressive bill that would name the lawmakers, like

Representative Meeks, who were the subject of past settlements, and make them repay them. This effort was dismissed, and in February 2018, Chairman Harper teamed with Representative Brady for a much more modest reform. But six months later, it was held up in secret talks in a departure from typical congressional procedures. Chairman Harper boasted that progress is being made nonetheless: members, staff, and even interns now have to sit through human resources "training" about harassment, as if a multiple-choice test asking whether harassment is good or bad would solve the whole thing. Aggressive oversight indeed.

At the belated hearing on congressional information security, before the committee were Sergeant at Arms Paul Irving, Chief Administrative Officer Phil Kiko, and the inspector general who replaced Theresa, Michael Ptasienski.

Ptasienski explained that system administrators like Awan "hold the 'keys to the kingdom,' meaning they can create accounts, grant access, view, download, update, or delete almost any electronic information within an office."

"A rogue system administrator could inflict considerable damage to an office and potentially disclose sensitive information, perform unauthorized updates, or simply export or delete files," he continued. "A rogue system administrator could take steps to cover up his or her actions and limit the possibility that their behavior being detected or otherwise traced back to them."

Kiko testified that experts found "two dozen" problems with the way the House supervised their computer administrators. "Enforcement gaps range from improper vetting of the employees themselves, to unfettered access to House accounts and use of non-approved software and/or cloud services, to the use of unauthorized equipment… far too many have privileged access to the House network with little to no supervision," he said.

Chairman Harper declared: "We just can't have this ever happen again."

The trio reminded him that, in a sense, this *was* again. Twice before, the committee had learned of procurement or IT scams that took advantage of the part-time "shared employee" system. They had pledged reforms and didn't follow through. In 2008, for example, "shared employee" bookkeeper Laura Flores was convicted of defrauding members of $200,000. The case included suspicion of unethical conduct by two congresswomen, sisters Loretta and Linda Sanchez. "I think this has been a great wake-up call," Republican Congressman Vernon Ehlers of Michigan, then the ranking member of the Administration Committee, said at the time. "I think all members should learn a lesson from this and I'm sure they will." They didn't.

This time around, Democrats had one favored solution: throwing money at the abstract problem of cybersecurity. Members of Congress pledged "$10 million in additional funding to the [CAO] in order to enhance their cybersecurity program."[1] The money did nothing to address the most serious known incident. And with no real punishment even for the Awans, anyone could see that there was no deterrent.

Kiko lectured: "The bookend to the outside threat is the insider threat. Tremendous efforts are dedicated to protecting the House against these outside threats, however these efforts are undermined when these employees do not adhere to and thumb their nose at our information security policy, and that's a risk in my opinion we cannot afford."

But Republican Congressman Barry Loudermilk of Georgia seemed to sense that these policies were toothless. "Especially if they disclose information we have on constituents or information we're working on. ... Does [the policy] spell out what penalties there are, i.e. you can go to jail?"

"There aren't any penalties," the CAO replied.

Kiko hid his frustration as he was forced to explain to members of Congress why there were no repercussions for bad actors he was supposed to be supervising, when those members knew full well that it was because their colleagues were protecting rulebreakers. "Termination, now it's the member's responsibility. ... We can revoke everything, but they could still be employed," he said in an obvious reference to Wasserman Schultz. "House officers cannot compel background checks or compliance with applicable House policies."

Months before, Chairman Harper and Representative Brady had offloaded their work— just as the committee had done in so many cases before—onto a group of unelected people working in secret, in this case a "working group" of Kiko, Irving, and the other usual suspects. They would tell the committee what to do, and the committee would presumably rubber-stamp it while giving members the ability to disavow any role in crafting it, should that become politically convenient.

The working group was clear that the vulnerabilities which emerged in the Awan affair would never go away unless the entire employment category that Imran exploited—that of the "shared" IT employee—was forever abolished. "It is impossible to eliminate the vulnerabilities posed by the use of shared employees without making significant changes to the employment structure itself," Kiko said. A lack of oversight was inherent to someone working part-time for many different members of Congress, and with disciplinary measures only possible with full consent of those members. "When risks and/or noncompliance with House policies have been identified," he said, "corrective actions by House officers is greatly delayed by the required coordination with shared employees' multiple employing authorities."

The answer was simple: hire companies to do the work, or better yet, have employees who reported to Central IT, rather than members, run the computer systems, Kiko said.

But the committee took the rare step of rejecting the proposal. And they did it in secret, with Committee Vice Chair Rodney Davis holding "listening sessions" in which members railed against fixing obvious cybersecurity holes by citing their need for autonomy. Republicans tend to use private contractors rather than shared employees, so it was no mystery where the objections came from: Democrats, the party who had for two years held up an abhorrence of cyber meddling as the cornerstone of their rhetoric. But the Illinois Republican Davis, who ranks near the top of Congress on a scorecard measuring bipartisanship, shielded their identities and took the hit for them. "Members expressed a strong desire to keep shared employees on as House employees instead of contract employees," he said.

Irving spoke up, saying those congressmen were putting their own selfish political desires over the security of the United States. "Ultimately it is the balance between the member interest and the governmental interest."

This time, it didn't even take a threatening finger jabbed in the chest to back Kiko down. Maybe "you could have it both ways" and the group of experts could dial back their proposal, he conceded. Even though he had just said it was "impossible" to close the loopholes while preserving the job category, and that his office would need the authority to override members who refused to fire people who made a mockery of the House's cyber-security rules, perhaps all of these things could be discarded while still billing it as a reform. "Members would be able to hire who they wanted, but as part of those employees' performance standards, maybe there could be something in there that said they had to comply with House policies, and then if they wouldn't, we could deny access or tell the member about it, or elevate it the committee," he offered lamely.

There you had it: nothing had been done to the Awans, so there was no deterrent to future bad actors. The major loopholes hadn't been closed. But maybe next time, if investigators detected someone hacking Congress, they could "tell the member about it" just as they had more than a year ago.

It sounded good and meant nothing, and Chairman Harper could take credit for it. It was perfect. He struck a tough pose, as if he had sided with the security experts instead of completely overriding them. "At the end of the day, you have to make sure you protect the House of Representatives, even if that upsets someone," the chairman said.

A few weeks later, Chairman Harper took his version of swift action: directing Kiko to write policies requiring certain things within the next six months. Largely, these were identical to what was already House policy: that shared employees file financial disclosures (the recommendations say nothing about whether they have to be accurate), and sign a piece of paper saying they won't break rules, just like the committee ordered in 2002 in a requirement that was entirely ignored.

There were pats on the back all around.

When Chairman Harper announced his retirement, Representative Brady commended him. "He has sought bipartisanship where it has been possible; he has managed the House in a truly professional manner. His polite, but results focused, approach has made this institution a better place."

INDEX OF AFFECTED CONGRESS MEMBERS

The Awan brothers had full access to all of the emails and files of the following members of Congress—all Democrats—and their staffs.

ARIZONA

Ex-Rep. Ron Barber
Ex-Rep. Gabrielle Giffords
Senator Kyrsten Sinema
Rep. Pete Aguilar

CALIFORNIA

Rep. Karen Bass
Attorney General Xavier Becerra
Rep. Julia Brownley
Rep. Tony Cardenas
Rep. Jim Costa
Rep. Ted Lieu
Ex-Rep. Hilda Solis

Rep. Jackie Speier
Rep. Mark Takano
Ex-Rep. Henry Waxman

COLORADO
Rep. Diana DeGette

DELAWARE
Governor John Carney
Rep. Lisa Blunt Rochester

FLORIDA
Rep. Charlie Crist
Rep. Ted Deutch
Rep. Lois Frankel
Ex-Rep. Joe Garcia
Ex-Rep. Gwen Graham
Ex-Rep. Ron Klein
Ex-Rep. Kendrick Meek
Ex-Rep. Patrick Murphy
Rep. Stephanie Murphy
Rep. Darren Michael Soto
Rep. Debbie Wasserman Schultz
Ex-Rep. Robert Wexler
Rep. Frederica Wilson

IOWA
Rep. Dave Loebsack

ILLINOIS
Ex-Rep. Melissa Bean
Senator Tammy Duckworth
Mayor Rahm Emanuel
Ex-Rep. Debbie Halvorson
Rep. Robin Kelly

INDIANA
Rep. Andre Carson
Senator Joe Donnelly
Ex-Rep. Baron Hill

KENTUCKY
Ex-Rep. Ben Chandler

LOUISIANA
Rep. Cedric Richmond

MASSACHUSETTS
Rep. Katherine Clark
Rep. Seth Moulton

MARYLAND
Rep. John Sarbanes

MICHIGAN
Rep. Dan Kildee
Rep. Sandy Levin

MISSOURI

Rep. Emanuel Cleaver

NEBRASKA

Ex-Rep. Brad Ashford

NEW MEXICO

Gov. Michelle Lujan Grisham

Sen. Martin Heinrich

NEVADA

Sen. Jacky Rosen

NEW YORK

Rep. Yvette Clarke

Ex-Rep. Joe Crowley

Rep. Hakeem Jeffries

Rep. Gregory Meeks

OHIO

Rep. Joyce Birdson Beatty

Rep. Marcia Fudge

Ex-Rep. Stephanie Tubbs Jones

Rep. Tim Ryan

TEXAS

Ex-Rep. Chris Bell

Rep. Joaquin Castro

VIRGINIA
Rep. Donald McEachin

ACKNOWLEDGMENTS

This book includes reporting by Wajid Ali Syed, a Washington-based correspondent for the GEO TV network in Pakistan. One of the savviest journalists I've ever met, he moves with astonishing grace through the Pakistani and Washington political scenes. Wajid traveled Pakistan and confronted witnesses at his physical peril, motivated only by his desire for truth. He is a kind and generous man who I consider a friend, and his easygoing style opened Urdu-speaking witnesses.

It also includes reporting by Kerry Picket—who undoubtedly falls under the category of strong, unshakable women—as well as Ethan Barton.

I am in awe of Sumaira Siddique, who left behind riches in Pakistan to follow her heart to the United States, only to wind up in a homeless shelter, and then rise from hardship based on nothing but her intelligence, integrity, and work ethic. A beautiful soul inside and out, she saw her first husband murdered, and faced violent threats from her second husband. Unlike so many others, she never wanted anything but selfless justice. She came forward, to me and to the FBI, despite perceiving imminent risk to her life.

The same cannot be said for the dozens, or hundreds, of Democratic staffers who have for a decade been keenly aware of serious problems relating to Imran Awan's activities in Congress, but who remained silent merely out of fear that their comfortable careers might, theoretically, be disrupted in the slightest way. To those who did come forward, placing the interests of the United States over those of particular politicians, my gratitude. The sheer number of people who remained silent shows that your commitment to principle over tribalism is uncommon.

This book relies at times by necessity on anonymous sources speaking on deep background to reconstruct scenes. I vetted the credentials of these sources thoroughly over two years, and their information, in every instance that it was possible to cross-reference, proved to be correct. Their insistence on anonymity was well-reasoned: they saw from the earliest days—long before I was convinced of it—that no good-faith investigation was being conducted, and that there was a deliberate concealment campaign. They told me again and again how if there was any chance that, by coming forward publicly, they would be listened to rather than merely retaliated against, they would do so. I pushed back hard against this reasoning at first, but as time went on, the accuracy of that assessment became clear to me.

My gratitude to the leadership of the Daily Caller News Foundation, including Neil Patel and Christopher Bedford, who understand that substantive investigative journalism can't be done on a tight timeframe; who don't find validation in following the pack; and who were never silenced by baseless threats from blustering lawyers, knowing that in this country, printing the truth can never be a problem. The Daily Caller News Foundation is an unstoppable pirate ship. While much of the mainstream media has recently, often rightfully, come under attack, organizations like the Daily Caller News Foundation provide a lesson I hope Americans don't forget: a free press is, and will always be, an essential force in the United States, without which our citizens would be entirely at the mercy of institutions. Though much of the media has fallen into a hive-minded echo chamber, working as a journalist still affords one the independence to be accountable to no one other than the truth, virtually free of the hierarchy and personality-driven forces that seem to corrupt so much else.

I extend my thanks to:

Politicians of all stripes who place principle over fealty to party leadership or institutions, like Louie Gohmert, Jim Jordan, Tim Canova, Scott Perry, Thomas Massie, Tom Coburn and Rand Paul.

Congressional staff who do the grunt work of oversight even when it is unglamorous.

Connie Hair, a veteran staffer, who helped a non-political animal like me understand how in Congress, truths are distorted by politics.

Roland Foster, who stands out among Republican congressional staff for his understanding of something that is better-known on the other side of the aisle: true, compelling stories are more effective political weapons than nearly any legislative tactic.

Regnery Publishing and its editors, who have a rare combination of brains and heart, and who believed in me fully while also making this work better with their experience and expertise.

Newt Gingrich, whose perceptiveness, tact, intelligence, and independence blew me away, and Kathy Lubbers, whose confidence and refreshingly straightforward manner kept me from drowning in the weeds and worry.

The "big" people who saw the truth from the earliest days when few others did: Dana Loesch, Tucker Carlson, Maria Bartiromo, Lou Dobbs, and Sean Hannity.

The "little" people whose lives were disrupted when they intersected randomly with something so much bigger than themselves, but who didn't shy away from talking with me.

Lauren and the cadre of online readers who made the effort to delve actively into the facts, including, to use their internet handles, Chillum and GreenIzeGirl.

Tom Anderson of the National Legal and Policy Center.

Jacob Fenton, for the initial spark that burned down the house.

Jerry Seper, a fearless editor and loyal mentor who was rattling the House and its members' penchant for covering for each other before I was born, and who taught me never to give up.

Matt Lavin, whose spiritual guidance strengthened my resilience, clarity, and emotional fortitude.

And most of all, my wife Eleanor, a woman whose versatility and intelligence keeps me in awe, and who became an essential encyclopedia of knowledge on this case—a case far too big for one man to handle—as I was nearly buried under the sheer volume of astonishing facts, none of which anyone else was examining. It was lonely being perhaps the only person who saw the big picture in a case of national importance for so long, but with her, I am never alone.

Paul Ryan's Republican leadership, the entire Democratic caucus, and the Department of Justice of the strongest nation on Earth did everything they could to prevent the information in this book from coming to light. They were not powerful enough to conceal these events—at least not entirely. Yet, the writing of this book would not have been possible without the Herculean efforts of Eleanor and my mother-in-law. These members of my family expertly, lovingly, and uncomplainingly sacrificed to manage a chaotic and growing household. In the end, only these two women in the Virginia suburbs wielded power sufficient to make the difference between this book being published or its findings remaining forever secret.

NOTES

ONE: "ONLY GOD CAN HELP ME"

1. http://www.documentcloud.org/documents/4493190-Pak-Shooting.html

TWO: FRAUD ON CAPITOL HILL

1. https://usasurvival.org/home/docs/Complaint_Against_Jesse_Jackson.pdf
2. https://www.washingtontimes.com/news/2013/jan/22/who-are-the-best-and-worst-bosses-on-capitol-hill/
3. https://s3-us-west-2.amazonaws.com/dailycaller/awan/fbi_memo.pdf

THREE: THE ELECTION SEASON HACK YOU NEVER HEARD ABOUT

1. http://thehill.com/blogs/blog-briefing-room/news/111969-pelosi-appoints-first-female-inspector-general

2. http://www.isaca.org/About-ISACA/Press-room/News-Releases/2015/Pages/Hon-Theresa-Grafenstine-of-Washington-DC-Re-elected-International-Vice-President-of-ISACA.aspx

FOUR: THE PUPPETEER

1. http://www.eisenhowerinstitute.org/about/national-advisory-council/fleet.dot
2. http://archive.is/q3iwK
3. https://www.politico.com/newsletters/playbook-power-briefing/2018/07/13/mueller-indicts-12-russians-285949
4. https://www.nytimes.com/2016/12/13/us/politics/russia-hack-election-dnc.html

FIVE: PANIC

1. http://www.documentcloud.org/documents/4493191-Restraining-Orders.html

SIX: A "THEFT INVESTIGATION"

1. https://s3-us-west-2.amazonaws.com/dailycaller/awan/cao_memo.pdf
2. http://archive.is/NpaGe

SEVEN: NEWS DUMP

1. https://www.buzzfeednews.com/article/johnstanton/feds-arrest-five-congressional-it-contractors-at-the-capitol
2. Stephen Taylor is a pseudonym, the only one used in this book. Taylor has seen what has happened to others who spoke out and is afraid of retaliation not only from the Awans, but from his employers in Congress.
3. https://wikileaks.org/dnc-emails/emailid/41311
4. https://wikileaks.org/dnc-emails/emailid/42803

EIGHT: FRIGHTENING CONNECTIONS

1. http://www.heraldscotland.com/news/14226329.Bizarre_
   extradition_case__The_Glasgow_sex_criminal__the_FBI_
   probe_and_the_religious_conversion/
2. https://www.documentcloud.org/documents/4332988-Cia-
   Lawsuits.html
3. https://www.nytimes.com/2003/04/11/us/nation-war-iraqi-
   americans-iraqis-us-prepare-return-rebuild-homeland.html
4. https://www.theamericanconservative.com/articles/paul-
   wolfowitzs-iran-connection/
5. https://www.politico.com/interactives/2017/obama-hezbollah-
   drug-trafficking-investigation/

NINE: PLAYING DUMB

1. https://www.documentcloud.org/documents/3983049-Scan.
   html
2. https://www.theindychannel.com/news/politics/fired-shared-
   congressional-it-employee-could-no-longer-perform-his-job-
   rep-carson-says
3. https://www.documentcloud.org/documents/5433625-
   Cybersecurity-Assistance-Legislation.html
4. https://www.congress.gov/bill/115th-congress/house-bill/244/
   text/eah?
5. https://www.congress.gov/bill/115th-congress/house-bill/2810/
   text#toc-H2859C6F8025E4DB9B701C3F7D4BD187FFmu

TEN: POWER OF ATTORNEY

1. https://www.documentcloud.org/documents/3516620-Abid-
   Awan-s-stepmother-calls-the-police-on-the.html

ELEVEN: "ROB YOU WITH THEIR TONGUES

1. http://www.dailymail.co.uk/news/article-4803884/Pictured-Dem-aide-charged-fraud-hacking-probe.html
2. https://freebeacon.com/politics/dem-rep-alcee-hastings-paid-convicted-money-launderer-75k-part-time-work-district-office/
3. https://www.opensecrets.org/personal-finances/top-net-worth?year=2008
4. https://www.opensecrets.org/personal-finances/top-net-worth?year=2015
5. https://s3-us-west-2.amazonaws.com/dailycaller/awan/Cleaver+OCE+Complaint+(1).pdf
6. https://www.citizensforethics.org/press-release/gregory-meeks-named-most-corrupt-member-of-congress/

TWELVE: PAKISTAN

1. https://www.dawn.com/news/944935
2. http://www.documentcloud.org/documents/4484560-Saif-College.html

THIRTEEN: BACK IN THE HOUSE

1. https://www.politico.com/story/2017/03/house-democrats-it-staffers-hina-alvi-imran-awan-235569
2. http://archive.is/bacX0

FOURTEEN: LAPTOP IN A PHONE BOOTH

1. https://www.opensecrets.org/personal-finances/top-net-worth?year=2015
2. http://clerk.house.gov/public_disc/financial-pdfs/2017/10023759.pdf
3. https://ethics.house.gov/gifts/house-gift-rule

4. https://www.youtube.com/watch?v=Cfby0FYLBkM&feature=youtu.be&t=1h26m40s
5. http://www.sun-sentinel.com/news/politics/fl-reg-wasserman-schultz-discusses-imran-awan-20170802-story.html

FIFTEEN: MEDIA MALPRACTICE: SEE SOMETHING, SAY NOTHING

1. https://www.nytimes.com/2017/11/21/us/politics/fbi-robert-brady-campaign-finance.html
2. https://www.news-leader.com/story/news/crime/2018/04/02/murder-hire-claim-legit-against-former-springfield-charity-executive-judge-says/479242002/

SIXTEEN: ARREST

1. https://www.wsj.com/articles/legal-fraud-of-the-century-1393978989
2. http://gowensilva.com/christopher-gowen/
3. http://www.sun-sentinel.com/news/politics/fl-reg-wasserman-schultz-questions-media-20170821-story.html
4. https://www.weeklystandard.com/jenna-lifhits/the-strange-case-of-debbie-wasserman-schulzs-it-guy
5. http://dailycaller.com/2017/09/20/like-a-slave-three-muslim-women-at-least-one-of-them-bloodied-called-police-on-imran-awan/
6. https://dailycaller.com/2017/12/12/federal-judge-recuses-herself-from-a-second-fusion-gps-case/

SEVENTEEN: INSIDER THREATS

1. https://www.washingtonpost.com/investigations/federal-probe-into-house-technology-worker-imran-awan-yields-intrigue-no-evidence-of-espionage/2017/09/16/100b4170-93f2-11e7-b9bc-

b2f7903bab0d_story.html?tid=sm_tw&utm_term
=.4a91d9f427a4

2. http://fullmeasure.news/news/cover-story/
cybersecurity-04-26-2018

3. http://www.documentcloud.org/documents/4390229-
20170901-Letter.html

4. https://www.youtube.com/watch?v=4RmDQQaOee8&featur
e=youtu.be

EIGHTEEN: INSURANCE

1. http://www.documentcloud.org/documents/4438429-10-4-17-
Samina-Gilani-Depo.html

NINETEEN: HELL HATH NO FURY LIKE A SHARIA WIFE SCORNED

1. http://fullmeasure.news/news/cover-story/
cybersecurity-04-26-2018

TWENTY: JEFF SESSIONS IS MR. MAGOO

1. https://www.realclearpolitics.com/video/2018/04/03/desantis_
oversight_committee_should_investigate_debbie_wasserman_
schultz_itawan_brothers_scandal.html

2. https://www.realclearpolitics.com/video/2017/10/14/gohmert_
hearing_imran_awan_wasserman_schultz_it_aide_managed_
house_cybersecurity_remotely_from_pakistan.html

3. https://twitter.com/realDonaldTrump/
status/987470932989050881

4. https://www.politico.com/story/2018/06/29/paul-manafort-
storage-locker-associated-press-687776

5. https://www.rollcall.com/news/politics/donor-accuses-
stockman-of-misspending-charitable-donation

TWENTY-TWO: THE PROSECUTION SLEEPS

1. https://www.cnn.com/2018/07/03/politics/imran-awan-debbie-wasserman-schultz-bank-fraud/index.html
2. https://www.nytimes.com/2018/07/03/us/politics/imran-awan-congress-bank-fraud.html
3. http://www.documentcloud.org/documents/4763619-Sentencingmemo.html
4. http://www.documentcloud.org/documents/4777841-Sentencing-Letters.html
5. https://www.investigativeproject.org/2190/rep-meeks-helped-jihad-flier
6. https://www.vox.com/2018/8/21/17766146/michael-cohen-guilty-plea-paul-manafort-day-explained
7. https://www.cnbc.com/2018/08/23/jeff-sessions-pushes-back-against-trump-actions-of-doj-will-not-be-improperly-influenced-by-political-considerations.html
8. https://twitter.com/realDonaldTrump/status/1033332301579661312

EPILOGUE

1. https://appropriations.house.gov/uploadedfiles/leg_report.pdf